LAW AND LEGAL ISSUES IN THE UNITED STATES:
ANALYSES AND DEVELOPMENTS

LAW AND LEGAL ISSUES IN THE UNITED STATES

ANALYSES AND DEVELOPMENTS

VOLUME 3

LAW AND LEGAL ISSUES IN THE UNITED STATES: ANALYSES AND DEVELOPMENTS

Additional books in this series can be found on Nova's website under the Series tab.

Additional e-books in this series can be found on Nova's website under the e-book tab.

LAW AND LEGAL ISSUES IN THE UNITED STATES:
ANALYSES AND DEVELOPMENTS

LAW AND LEGAL ISSUES IN THE UNITED STATES

ANALYSES AND DEVELOPMENTS

VOLUME 3

LAURENT B. LANDERS
EDITOR

nova publishers
New York

For permission to use material from this book please contact us:
Telephone 631-231-7269; Fax 631-231-8175
Web Site: http://www.novapublishers.com

Library of Congress Cataloging-in-Publication Data

ISBN: 978-1-63117-827-6

Published by Nova Science Publishers, Inc. † New York

CONTENTS

PREFACE

This series provides an overview of current analyses and developments pertaining to the law and legal issues in the United States. Topics covered in this volume include oversight and legal enforcement of the national mortgage settlement; public charge grounds of inadmissibility and deportability; an overview of judicial review of immigration matters; congressional authority to enact criminal law; judicial activity concerning enemy combatant detainees; the Iran hostages; and federal criminal offenses of sexual abuse of children.

Chapter 1 - In Autumn 2010, all 50 state attorneys general, the attorney general for the District of Columbia, the Conference of State Bank Supervisors, the U.S. Department of Justice (DOJ), the U.S. Department of Housing and Urban Development (HUD), and the U.S. Department of the Treasury (Treasury Department) initiated an investigation into foreclosure-related state and federal law violations by the nation's top five mortgage servicers: Ally Financial, Inc. (formerly GMAC, Inc.); Bank of America, Corp.; Citigroup, Inc.; JP Morgan Chase & Co.; and Wells Fargo & Co. On February 8, 2012, these state and federal officials, with the exception of Oklahoma's attorney general, announced a "National Mortgage Settlement" of certain legal claims with these five institutions. The settlement is to result in the servicers providing about $25 billion of relief, primarily to homeowners and individuals who recently lost their homes through foreclosure. In financial terms, it constitutes the second largest legal settlement ever reached by the attorneys general, behind only the 1998 settlement with tobacco companies.

The agreements stipulate that, in exchange for a release of liability for legal claims that otherwise could have been raised against the servicers by the participating regulators, these five mortgage companies will provide five distinct forms of relief. Under the agreements, the mortgage companies shall

- comply with specified servicing standards going forward;
- provide various forms of mortgage-related consumer relief to current borrowers whose mortgages are owned and serviced by the five servicers ("Consumer Relief" component);
- provide relief to servicemembers who may have been harmed by violations of the Servicemembers Civil Relief Act (SCRA) and to improve the servicing of soldiers' mortgages to prevent future SCRA violations ("SCRA" component);
- provide compensation to certain individuals whose homes were previously foreclosed by the five servicers ("Borrower Payment" component); and
- make direct payments to federal and state governments to cover the resolution of legal claims ("Direct Settlement Payment" component).

With the exception of the Direct Settlement Payment component, the agreements also provide explicit mechanisms by which compliance of each distinct relief component will be overseen and enforced. The agreements establish an independent monitor with the primary authority to conduct oversight of the servicers' compliance with Consumer Relief and Servicing Standards of the settlement, while the enforcement powers primarily are provided to a Monitoring Committee that is composed of representatives of the state and federal regulators that are parties to the agreements. Primary oversight and enforcement of the SCRA terms reside with the DOJ. A Special Administrator is charged with identifying individuals who qualify for monetary relief under the Borrower Payment terms and with distributing those funds, while the state members of the Monitoring Committee have the authority to oversee the Special Administrator's operations.

Individual homeowners are not parties to the agreements, and the terms of the agreements do not provide individual borrowers a private right of action to enforce the agreements. Similarly, the settlement agreements do not, in any way, limit any enforcement power held by state or federal regulators that are not parties to the agreements, including the authorities of the federal banking regulators.

Chapter 2 - The Immigration and Nationality Act (INA) has long provided for aliens' exclusion and deportation from the United States on "public charge" grounds. Under current law, aliens outside the United States who seek to obtain visas at U.S. consulates overseas, or admission at U.S. ports of entry, are generally denied entry if they are deemed "likely at any time to become a public charge." Aliens within the United States who seek to adjust their status to that of lawful permanent resident (LPR), or who entered the United States without inspection, are also generally subject to this ground of inadmissibility. Similarly, LPRs and other aliens who have been admitted to the United States are removable if they become a public charge within five years after the date of their entry due to causes that pre-existed their entry. These public charge grounds have recently been of interest because of concerns, among some Members of Congress and the public, regarding noncitizens' receipt of public assistance.

The INA does not expressly define what it means for an alien to be a public charge, and, prior to 1996, there was no statutory guidance on what was to be considered in determining whether an alien is inadmissible or deportable (removable) on public charge grounds. Then, in 1996, the INA was amended to require that certain factors be taken into account when determining whether aliens are inadmissible on public charge grounds, including the alien's age, health, family status, financial resources, education, and skills. There still is no similar guidance on the public charge ground of deportability.

Given this general lack of statutory guidance, the executive and judicial branches initially construed the meaning of *public charge* in adjudicating cases involving individual aliens. In so doing, administrative authorities interpreted *public charge* differently for purposes of the grounds of inadmissibility than for the grounds of deportability. Specifically, *public charge* was construed broadly in the context of admissibility, with determinations based on a "totality of the circumstances" test that considered factors like those codified in the INA in 1996. In contrast, in the context of deportability, "public charge" was construed more narrowly. Aliens could only be found to be deportable on public charge grounds if (1) they received government assistance that they were legally obligated to repay, (2) the government entity providing the assistance demanded repayment, and (3) the alien or the alien's sponsor was unable to pay.

Following the enactment of the Personal Responsibility and Work Opportunity Reconciliation Act (PRWORA) of 1996, executive agencies issued guidance regarding the public charge grounds. While PRWORA generally restricts noncitizens' eligibility for "public benefits," it permits them to receive specified benefits, and its enactment raised questions about whether aliens who receive benefits for which they are eligible under PRWORA could potentially be removable on public charge grounds. Immigration officials addressed these questions in a 1999 policy letter that defined *public charge*, and identified which benefits are considered in public charge determinations.

This policy letter underlies current regulations and other guidance on the public charge grounds of inadmissibility and deportability.

Collectively, the various sources addressing the meaning of *public charge* suggest that an alien's receipt of public benefits, per se, is unlikely to result in the alien being deemed removable on public charge grounds. Neither the INA nor implementing regulations address the role that receipt of public benefits plays in public charge determinations. Other agency guidance and court decisions indicate that, while receipt of certain public benefits could be considered in public charge determinations, other factors are also considered (e.g., age, obligation to repay).

Chapter 3 - Congress has plenary or sovereign power over the conditions for admitting aliens into the United States and permitting them to remain. This power is so completely entrusted to the political branch to legislate and implement as to be largely free from judicial review. However, this power is still subject to constitutional limitations, including substantive and procedural due process protections. In immigration cases, due process may be a flexible concept and the particular procedures that may be constitutionally required depend on the relative interests involved.

Historically, immigration policy has sought to encourage and enable the admission and integration of desirable immigrants (workers, family, refugees/asylees), while discouraging and preventing the entry of undesirable aliens (national security risks/terrorists, criminals, public charges). Accordingly, in deciding what degree of judicial review is appropriate in immigration matters, Congress has sought a balance between a system that is fair to desired immigrants, yet facilitates the removal of undesired aliens. Initially, a *habeas corpus* proceeding provided the primary avenue of judicial review of various immigration determinations. In the wake of Supreme Court decisions construing the Administrative Procedure Act as applying to and providing an avenue for judicial review of immigration adjudications, Congress amended the Immigration and Nationality Act (INA) of 1952 by adding a judicial review provision in 1961 that provided for review by federal courts of appeal for deportation orders, but only for habeas corpus review of exclusion orders by federal district courts.

Beginning with the Antiterrorism and Effective Death Penalty Act of 1996 (AEDPA) and the Illegal Immigration Reform and Immigrant Responsibility Act of 1996 (IIRIRA), legislation and administrative actions have focused on reducing immigration litigation by limiting and streamlining both administrative appeal and judicial review procedures regarding removal of aliens and by rendering aliens in certain categories ineligible for certain types of relief from removal. Even when an alien may be considered for discretionary relief, judicial review of denials of relief from removal is restricted, as is review of removal orders issued to criminal aliens or national security risks. Also, the REAL ID Act restricted habeas review and certain other non-direct judicial review in response to U.S. Supreme Court holdings that such review was still available after the 1996 acts. In the 113th Congress, S. 744 and H.R. 2278, among other bills, would generally continue the trend of limiting judicial review; however, S. 744 provides for judicial review of its legalization programs.

This report will summarize judicial review for immigration matters, including visa denials and revocations; removal orders and detention; naturalization delays, denials, and revocations; expatriation; and legalization denials. Administrative adjudications such as removal proceedings or determination of immigration benefits such as naturalization are beyond the scope of this report.

Chapter 4 - The powers of Congress begin and end with the Constitution. The Constitution vests Congress with explicit authority to enact criminal laws relating to counterfeiting, piracy, crimes on the high seas, offenses against the law of nations, and treason. It grants Congress other broad powers, such as the power to regulate interstate commerce. The Constitution's Necessary and Proper Clause allows Congress to enact criminal laws when reasonably related to the regulation of commerce or to one of the other constitutionally enumerated powers. The Constitution also imposes limits on the powers of Congress, however. It places those limits in the terms it uses in its grants of authority, in explicit prohibitions, and in the Tenth Amendment reminder of the restrictions implicit in the federal union. Recently, the Supreme Court and the lower federal appellate courts have supplied several examples of the scope and limits of congressional authority.

In the case of the Commerce Clause, seven Justices of the Supreme Court endorsed separate opinions in *National Federation* explaining that the power to regulate interstate commerce does not include the power to require participation in commerce. The Fifth Circuit held in *Kebodeaux* that the Commerce Clause does not embody the power to outlaw purely intrastate movement with only an attenuated nexus to commercial activity. As for foreign commerce, the circuits disagree on whether Congress's regulatory authority is subject to the same constraints that apply to its powers over domestic commerce. The Ninth Circuit (*Clark*) believes it is not. The Third Circuit (*Pendleton*) disagrees. (The Violence Against Women Reauthorization

Act, P.L. 113-4 (S. 47), eliminates the need to prove a foreign commerce element in the law that gave rise to the circuit split.)

In the realm of the Necessary and Proper Clause, the Eleventh Circuit in *Belfast* observed that Congress may pass criminal legislation in order to implement a treaty obligation, and the Third Circuit in *Bond* held that it may do so without regard to federalism concerns. Moreover, the Ninth Circuit Court of Appeals concluded in *Elk Shoulder* that Congress may outlaw the unregistered movement within a state of a federally convicted sex offender who is on supervised release. The Fifth Circuit held in *Kebodeaux*, however, that the Clause does not permit enactment of a statute that outlaws such movement after the offender has been fully discharged.

Although they did not join in a single opinion, seven Justices in *National Federation* concluded that Congress's power under the Spending Clause may not be used to compel the states to accept expansion of a federal regulatory regime or to face draconian economic consequences. The case did not involve criminal penalties, but a limit on Congress's Spending Clause power is a limit on its authority to enact implementing necessary and proper criminal legislation.

Article I, Section 8, clause 10 grants Congress the power "to define and punish Piracies and Felonies committed on the high Seas, and Offenses against the Law of Nations." Federal appellate courts have looked to customary international law for explanations of the power over offenses against the law of nations (*Bellaizac-Hurtado*) and piracy (*Dire*). The High Seas cases (*Saac* and *Ibarguen-Mosquera*) continue to acknowledge congressional authority to outlaw drug trafficking in international waters subject only to an elusive due process limitation. The Constitution's Military Clauses permit Congress to criminalize overseas assaults by Defense Department foreign contractors (*Brehm*), but do not permit it to punish an individual's conduct based solely on his status as a former member of the Armed Forces even when supplemented by the Necessary and Proper Clause (*Kebodeaux*).

Chapter 5 - As part of the conflict with Al Qaeda and the Taliban, the United States has captured and detained numerous persons believed to have been part of or associated with enemy forces. Over the years, federal courts have considered a multitude of petitions by or on behalf of suspected belligerents challenging aspects of U.S. detention policy. Although the Supreme Court has issued definitive rulings concerning several legal issues raised in the conflict with Al Qaeda and the Taliban, many others remain unresolved, with some the subject of ongoing litigation.

This report discusses major judicial opinions concerning suspected enemy belligerents detained in the conflict with Al Qaeda and the Taliban. The report addresses all Supreme Court decisions concerning enemy combatants. It also discusses notable circuit court opinions addressing issues of ongoing relevance. In particular, it summarizes notable decisions which have (1) addressed whether the Executive may lawfully detain only persons who are "part of" Al Qaeda, the Taliban, and affiliated groups, or also those who provide support to such entities in their hostilities against the United States and its allies; (2) adopted a functional approach for assessing whether a person is "part of" Al Qaeda; (3) decided that a preponderance of evidence standard is appropriate for detainee habeas cases, but suggested that a lower standard might be constitutionally permissible, and instructed courts to assess the cumulative weight of evidence rather than each piece of evidence in isolation; (4) determined that Guantanamo detainees have a limited right to challenge their proposed transfer to foreign custody, but denied courts the authority to order detainees released into the United States; and (5) held that the constitutional writ of habeas does not presently extend to noncitizen detainees held at U.S.-operated facilities in Afghanistan. Finally, the report discusses a few criminal cases involving persons who were either involved in the 9/11 attacks (Zacarias Moussaoui) or were captured abroad by U.S. forces or allies during operations against Al Qaeda, the Taliban, and associated entities (John Walker Lindh and Ahmed Ghailani).

For over a decade, the primary legal authority governing the detention of enemy belligerents in the conflict with Al Qaeda was the 2001 Authorization for Use of Military Force ("AUMF," P.L. 107-40. In December 2011, Congress passed the National Defense Authorization Act for FY2012 ("2012 NDAA," P.L. 112-81), which contains a provision that is largely intended to codify the current understanding of the detention authority conferred by the AUMF, as has been interpreted and applied by the Executive and the D.C. Circuit. The full implications of the 2012 NDAA upon wartime detention jurisprudence remain to be seen. In any event, the act does not address many of the legal issues involving wartime detention that have not been squarely resolved by the Supreme Court. Among other things, these unresolved issues include the precise scope of the Executive's wartime detention authority, including the circumstances in which U.S. citizens may be detained; the degree to which noncitizens (or in one case, U.S. citizens) held abroad are entitled to protections under the Constitution; the authority of federal habeas courts to compel the release into the United States of detainees determined to be unlawfully held; and the ability of detainees to receive advance notice and to challenge their proposed transfer to foreign custody.

Chapter 6 - Even today, after the passage of some three decades, the 1979-1981 Iran Hostage Crisis remains an event familiar to most Americans. Many might be unaware that the 52 American mostly military and diplomatic personnel held hostage in Tehran for 444 days continue to strive for significant compensation for their ordeal. The former hostages and their families did receive a number of benefits under various civil service laws, and each hostage received from the U.S. government a cash payment of $50 for each day held hostage. The hostages have never received any compensation from Iran through court actions, all efforts having failed due to foreign sovereign immunity and an executive agreement known as the Algiers Accords, which bars such lawsuits. Congress took action to abrogate Iran's sovereign immunity in the case *Roeder v. Islamic Republic of Iran*, but never successfully abrogated the executive agreement, leaving the plaintiffs with jurisdiction to pursue their case but without a judicial cause of action.

Having lost their bids in the courts to obtain recompense, the former hostages have turned to Congress for relief. This report outlines the history of various efforts, including legislative efforts and court cases, and describes three bills currently before Congress (H.R. 904, S. 559, H.R. 3200).

Chapter 7 - Over the past 100 years, Congress has sought to prohibit acts of sexual abuse of minors and punish those who harm the nation's children. These efforts began in the early 20th century when Congress prohibited the transportation of a minor in interstate commerce for the purpose of sexual exploitation, and continue to more modern measures such as outlawing the use of the Internet to lure children for sexual purposes. Nevertheless, Congress's power in this area does have constitutional limits.

The power to create criminal laws in the United States resides most broadly with the states. The states retain a general police power to regulate for the health, safety, and welfare of their citizens. By contrast, Congress may only act within its express and implied powers, including the power to legislate for federal enclaves and in areas within its enumerated powers (e.g., commerce, spending, taxing). Congress has exercised both strands of authority to criminalize sexual abuse of children.

Congress began outlawing sexual abuse of minors in 1910 with the Mann Act, which outlawed the use of a common carrier to transport a minor in interstate commerce for an illegal sexual purpose. In subsequent enactments, including the Sexual Exploitation of Children Act of 1977, the Sexual Abuse Act of 1986, and the Protection of Children from Sexual Predators Act of

1998, Congress increased penalty provisions (including repeat offender provisions), expanded jurisdictional clauses, and broadened the list of prohibited acts, including aggravating factors warranting an increased penalty.

Presently, federal sexual abuse law is a hierarchy based on the age of the victim and whether the act involved aggravating circumstances. The most serious offense is when a child is murdered during the commission of a sexual offense. The penalty is death or up to life imprisonment. The least serious is sexual *contact* (as opposed to a sexual *act*) with a minor at least 12 years of age but younger than 16. This crime requires no aggravating circumstances and carries a possible four-year maximum prison sentence. Between these two crimes falls a host of other offenses prohibiting sexual abuse or contact. These include sexual abuse of a child at least 12 years of age but younger than 16, sexual contact with a child under the age of 12 years, and use of the mail or other facility of interstate commerce to persuade a minor under the age of 18 to engage in an illegal sexual act.

Because much of the prohibited conduct in these statutes overlaps, courts must consider the lesser-included offense doctrine when handling sexual abuse cases. This doctrine permits a court to instruct the jury on not only the offense charged by the government, but also a lesser offense that is "necessarily included" in the charged offense. This doctrine has been used to aid the prosecution in obtaining a conviction when proof of the charged offense is insufficient, but also assists defendants by allowing the jury to convict on the lesser included offense.

In: Law and Legal Issues in the United States
Editor: Laurent B. Landers
ISBN: 978-1-63117-827-6

Chapter 1

OVERSIGHT AND LEGAL ENFORCEMENT OF THE NATIONAL MORTGAGE SETTLEMENT*

David H. Carpenter

SUMMARY

In Autumn 2010, all 50 state attorneys general, the attorney general for the District of Columbia, the Conference of State Bank Supervisors, the U.S. Department of Justice (DOJ), the U.S. Department of Housing and Urban Development (HUD), and the U.S. Department of the Treasury (Treasury Department) initiated an investigation into foreclosure-related state and federal law violations by the nation's top five mortgage servicers: Ally Financial, Inc. (formerly GMAC, Inc.); Bank of America, Corp.; Citigroup, Inc.; JP Morgan Chase & Co.; and Wells Fargo & Co. On February 8, 2012, these state and federal officials, with the exception of Oklahoma's attorney general, announced a "National Mortgage Settlement" of certain legal claims with these five institutions. The settlement is to result in the servicers providing about $25 billion of relief, primarily to homeowners and individuals who recently lost their homes through foreclosure. In financial terms, it constitutes the second largest legal settlement ever reached by the

* This is an edited, reformatted and augmented version of Congressional Research Service Publication, No. R42919, dated January 9, 2013.

attorneys general, behind only the 1998 settlement with tobacco companies.

The agreements stipulate that, in exchange for a release of liability for legal claims that otherwise could have been raised against the servicers by the participating regulators, these five mortgage companies will provide five distinct forms of relief. Under the agreements, the mortgage companies shall

- comply with specified servicing standards going forward;
- provide various forms of mortgage-related consumer relief to current borrowers whose mortgages are owned and serviced by the five servicers ("Consumer Relief" component);
- provide relief to servicemembers who may have been harmed by violations of the Servicemembers Civil Relief Act (SCRA) and to improve the servicing of soldiers' mortgages to prevent future SCRA violations ("SCRA" component);
- provide compensation to certain individuals whose homes were previously foreclosed by the five servicers ("Borrower Payment" component); and
- make direct payments to federal and state governments to cover the resolution of legal claims ("Direct Settlement Payment" component).

With the exception of the Direct Settlement Payment component, the agreements also provide explicit mechanisms by which compliance of each distinct relief component will be overseen and enforced. The agreements establish an independent monitor with the primary authority to conduct oversight of the servicers' compliance with Consumer Relief and Servicing Standards of the settlement, while the enforcement powers primarily are provided to a Monitoring Committee that is composed of representatives of the state and federal regulators that are parties to the agreements. Primary oversight and enforcement of the SCRA terms reside with the DOJ. A Special Administrator is charged with identifying individuals who qualify for monetary relief under the Borrower Payment terms and with distributing those funds, while the state members of the Monitoring Committee have the authority to oversee the Special Administrator's operations.

Individual homeowners are not parties to the agreements, and the terms of the agreements do not provide individual borrowers a private right of action to enforce the agreements. Similarly, the settlement agreements do not, in any way, limit any enforcement power held by state or federal regulators that are not parties to the agreements, including the authorities of the federal banking regulators.

BACKGROUND ON THE NATIONAL MORTGAGE SETTLEMENT

The National Mortgage Settlement is an outgrowth of state and federal regulatory investigations into the foreclosure practices of large mortgage servicers that were initiated in late 2010 and early 2011. As is described in detail in CRS Report R41491, *"Robo-Signing" and Other Alleged Documentation Problems in Judicial and Nonjudicial Foreclosure Processes*, by David H. Carpenter, in the fall of 2010, the sworn statements of employees from several large mortgage servicers raised concerns that the companies were systematically engaged in documentation and procedural improprieties, especially when handling mortgages in default. These alleged transgressions included signing affidavits without personal knowledge of the facts presented in the legal documents submitted to courts to support the right to foreclose; backdating mortgage documents to fabricate evidence to give the appearance of compliance with state foreclosure requirements; failing to adhere to notarization requirements for foreclosure-related documents filed with courts; losing mortgage paperwork; assessing excessive fees against borrowers; failing to properly account for borrower mortgage payments; and failing to properly consider borrowers for eligibility in mortgage modification and other loss mitigation programs. Concerns about these illicit acts provoked a number of state and federal regulators to initiate multiple investigations, enforcement actions, lawsuits, and legal settlement negotiations.

Of particular relevance to this report, all 50 state attorneys general, the attorney general for the District of Columbia, the Conference of State Bank Supervisors, the U.S. Department of Justice (DOJ), the U.S. Department of Housing and Urban Development (HUD), and the U.S. Department of the Treasury (Treasury) initiated an investigation into foreclosure-related state and federal law violations by the nation's top five mortgage servicers.[1] On February 8, 2012, these state and federal officials,[2] with the exception of Oklahoma's attorney general,[3] announced a "National Mortgage Settlement" of certain legal claims with these five institutions.[4] The settlement is to result in the servicers providing about $25 billion of relief, primarily to homeowners and individuals who recently lost their homes through foreclosure. In financial terms, it constitutes the second largest legal settlement ever reached by the attorneys general, behind only the settlement with tobacco companies in 1998.[5]

The agreements stipulate that, in exchange for a release of liability for legal claims[6] that otherwise could have been raised against the servicers by the participating regulators, these five mortgage companies will provide five distinct forms of relief.[7] Under the agreements, the mortgage companies shall

- comply with specified servicing standards going forward ("Servicing Standards" component); [8]
- provide various forms of mortgage-related consumer relief to current borrowers whose mortgages are owned and serviced by the five servicers ("Consumer Relief" component);[9]
- provide certain relief to servicemembers who may have been harmed by violations of the Servicemembers Civil Relief Act (SCRA) and to improve the servicing of soldiers' mortgages to prevent future SCRA violations ("SCRA" component);[10]
- provide compensation to certain individuals whose homes were previously foreclosed by the five servicers ("Borrower Payment" component); [11] and
- make direct payments to federal and state governments to cover the resolution of legal claims ("Direct Settlement Payment" component).[12]

Individual homeowners are not parties to the agreements, and the terms of the agreements do not provide individual borrowers a private right of action to enforce the agreements. Similarly, the settlement agreements do not, in any way, limit any enforcement power held by state or federal regulators that are not parties to the agreements, including the authorities of the federal banking regulators, the Office of the Comptroller of the Currency (OCC), the Board of Governors of the Federal Reserve System (Federal Reserve Board), and the Federal Deposit Insurance Corporation (FDIC).[13]

The National Mortgage Settlement is just one of several avenues by which mortgage servicers are being held accountable for alleged mortgage-related transgressions. Notably, beginning in the fourth quarter of 2010, the federal banking regulators[14] began on-site examinations of the foreclosure processes and governance protocols of the 14 largest U.S. mortgage servicers.[15] The regulators reviewed a sampling of mortgage files for which there were foreclosure actions pending during calendar years 2009 and 2010.[16] The examinations revealed "critical weaknesses in [the] servicers' foreclosure governance processes, foreclosure document preparation processes, and oversight and monitoring of third-party vendors, including foreclosure attorneys."[17] As a result of these findings, the banking regulators, in April 2011, entered into binding consent orders with all 14 mortgage servicers and several of the third-party service providers that the servicers used in various ways during foreclosure processes (hereinafter, the "Federal Banking Consent Orders").[18] Numerous aspects of the Federal Banking Consent Orders overlap with the terms of the National Mortgage Settlement.[19] Although the focus of this report is on the National Mortgage Settlement, at times, it will highlight the points of intersection with the Federal Banking Consent Orders.

The following is a synthesis of the substantive provisions of the National Mortgage Settlement's Servicing Standards, Consumer Relief, SCRA, Borrower Payment, and Direct Settlement Payment and an analysis of how compliance with these substantive provisions may be overseen and enforced.[20]

THE SERVICING STANDARDS AND CONSUMER RELIEF TERMS

The Servicing Standards and Consumer Relief components are discussed together because they have similar oversight and enforcement terms.

Overview of the Servicing Standards

The Servicing Standards of the agreements are designed to correct alleged servicing improprieties that prompted the National Mortgage Settlement. The agreements require the servicers to implement more than 300 specific Servicing Standards, including requirements that servicers: establish a single point of contact for each delinquent mortgage borrower; hire and maintain adequate levels of loss mitigation staff that meet minimum education, training, and experience standards; and maintain electronic documentation of servicing files and interactions with borrowers.[21] The Servicing Standards also require the servicers to take steps to ensure that they are adhering to the mortgage-related protections of the SCRA, which are discussed more fully below.[22] The Servicing Standards of the settlement generally only apply to the owner-occupied, single-family, residential mortgages that are serviced by the five mortgage companies.[23] Each of the servicers was required to have implemented all of the Servicing Standards by no later than October 2, 2012.[24]

Overview of the Consumer Relief Terms

The Consumer Relief component of the agreements is designed to help borrowers who are struggling to keep up with their mortgage payments and who are contending with a precarious housing market—circumstances that may have been caused in part, or exacerbated by, the alleged transgressions of the mortgage servicers. The Consumer Relief provisions of the agreements require the servicers to provide homeowners principal reductions and other types of mortgage modifications, short sales, refinancings, and similar mortgage-related relief.[25] The agreements require that each servicer provide minimum levels of Consumer Relief, referred to as the "Commitment Amount." The combined minimum Commitment Amount equals approximately $20 billion of relief. Servicers earn varying levels of credit towards the Commitment Amount for each type of relief provided based on a complex scoring system explained in Exhibit D-1 of the agreements.[26] The scoring system is structured to encourage servicers to deliver types of relief that are deemed most beneficial to consumers and to do so sooner rather than later.[27] For example, servicers generally will get $1.00 of credit for every $1.00 of principal forgiveness on first lien mortgages, but they will only receive $0.10 of credit for every $1.00 of waived deficiency claims against borrowers.[28] As a result, servicers likely will not get a dollar-for-dollar credit for the gross amount of relief provided.[29]

The Consumer Relief terms of the settlement generally only apply to the owner-occupied, single-family, residential mortgages that are *owned and serviced* by the five mortgage companies.[30] As a result, borrowers of mortgages that are serviced by one of the five servicers but that are owned or guaranteed by others, such as Fannie Mae or Freddie Mac, do not qualify for the settlement's Consumer Relief.

Oversight of the Servicing Standards and Consumer Relief Terms

The agreements establish an independent Monitor with the primary authority to conduct oversight of the servicers' compliance with the Servicing Standards and Consumer Relief terms.[31] Each servicer and the Monitor must agree on a Work Plan that details both how the servicers will implement the Servicing Standards and the Consumer Relief requirements, as well as how the

Monitor will evaluate the servicers' compliance with these aspects of the agreements.[32]

Exhibit E-1 of the settlement agreements outlines specific Metrics that the Monitor will use to measure compliance with the Servicing Standards. Exhibit E-1 also establishes a maximum permissible cushion of error, called a "Threshold Error Rate," associated with each Metric.[33] The Threshold Error Rates play an important role in the enforcement of the Servicing Standards and Consumer Relief provisions of agreements, which are discussed in the following section of this report. The terms of the agreements also allow the Monitor to impose additional Metrics and Threshold Error Rates beyond those provided in Exhibit E-1, under certain circumstances.[34]

The Consumer Relief requirements of the Work Plans generally detail how each servicer plans to satisfy its minimum Commitment Amount based on the credit scoring system provided in Exhibit D-1 of the agreements.

Each servicer is required to establish an Internal Review Group to conduct compliance reviews of its progress in implementing the Metrics and satisfying the Consumer Relief requirements, and to provide "general statistical data on Servicer's overall servicing performance."[35] Servicers must publish the findings of those reviews in quarterly Compliance Reports.[36] Individuals comprising the Internal Review Groups must be "independent from the line of business whose performance is being measured."[37]

The Monitor generally must be provided access to the Internal Review Groups' reports, consumer complaint documents, work papers, and other information held by the servicers to allow him to independently evaluate each servicer's compliance with the settlement terms and to verify the accuracy of the information provided in the Compliance Reports.[38] The Monitor may have the work of each Internal Review Group independently reviewed.[39] The Monitor also must generate regular reports on his oversight activities and the servicers' compliance. The Monitor Reports are to be filed with federal District Court for the District of Columbia (D.C. federal District Court) and distributed to the Servicers and the Monitoring Committee.[40] The Monitor expects to file the first Monitor Report during the second quarter of 2013.

To date, the Monitor has issued two reports designed to inform the public of the progress the servicers have made to implement the Servicing Standards and Consumer Relief components of the settlement.[41] These Progress Reports offer the raw data of Consumer Relief provided, as self-reported by the servicers, that the Monitor ultimately will audit and verify.[42]

Enforcement of the Servicing Standards and Consumer Relief Terms

Generally

A Monitoring Committee that is composed of representatives of the state and federal regulators that are parties to the agreements primarily are responsible for enforcing the Servicing Standards and Consumer Relief terms.[43] The state and federal parties, acting through the Monitoring Committee or individually, have the authority to enforce the Servicing Standards and Consumer Relief terms.[44] "Unless immediate action is necessary in order to prevent irreparable harm," one or more of the parties must provide advanced notice to the Monitoring Committee about the desire to initiate an enforcement action.[45] The Monitoring Committee has 21 days to determine whether or not to initiate the enforcement action.[46] If the Monitoring Committee decides to not initiate the action, the individual party (or parties) may bring the enforcement action no sooner than 21 days after the Committee's decision.[47]

The Monitor, the Monitoring Committee, and each servicer have the right to petition the D.C. federal District Court to settle disagreements over the enforcement and implementation of the agreements.[48]

Servicing Standards

If a quarterly Compliance Report shows that a servicer has exceeded a Threshold Error Rate for a particular Metric in its Work Plan, the servicer is considered to be in Potential Violation of the Servicing Standards of the agreement.[49] Upon the discovery of a Potential Violation of the settlement terms, the servicer has a chance to cure the Potential Violation by implementing a corrective action plan and getting back within the acceptable Threshold Error Rate.[50] The servicer generally has until the next quarterly Compliance Report to cure the Potential Violation.[51] The servicer also is responsible for providing remediation to individuals who are materially harmed by a Potential Violation.[52]

If a servicer fails to cure a Potential Violation, it may be subject to additional penalties. A servicer that violates the same Metric during the cure period or the quarter following the Potential Violation is considered to have committed an Uncured Violation.[53] In addition to providing remediation, servicers may be assessed court-ordered civil penalties of up to $1 million for each Uncured Violation and up to $5 million for subsequent violations of the same Metric.[54] Any such penalties generally will be distributed to reimburse the Monitoring Committee or the individual parties for the costs of raising the enforcement action and then to the states in accordance with the same formula for distribution of the states' Direct Settlement Payment pursuant to Exhibit B of the agreements, which is discussed below.[55]

Additionally, if the Monitor "reasonably conclude[s]," based on any facts or information received, that the servicer "may be engaged in a pattern of noncompliance with a material term of the Servicing Standards that is reasonably likely to cause harm to borrowers," the Monitor is required to investigate the veracity of the matter.[56] If the Monitor's initial conclusions are confirmed by the review, he may add new Metrics to the noncompliant servicer's Work Plan and may require the servicer to initiate a corrective action plan to rectify the problems.[57]

Consumer Relief

The agreements stipulate that the servicers must satisfy 75% of their Consumer Relief requirements within two years of the settlement start date (March 1, 2012) and 100% of the Consumer Relief requirements within three years of the settlement start date.[58] If a servicer fails to comply with both the two- and three-year targets, the servicer must pay a sum equal to 140% of the unmet Commitment Amount.[59] If a servicer meets the two-year target but fails to meet the three-year target, the servicer must pay an amount equal to 125% of the unmet Commitment Amount.[60] Half of any payments made for failure to satisfy the Consumer Relief requirements are to be made to the federal government, while the other half of the payments will go to the state parties and be distributed in accordance with the same formula that applies to the Direct Settlement Payment established by Exhibit B.[61]

THE SERVICEMEMBERS CIVIL RELIEF ACT TERMS

The SCRA, Generally

The Servicemembers Civil Relief Act (SCRA), enacted in 2003, is an expansion of a precursor, the Soldiers' and Sailors' Civil Relief Act of 1940. The SCRA provides protections from certain financial burdens incurred before individuals enter active military duty.[62] The SCRA is designed "to enable [servicemembers] to devote their entire energy to the defense needs of the Nation; and to provide for the temporary suspension of judicial and administrative proceedings and transactions that may adversely affect the civil rights of servicemembers during their military service."[63]

Sections 533, 521, and 527 of the SCRA provide mortgage-related protections. Section 533 restricts the ability of lenders to initiate foreclosures on properties acquired before active duty service without prior court approval during and one year after the homeowners' active duty service.[64] SCRA section 521 requires lenders, prior to securing an uncontested default judgment on a mortgage (or another debt), to file an affidavit with a court attesting to the fact that the debtor is not an active duty servicemember or that the lender was unable to confirm that the debtor was not an active duty servicemember.[65] Additionally, section 527 of the SCRA caps interest rates that may be assessed on mortgages (and other debts) incurred before active duty at 6%.[66] The SCRA is enforceable by the U.S. Attorney General,[67] as well as through private rights of action.[68]

Overview of the Settlement's SCRA Terms

The National Mortgage Settlement builds on the statutory protections of the SCRA by requiring each of the servicers to review its mortgage files to identify and provide financial compensation to any individual whose SCRA rights were violated over a specified period. Through the agreements, the five servicers also agreed to expand the class of individuals who are eligible for SCRA protections and to implement policies, procedures, and employee training programs to ensure SCRA-compliance in the future.[69]

The settlement agreements stipulate that the servicers must provide compensation to any servicemember who was subject to a completed foreclosure between January 1, 2006 and March 2012 in violation of the SCRA section 533[70] or section 521.[71] To accomplish this, the agreements require the servicers to hire an independent consultant to review all foreclosures that took place over the more than five-year span that are known to have involved a servicemember who was eligible for SCRA protections in order to verify SCRA compliance.[72] The independent consultant also must conduct a similar review of *a sampling of all* foreclosures initiated during that five-year period for SCRA compliance.[73] The servicers must provide compensation to any servicemember harmed by SCRA violations during that time.[74] The settlement's SCRA restitution requirements expand on what is required under the Federal Banking Consent Orders, which mandate a similar independent review of mortgage files that were subject to foreclosure actions in 2009 and 2010.[75]

The National Mortgage Settlement Agreements also require the servicers to provide compensation to mortgage borrowers harmed by violations of SCRA section 527's interest rate cap.[76] To find these individuals, the agreements call for an independent consultant to review either all or a sampling of all mortgage files from January 1, 2008 on in which a mortgage borrower requested rate cap relief under section 527.[77]

The financial relief that is to be provided for violations of sections 533, 521, and 527 is explicitly specified in the agreements.[78] For wrongful foreclosures in violation of either sections 533 or 521, each servicer is required to pay: (1) the higher of either $116,785 or an amount consistent with what is required to be paid for violations of section 533 or 521 under the Federal Banking Consent Orders; plus (2) an amount equal to the equity lost as a result of the wrongful foreclosure; plus (3) interest on the lost equity.[79] Under the settlement terms, the amount calculated in (1) will go exclusively to the relevant servicemember, while the amounts in (2) and (3) will be shared between the servicemember and any co-borrowers on the mortgage.[80]

For violations of SCRA section 527's rate cap, the servicers must pay: an amount equal to all charges in excess of the rate cap, plus interest on that amount; and (2) the higher of either $500 or three times the amount of refund calculated in (1).[81] The settlement agreements specify that the amount in (1) will be shared among the servicemember and all co-borrowers on the promissory note that secures the mortgage, while all amounts calculated in (2) will be paid exclusively to the servicemember.[82]

When calculating how much is owed under the settlement agreements for violations of sections 533, 521, and 527, the DOJ will take into account any relief provided pursuant to private SCRA litigation and the Federal Banking Consent Orders.[83] In other words, to the extent that a covered servicer provided payments to a borrower for violations of the mortgage-related SCRA provisions in compliance with the Federal Banking Consent Orders or any other action, that servicer generally will not have to pay the same servicemember the same financial compensation twice.[84] However, the servicer will be required to provide any additional compensation owed to the servicemember based on the terms of the settlement agreements that exceed that which previously was provided.

In addition to the financial relief, the National Mortgage Settlement agreements also require the servicers to take concrete steps to ensure their employees comply with the SCRA going forward[85] and to mandate that their employees take courses designed to teach them how to service mortgages owned by servicemembers.[86]

Oversight and Enforcement of the SCRA Terms

The DOJ holds the authority to oversee compliance with the National Mortgage Settlement's SCRA terms. The DOJ must approve of the independent consultants chosen to conduct the settlements' SCRA reviews, as well as their analytical methodologies.[87] The independent consultants also are required to provide the DOJ the data they use to conduct the reviews so that the DOJ may conduct its own analysis of compliance.[88] Based on the reviews of the independent consultants and on its own analysis, the DOJ will identify who has suffered violations of the SCRA.[89] The servicers will have 30 days to rebut the DOJ's conclusions.[90] The DOJ then will determine the level of compensation that must be provided to borrowers in accordance with the standards spelled out in the agreements, while also taking into account any relief already provided as a result of the Federal Banking Consent Orders or other measures. Servicers will have 10 days after the DOJ makes a final determination to petition for judicial review of the DOJ's conclusions.[91] The court generally may only review the record for "clearly erroneous factual determination[s]" made by the DOJ.[92] Upon finding a violation, servicers will be required to contact the three major credit bureaus (Experian, Equifax, and TransUnion) to ask that any negative information associated with the violation be removed from the servicemembers' and their co-borrowers' credit reports.[93] The agreements also require the servicers "to indemnify the servicemember and his or her co-borrower(s) against any third-party pursuing any deficiency that was remaining on the servicemember's SCRA-protected mortgage or junior lien after a foreclosure was completed in violation of the SCRA."[94]

The agreements place the onus on the servicers to contact borrowers using form letters (provided in Exhibits H-1 and H-2 of the agreements)[95] that are due financial relief for violations of the SCRA.[96] The servicers must maintain and provide the DOJ an accounting of all letters mailed, checks sent, and credit report changes requested.[97] The servicers must also submit quarterly reports to the DOJ that provide analysis of their compliance with the SCRA terms of the settlement agreements.[98]

In addition, the servicers must provide the DOJ with the company policies and procedures that they will put in place to ensure servicing compliance with the SCRA going forward, as well as any future changes to those policies and procedures, for the DOJ's approval.[99] Similarly, the DOJ must approve of proposed SCRA training programs.[100]

BORROWER PAYMENT TERMS

Overview of the Borrower Payment Terms

The settlement agreements require the five servicers to pay just under $1.5 billion to an interest bearing escrow account to be distributed by a Special Administrator to provide remedial relief to qualifying mortgage borrowers whose homes were foreclosed between January 1, 2008 and December 31, 2011 and, in the process, may have suffered harm as a result of the alleged misconduct detailed in the agreements.[101]

The Special Administrator charged with distributing the Borrower Payments was appointed by the state members of the Monitoring Committee.[102]

In order to receive a Borrower Payment, borrowers must submit a claim requesting such relief, but they do not need to prove that they were actually harmed.[103]

The Special Administrator mailed notices and claim forms to all individuals believed to be eligible for relief.[104] Individuals also could submit a claim form electronically through the National Mortgage Settlement's website.[105] Each qualified claimant is to receive a uniform payment, which will vary depending on how many claims are submitted.[106]

Oversight and Enforcement of the Borrower Payment Terms

The servicers are required to give the Special Administrator "all information ... reasonably necessary" to implement the Borrower Payment component of the agreements.[107]

The Special Administrator must issue a final report detailing which claimants received payment.[108] The servicers also may request interim reports from the Special Administrator to help ensure that specific borrowers are not receiving duplicative payments through other means, such as private litigation or regulatory enforcement actions.[109]

The state members of the monitoring committee may conduct on-site examinations of the Special Administrator to ensure compliance with the Borrower Payment component of the settlement agreements.[110]

DIRECT SETTLEMENT PAYMENT TO THE STATE AND FEDERAL PARTIES

Overview of the Direct Settlement Payment

The servicers' Direct Settlement Payment to both the state and federal parties is approximately $5 billion.[111] The payment is intended to cover the release of the state and federal legal claims that the parties could have raised against the servicers, as well as to resolve certain specific lawsuits previously initiated against some of the servicers named in the settlement.[112]

The payments to the federal government generally will be distributed to: the Federal Housing Administration's Capital Reserve Account; the Veteran Housing Benefit Program Fund, which is administered by the Department of Veterans Affairs; and the Rural Housing Service, which is administered by the Department of Agriculture.[113]

Each individual state is to receive a specific amount of the Direct Settlement Payment, as established in Exhibit B1.[114] Exhibit B of the settlement agreements provides the general parameters by which the states may use these funds. Exhibit B states that, "[t]o the extent practicable," the state's portion of Direct Settlement Payment "shall be used for purposes intended to avoid preventable foreclosures, to ameliorate the effects of the foreclosure crisis, to enhance law enforcement efforts to prevent and prosecute financial fraud, or unfair or deceptive acts or practices and to compensate the States for costs resulting from the alleged unlawful conduct of the [servicers]."[115]

Additionally, each state party negotiated state-specific parameters, provided for in Exhibit B2 of the agreements, that guide how the Direct Settlement Payment is to be allocated. The state-specific parameters vary widely in both specificity and flexibility.[116]

For example, the approximately $100 million allocated for the State of Georgia is to go to the state's general treasury fund, where it may be appropriated by the state's general assembly "for any purposes permitted under state law.... "[117] In contrast, the terms of Exhibit B2 detail specific allocations and the purposes of those allocations for North Carolina's portion of the Direct Payment Amount. Of the approximately $60 million allocated to North Carolina, $5.74 million will go to a civil penalty fund established under state law; $30.6 million will go to the North Carolina Housing Finance Agency for specified purposes; $6.69 million will go to Conference of District

Attorneys of the North Carolina Administrative Office of the Courts for certain specified purposes; $2.87 million will go to the state Bureau of Investigation to enhance its ability to investigation financial crimes; $4.78 million will go to the Consumer Protection Division of the state's Department of Justice for certain purposes; and $8.6 million will go to the state's general treasury fund "as compensation for costs and economic losses sustained by the State due to mortgage fraud and foreclosure misconduct."[118]

Oversight and Enforcement of the Direct Settlement Payment

The agreements do not explicitly establish a means of enforcing or overseeing the Direct Settlement Payment terms.[119] As a result, the agreements seem to leave oversight and enforcement of the Direct Settlement Payment terms to the political processes that typically apply to government spending at the federal level and within each of the 49 states and the District of Columbia.[120]

End Notes

[1] *50 States Sign Mortgage Foreclosure Joint Statement*, Nat'l Ass'n. of Attorneys Gen. Press Release, Oct. 13, 2010, available at http://www.naag.org/joint-statement-of-the-mortgage-foreclosure. The five largest U.S. mortgage servicers are Ally Financial, Inc. (formerly GMAC, Inc.); Bank of America, Corp.; Citigroup, Inc.; JP Morgan Chase & Co.; and Wells Fargo & Co. *Interagency Review of Foreclosure Policies and Practices*, Fed. Reserve Sys., Office of the Comptroller of the Currency, Office of Thrift Supervision, at 5, Apr. 2011, available at http://www.occ.gov/news-issuances/news-releases/2011/nr-occ-2011-47a.pdf.

[2] In addition to the parties listed above, the Bureau of Consumer Financial Protection and the Federal Trade Commission also signed as parties to the agreements, but only with respect to Exhibit F, which details the federal release of legal claims.

[3] The Oklahoma attorney general entered into a separate settlement agreement. *Oklahoma Mortgage Settlement Information*, Okla. Office of the Attorney Gen., available at http://www.oag.ok.gov/oagweb.nsf/mortgageinfo.html.

[4] Consent Judgments With Bank of America, *et al.*, available at http://www.nationalmortgage settlement.com/. The National Mortgage Settlement is just one of several distinct legal settlements and enforcement actions entered into/issued in response to alleged mortgage servicing misconduct.

[5] Executive Summary of Multistate/Federal Settlement of Foreclosure Misconduct Claims, July 23, 2012, available at https://d9klfgibkcquc.cloudfront.net/NMS_Executive_Summary-7-23-2012.pdf.

[6] The legal claims that are released generally arise out of traditional servicing activities such as: payment processing; engaging in loss mitigation activities; performing foreclosure actions;

escrow account administration; and maintaining and processing mortgages, promissory notes, assignments, and other legal documents. Importantly, legal claims arising out of securitization activities, criminal activities, and the actions of the Mortgage Electronic Registration Systems, Inc., a third-party service provider used by all five servicers, are not released by the agreements. Consent Judgments With Bank of America, *et al.*, at Exhibits F (release of federal claims) and G (release of state claims), available at http://www.nationalmortgagesettlement.com/. See also *Fact Sheet: Mortgage Servicing Settlement*, National Mortgage Settlement, at 4, available at https://d9klfgibkcquc.cloudfront.net/Mortgage_Servicing_Settlement_Fact_Sheet.pdf.

[7] Consent Judgments With Bank of America, *et al.*, at Exhibits F (release of federal claims) and G (release of state claims), available at http://www.nationalmortgagesettlement.com/. The servicers did not admit to any wrongdoing. *Id.* at 2.

[8] *Id.* at Exhibit A.

[9] *Id.* at Exhibit D.

[10] *Id.* at Exhibit H.

[11] *Id.* at Exhibit C.

[12] *Id.* at Exhibit B.

[13] *Id.* at Exhibit E.I.

[14] Each these servicers is organized as a depository institution that is primarily regulated by either the Office of the Comptroller of the Currency (OCC) or the Board of Governors of the Federal Reserve System (FRB). *Interagency Review of Foreclosure Policies and Practices*, Fed. Res. Sys., Off. of the Comptroller of the Currency, Off. of Thrift Supervision, Apr. 2011, available at http://www.occ.gov/news-issuances/news-releases/2011/nr-occ-2011-47a.pdf. Some of these institutions had been primarily regulated by the Office of Thrift Supervision (OTS) until the agency was recently eliminated in accordance with the Dodd-Frank Wall Street Reform and Consumer Protection Act (P.L. 111- 203). Both the OCC and the FRB have the duty to ensure that the depositories under their jurisdictions are being run in a safe and sound manner in all respects, including in their mortgage servicing activities. To reach this end, these federal banking regulators have the authority to conduct examinations of the institutions under their jurisdictions and have very strong and flexible enforcement powers to rectify any problems, practices, or governing controls found during the course of those examinations that may jeopardize the financial soundness of an institution. See, e.g., 12 U.S.C. § 1818.

[15] The 14 largest U.S. mortgage servicers, which service close to 70% of the total volume of mortgages in the country, are: "Ally Bank/GMAC, Aurora Bank, Bank of America, Citibank, EverBank, HSBC, JPMorgan Chase, MetLife, OneWest, PNC, Sovereign Bank, SunTrust, U.S. Bank, and Wells Fargo." *Interagency Review of Foreclosure Policies and Practices*, Fed. Res. Sys., Off. of the Comptroller of the Currency, Off. of Thrift Supervision, at 1, Apr. 2011, available at http://www.occ.gov/news-issuances/news-releases/2011/nr-occ-2011-47a.pdf.

[16] *Interagency Review of Foreclosure Policies and Practices*, Fed. Res. Sys., Off. of the Comptroller of the Currency, Off. of Thrift Supervision, Apr. 2011, available at http://www.occ.gov/news-issuances/news-releases/2011/nr-occ2011-47a.pdf.

[17] *Id.* at 2-3 (internal citations omitted).

[18] The third parties with which consent orders were entered included Mortgage Electronic Registration Systems, Inc. (MERS), DocX, LLC, and Lender Processing Services, Inc.

[19] *Interagency Review of Foreclosure Policies and Practices*, Fed. Res. Sys., Off. of the Comptroller of the Currency, Off. of Thrift Supervision, at 13, Apr. 2011, available at

http://www.occ.gov/news-issuances/news-releases/2011/nrocc-2011-47a.pdf. On January 7, 2013, the OCC and Federal Reserve Board announced that they had "reached an agreement in principal" with 10 of the 14 servicers to make significant changes to the April 2011 consent orders. *Independent Foreclosure Review to Provide $3.3 Billion in Payments, $5.2 Billion in Mortgage Assistance*, Joint Press Release, Fed. Res. Sys., Off. of the Comptroller of the Currency, Jan. 7, 2013, available at http://www.federal reserve.gov/newsevents/press/bcreg/20130107a.htm. More information about the agreements announced on January 7, 2013 is available at *Corrective Foreclosure Practices*, Off. of the Comptroller of the Currency, available at http://www.occ.gov /topics/consumer-protection/

[20] It should be noted that several states secured commitments from one or more of the servicers that provide state-specific relief on top of what is required by the National Mortgage Settlement. For example, California entered into separate agreements with the servicers that require the companies to provide a minimum amount of principal forgiveness for state borrowers or else pay the state up to $800 million. *Attorney General Kamala D. Harris Secures $18 Billion California Commitment for Struggling Homeowners*, State of California Dept. of Justice, Press Release, Feb. 9, 2012, available at http://oag.ca.gov/news/press-releases/attorney-general-kamala-d-harris-secures-18-billioncalifornia-commitment. These separate agreements generally are outside the scope of this report. For more information these side agreements, see Kevin Wack, *The State That Ate the National Mortgage Settlement*, American Banker, Dec. 27, 2012, available at http://www.american banker.com/countdown2013/news/california-the-state-that-ate-the-nationalmortgage-settlement-1055479-1.html.

[21] *Id.* at Exhibit A.

[22] *Id.* at Exhibit A.V.

[23] *Id.* at Exhibit A.IX.B. and Exhibit D.

[24] *Id.* at Exhibit E.A.

[25] *Id.* at Exhibit D.

[26] *First Take: Progress Report from the Monitor of the National Mortgage Settlement*, Office of Mortgage Settlement Oversight, at 4, Aug. 29, 2012, available at https://www.mortgage oversight ProgressReport08292012.pdf.

[27] Consent Judgments With Bank of America, *et al.*, at Exhibit D-1, available at http://www.nationalmortgagesettlement.com/.

[28] *Id.*

[29] *First Take: Progress Report from the Monitor of the National Mortgage Settlement*, Office of Mortgage Settlement Oversight, at 4, Aug. 29, 2012, available at https://www.mortgage oversight ProgressReport08292012.pdf.

[30] Consent Judgments With Bank of America, *et al.*, at Exhibit A.IX.B. and Exhibit D, available at http://www.nationalmortgagesettlement.com/.

[31] *Id.* at Exhibit E.C.5. Exhibit E also outlines how servicers must implement the agreements. Each servicer must establish timeline for the implementation of the settlement's Servicing Standards and Consumer Relief requirements, prioritized based on their complexity and importance to borrowers. *Id.* at Exhibit E.A. Servicers must make reasonable attempts to comply with these timelines, but may request extensions from the Monitor. *Id.*

[32] *Id.* at Exhibit E.C.11-15. The Monitoring Committee has the power to object to Work Plans. *Id.* If the parties cannot agree on a Work Plan, they may petition the federal District Court for the District of Columbia (D.C. federal District Court) to resolve their disputes *Id.* at Exhibit E.C.13. According to the Monitor, the Work Plans were "largely agreed to" as of

late September 2012. *Continued Progress: A Report from the Monitor of the National Mortgage Settlement*, Office of Mortgage Settlement Oversight, at 4, Nov. 19, 2012, available at https://www.mortgageoversight.com/wpcontent/uploads/2012/11/Continued-Progress_11.19.12.pdf.

[33] Consent Judgments With Bank of America, *et al.*, at Exhibit E.C.11, available at http://www.nationalmortgagesettlement.com/.

[34] *Id.* at Exhibit E.C.12.

[35] *Id.* at Exhibit E.D.1.

[36] *Id.*

[37] *Id.* at Exhibit E.C.7.

[38] *Id.* at Exhibit E.C.16-18.

[39] *Id.* at Exhibit E.C.23.

[40] *Id.* at Exhibit E.D.4.

[41] *Continued Progress: A Report from the Monitor of the National Mortgage Settlement*, Office of Mortgage Settlement Oversight, at 4, Nov. 19, 2012, available at https://www.mortgage oversight.com/wp-content/uploads/2012/11/Continued-Progress_ 11.19.12.pdf.; *First Take: Progress Report from the Monitor of the National Mortgage Settlement*, Office of Mortgage Settlement Oversight, at 4, Aug. 29, 2012, available at https://www.mortgageoversight.com /wpcontent /uploads/2012/08/Progress Report08292012.pdf.

[42] *Id.* For more information on the two Progress Reports, see CRS Report WSLG345, *More Than $26 Billion in Consumer Relief Reported Thus Far As Part of the National Mortgage Settlement*, by David H. Carpenter and CRS Report WSLG221, *$10.5 Billion in Consumer Relief Delivered Thus Far*, by David H. Carpenter.

[43] Consent Judgments With Bank of America, *et al.*, at IV.8. and Exhibit E, available at http://www.nationalmortgagesettlement.com/.

[44] *Id.* at Exhibit E.J.2.

[45] *Id.*

[46] *Id.*

[47] *Id.*

[48] *Id.* at Exhibit E.G. and Exhibit E.J.2.

[49] *Id.* at Exhibit E.E.

[50] *Id.* at Exhibit E.2-3.

[51] *Id.* at Exhibit E.E.3.

[52] *Id.* at Exhibit E.E.5.

[53] *Id.* at Exhibit E.4.

[54] *Id.* at Exhibit E.J.3. Servicers that commit Uncured Violations also may be required to provide non-monetary equitable relief, such as specific performance. *Id.*

[55] *Id.* at Exhibit E.J.3.(c). "In the event of a penalty based on a violation of a term of the Servicing Standards that is specifically related to conduct in bankruptcy, the penalty shall be allocated to the United States or as otherwise directed by the Director of the United States Trustee Program." *Id.* at Exhibit E.J.3.(c)2.

[56] *Id.* at Exhibit E.C.19.

[57] *Id.* at Exhibit E.C.23.

[58] *Id.* at Exhibit D.10.a-b.

[59] *Id.* at Exhibit D.10.d.

[60] *Id.*

[61] *Id.* at Exhibit E.J.3.(c)3.

[62] For an in-depth analysis, see CRS Report RL34575, *The Servicemembers Civil Relief Act (SCRA): An Explanation*, by R. Chuck Mason.
[63] 50 U.S.C. app. § 502.
[64] 50 U.S.C. app. § 533.
[65] 50 U.S.C. app. § 521.
[66] 50 U.S.C. app. § 527.
[67] 50 U.S.C. app. § 597.
[68] 50 U.S.C. app. § 597a.
[69] Consent Judgments With Bank of America, *et al.*, at Exhibit H and Exhibit A.V., available at http://www.nationalmortgagesettlement.com/.
[70] The federal government resolved SCRA section 533 claims against Bank of America through a consent order entered into prior to the National Mortgage Settlement agreements. United States v. BAC Home Loans Servicing, L.P. (C.D. Cal. 2011), available at http://www.justice.gov/crt/about/hce/documents/bacsettle.pdf. As a result, the National Mortgage Settlement agreement with Bank of America does not cover section 533 claims. However, claims arising under sections 533, 521, and 527 against the other four servicers, as well as claims arising under SCRA sections 521 and 527 against Bank of America are dealt with in the National Mortgage Settlement agreements.
[71] Consent Judgments With Bank of America, *et al.*, at Exhibit H.II.a., available at http://www.nationalmortgagesettlement.com/.
[72] *Id.*
[73] *Id.*
[74] *Id.*
[75] *Interagency Review of Foreclosure Policies and Practices*, Fed. Res. Sys., Off. of the Comptroller of the Currency, Off. of Thrift Supervision, at 3, Apr. 2011, available at http://www.occ.gov/news-issuances/news-releases/2011/nr-occ2011-47a.pdf. See, also, the text associated with notes 16-19 above. Each of the individual consent orders is available at http://www.occ.gov/topics/consumer-protection and rhttp://www.federalreserve.gov/news events/press/enforce ment/20110413a.htm. On January 7, 2013, the Federal Reserve Board and OCC announced that they had reached agreements with 10 of the 14 servicers through which the foreclosure reviews that were mandated by the April 2011 consent orders will be replaced by a remediation and borrower assistance framework. *Independent Foreclosure Review to Provide $3.3 Billion in Payments, $5.2 Billion in Mortgage Assistance*, Joint Press Release, Fed. Res. Sys., Off. of the Comptroller of the Currency, Jan. 7, 2013, available at http://www.federalreserve.gov /newsevents/press/bcreg/20130107a.htm. More information about the agreements announced on January 7, 2013 is available at *Corrective Foreclosure Practices*, Off. of the Comptroller of the Currency, available at http://www.occ.gov/topics/consumer-protection/foreclosure-prevention/correctingfore closure-practices.html.
[76] Consent Judgments With Bank of America, *et al.*, Exhibit H.II.b., available at http://www.nationalmortgagesettlement.com/.
[77] *Id.*
[78] In some instances what is to be provided pursuant to the terms of the settlement agreements exceeds potential compensation available under the ordinary provisions of the SCRA and the remediation requirements under the Federal Banking Consent Orders.
[79] Consent Judgments With Bank of America, *et al.*, Exhibit H.II.a., available at http://www.nationalmortgagesettlement.com/.
[80] *Id.*

[81] *Id.* at Exhibit H.II.b.

[82] *Id.*

[83] *Id.* at Exhibit H, notes 6 and 8.

[84] Any payment received under the National Mortgage Settlement "will not be offset by payments" made pursuant to the terms of the Federal Banking Consent Orders. *Financial Remediation Framework Frequently Asked Questions*, Fed. Res. Sys. and Off. of the Comptroller of the Currency, at 11, June 21, 2012 (Updated Nov. 20, 2012), available at http://www.federalreserve.gov/newsevents/press/bcreg/bcreg20120621b1.pdf.

[85] Consent Judgments With Bank of America, *et al.*, Exhibit H.III and Exhibit A.V., available at http://www.nationalmortgagesettlement.com/.

[86] *Id.* at Exhibit H.IV.

[87] *Id.* at Exhibit H.II.a-b.

[88] *Id.*

[89] *Id.*

[90] *Id.*

[91] *Id.* at Exhibit H.II.d.

[92] *Id.*

[93] *Id.* at Exhibit H.II.c.

[94] *Id.*

[95] *Id.* at Exhibit H-1 and Exhibit H-2.

[96] *Id.* at Exhibit H.II.a-b.

[97] *Id.*

[98] *Id.* at Exhibit H.III.b.

[99] *Id.* at Exhibit H.III.

[100] *Id* at Exhibit H.IV.

[101] *Id.* at III.4., Exhibit B.2.a., and Exhibit C.

[102] *Id.* at Exhibit C.2.

[103] *Id.* at Exhibit B.2.a.

[104] See *Payment to borrowers who lost their homes to foreclosure*, available at http://www. nationalmortagesettlement.com.

[105] National Mortgage Settlement Claim Filing Site, available at https://national mortgagesettlementclaim.com/.

[106] Executive Summary of Multistate/Federal Settlement of Foreclosure Misconduct Claims, July 23, 2012, available at https://d9klfgibkcquc.cloudfront.net/NMS_Executive_Summary-7-23-2012.pdf.

[107] Consent Judgments With Bank of America, *et al.*, at Exhibit C.3., available at http://www.nationalmortgagesettlement.com/.

[108] *Id.*

[109] *Id.* The Special Administrator must only issue those interim reports that the state members of the Monitoring Committee "deem[] reasonable." *Id.*

[110] *Id.* at Exhibit C.4.

[111] *Id.* at Exhibit B. See also Executive Summary of Multistate/Federal Settlement of Foreclosure Misconduct Claims, July 23, 2012, available at https://d9klfgibkcquc.cloudfront.net/NMS_Executive_Summary-7-23-2012.pdf.

[112] Consent Judgments With Bank of America, *et al.*, at Exhibit B, available at http://www. nationalmortgagesettlement.com/.

[113] *Id.* at Exhibit B.1.a.

[114] *Id.* at Exhibit B1.

[115] *Id.* at Exhibit B.1.b. The maximum of 10% of the states' Direct Settlement Payment "may be designated as a civil penalty, fine, or similar payment." *Id.*

[116] *Id.* at Exhibit B2.

[117] *Id.*

[118] *Id.*

[119] *Id.* at Exhibit B and Exhibit C.

[120] The Oklahoma attorney general entered into a separate settlement agreement. *Oklahoma Mortgage Settlement Information*, Okla. Office of the Attorney Gen., available at http://www.oag.ok.gov/oagweb.nsf/mortgageinfo.html.

In: Law and Legal Issues in the United States ISBN: 978-1-63117-827-6
Editor: Laurent B. Landers

Chapter 2

PUBLIC CHARGE GROUNDS OF INADMISSIBILITY AND DEPORTABILITY: LEGAL OVERVIEW*

Kate M. Manuel

SUMMARY

The Immigration and Nationality Act (INA) has long provided for aliens' exclusion and deportation from the United States on "public charge" grounds. Under current law, aliens outside the United States who seek to obtain visas at U.S. consulates overseas, or admission at U.S. ports of entry, are generally denied entry if they are deemed "likely at any time to become a public charge." Aliens within the United States who seek to adjust their status to that of lawful permanent resident (LPR), or who entered the United States without inspection, are also generally subject to this ground of inadmissibility. Similarly, LPRs and other aliens who have been admitted to the United States are removable if they become a public charge within five years after the date of their entry due to causes that pre-existed their entry. These public charge grounds have recently been of interest because of concerns, among some Members of Congress and the public, regarding noncitizens' receipt of public assistance.

---

* This is an edited, reformatted and augmented version of Congressional Research Service Publication, No. R43220, dated September 9, 2013.

The INA does not expressly define what it means for an alien to be a public charge, and, prior to 1996, there was no statutory guidance on what was to be considered in determining whether an alien is inadmissible or deportable (removable) on public charge grounds. Then, in 1996, the INA was amended to require that certain factors be taken into account when determining whether aliens are inadmissible on public charge grounds, including the alien's age, health, family status, financial resources, education, and skills. There still is no similar guidance on the public charge ground of deportability.

Given this general lack of statutory guidance, the executive and judicial branches initially construed the meaning of *public charge* in adjudicating cases involving individual aliens. In so doing, administrative authorities interpreted *public charge* differently for purposes of the grounds of inadmissibility than for the grounds of deportability. Specifically, *public charge* was construed broadly in the context of admissibility, with determinations based on a "totality of the circumstances" test that considered factors like those codified in the INA in 1996. In contrast, in the context of deportability, "public charge" was construed more narrowly. Aliens could only be found to be deportable on public charge grounds if (1) they received government assistance that they were legally obligated to repay, (2) the government entity providing the assistance demanded repayment, and (3) the alien or the alien's sponsor was unable to pay.

Following the enactment of the Personal Responsibility and Work Opportunity Reconciliation Act (PRWORA) of 1996, executive agencies issued guidance regarding the public charge grounds. While PRWORA generally restricts noncitizens' eligibility for "public benefits," it permits them to receive specified benefits, and its enactment raised questions about whether aliens who receive benefits for which they are eligible under PRWORA could potentially be removable on public charge grounds. Immigration officials addressed these questions in a 1999 policy letter that defined *public charge*, and identified which benefits are considered in public charge determinations. This policy letter underlies current regulations and other guidance on the public charge grounds of inadmissibility and deportability.

Collectively, the various sources addressing the meaning of *public charge* suggest that an alien's receipt of public benefits, per se, is unlikely to result in the alien being deemed removable on public charge grounds. Neither the INA nor implementing regulations address the role that receipt of public benefits plays in public charge determinations. Other agency guidance and court decisions indicate that, while receipt of certain public benefits could be considered in public charge determinations, other factors are also considered (e.g., age, obligation to repay).

INTRODUCTION

Congress has long sought to ensure that aliens immigrating to the United States are able to support themselves. The country's first general immigration law, enacted in 1882, excluded aliens who were deemed "likely to become a public charge" after they came to the United States.[1] A little over 20 years later, in 1903, Congress made aliens who had migrated to the United States deportable if they became public charges within two years after entry (subsequently increased to five years).[2] Both provisions have been modified somewhat over the years, but remain part of the Immigration and Nationality Act (INA). Congress has also enacted other provisions designed to promote the "national policy" that "aliens within the Nation's borders not depend on public resources to meet their needs, but rather rely on their own capabilities and the resources of their families, their sponsors, and private organizations."[3] Key among these is the Personal Responsibility and Work Opportunity Reconciliation Act (PRWORA) of 1996, which generally restricts noncitizens' eligibility for public benefits.[4] The public charge grounds of inadmissibility and deportability have recently been of interest because of concerns, among some Members of Congress and the public, regarding noncitizens' receipt of public assistance.[5]

This report provides an overview of the public charge grounds of inadmissibility and deportability. In particular, it describes the statutory basis for the public charge grounds; seminal administrative and judicial decisions construing the meaning of *public charge*; and regulations and other guidance promulgated by executive agencies after the enactment of PRWORA to address questions about whether aliens who receive public benefits that they are permitted to receive under PRWORA could potentially be subject to removal on public charge grounds. The report concludes by discussing why an alien's previous or present receipt of public benefits, in itself, would generally not suffice to result in the alien being found to be removable under current law.

THE IMMIGRATION AND NATIONALITY ACT

Since 1903, the INA has contained two separate provisions addressing the public charge grounds. One provision, currently in Section 212 of the INA, addresses the public charge grounds of *inadmissibility* (formerly, excludability), and specifies that "[a]ny alien who ... is likely at any time to become a public charge is inadmissible."[6] This provision generally applies to

- aliens seeking to obtain visas or admission at ports of entry;
- aliens within the United States who seek to adjust their status to that of lawful permanent resident (LPR); and
- aliens who entered the United States without inspection.[7]

If such aliens are found to be inadmissible on public charge grounds, they are, respectively, barred from entering the United States, denied adjustment of status, or subject to removal from the country.

Another provision, currently in Section 237 of the INA, addresses the public charge ground of *deportability*, and specifies that "[a]ny alien who, within five years after the date of entry, has become a public charge from causes not affirmatively shown to have arisen since entry is deportable."[8] This provision applies to LPRs and other aliens admitted to the United States.[9]

However, while the INA provides that an alien may be inadmissible or deportable on public charge grounds, it does not define what it means for an alien to be a public charge. Such determinations were historically made using certain tests developed by the case law, discussed below. Then, in 1996, Congress amended the INA provisions regarding the public charge ground of *inadmissibility* to require that consular and immigration officers take certain factors "into account" when determining whether aliens are inadmissible or ineligible for adjustment of status on public charge grounds.[10] These factors include, "at a minimum," the alien's age; health; family status; assets, resources, and financial status; and education and skills.[11] In addition, the 1996 amendments also authorize consular and immigration officers to consider any affidavit of support furnished on behalf of an alien,[12] and provide that certain family-sponsored and employment-based immigrants are inadmissible if they do not have the requisite affidavit of support.[13]

No similar amendments have been made as to the public charge ground of *deportability*, which is still assessed based upon a three-part test developed by the case law, discussed below. It is important to note, however, that *public charge* has been construed more narrowly for purposes of the grounds of deportability than it has been construed for purposes of the grounds of inadmissibility, in part, due to the differences between deportation and exclusion. Because the "deportation statute dislodges an established residence" in the United States, it "must be strictly construed." The same is not true with the INA's provisions regarding inadmissibility.[14]

EARLY ADMINISTRATIVE AND JUDICIAL DECISIONS

Given this general lack of statutory guidance, the executive and judicial branches initially construed the term *public charge* in adjudicating cases involving individual aliens. Immigration officers would consider certain factors in determining whether particular aliens were inadmissible or deportable on public charge grounds. If the alien appealed, the determinations of these officers were subject to review by the Board of Immigration Appeals (BIA or Board), the highest administrative body for interpreting and applying immigration law. Then, if appealed, the BIA's decisions were subject to review by the federal courts. Numerous decisions, dating back to at least 1903, address the applicability of the public charge grounds to particular aliens.[15] However, two BIA decisions, in particular, helped establish what it means for an alien to be a public charge.

First, in its 1948 decision in *Matter of B—*, the BIA established the prevailing test for determining whether an alien is *deportable* on public charge grounds.[16] There, a majority of the Board granted the INS's motion to withdraw the order and warrant of deportation and dismiss removal proceedings against an alien who had been committed by the courts to a state hospital.[17] In so doing, the BIA articulated a three-part test for determining whether an alien is deportable on public charge grounds that, it said, had been "implicit" in prior judicial decisions and "applied administratively over a long period of time."[18] For an alien to be deportable as a public charge under this test,

1) The State or other governing body must, by appropriate law, impose a charge for the services rendered to the alien. ...
2) The authorities must make demand for payment of the charges upon those persons made liable under State law.
3) [T]here must be a failure to pay for the charges.[19]

Applying this test to the alien in question, the BIA found that the alien could not be deemed a public charge because the Illinois statute governing commitment at the state hospital provided that hospital residents were entitled to receive free maintenance, care, and treatment.[20] Residents were only legally liable for their clothing, transportation, and other incidental expenses, which the record "clearly show[ed]" that the alien's sister had paid.[21] In its decision, the Board also emphasized that "[t]he fact that the State or municipality pays for the services accepted by the alien is not, ... by itself, the test of whether the alien has become a public charge."[22]

Subsequently, in its 1974 decision in *Matter of Harutunian*, the BIA reaffirmed that a "totality of the circumstances" test—as opposed to the three-part test of *Matter of B—* applies in determining when an alien is *inadmissible* on public charge grounds.[23] In *Harutunian*, the Board affirmed immigration officials' determination that a 70-year-old alien who had relied on state "old-age assistance benefits" for support was ineligible for adjustment of status on public charge grounds.[24] The alien had sought to overturn this decision by citing the precedent of *Matter of B—*, since California did not require repayment of old-age assistance benefits of the type the alien received.[25] The BIA rejected this argument, primarily because it construed *public charge* as having a different meaning in Section 212 of the INA than it does in Section 237.[26] In support of this conclusion, the Board first noted the differences between deportation and exclusion, particularly that deportation "dislodges an established residence" in the United States, while aliens outside the United States generally have no constitutional right to enter the country.[27] Thus, the Board concluded that the grounds of deportability must be more "strictly construed" than the grounds of inadmissibility.[28] The Board also noted that the legislative history of the public charge ground of inadmissibility supported the view that Congress intended "elements" such as age, financial status, and family support be considered in determining whether an alien is a public charge.[29] The Board further emphasized that administrative authorities had historically taken the view that the alien's physical and mental condition, as well as economic circumstances, was to be considered in determining whether the alien is inadmissible on public charge grounds.[30] In addition, the BIA viewed the three-part test of *Matter of B—* as inappropriate in determining inadmissibility, since the public charge ground of inadmissibility is concerned with whether the alien is "likely to become a public charge at some time in the future, a prediction which necessarily precludes the element of reimbursement."[31]

Applying this "totality of the circumstances" test to the alien in question, the BIA found in *Harutunian* that immigration officials had properly determined that the alien was ineligible for adjustment of status on public charge grounds. The alien had been on welfare since her arrival in the United States, and was receiving such assistance at the time she applied for adjustment of status.[32] In addition, the alien was aged, unskilled, uneducated, and without family or other support.[33] In light of these circumstances, the Board concluded that the alien could be deemed a public charge, "even though the state from which she will receive old age assistance may not permit reimbursement."[34]

PRWORA AND RESULTING GUIDANCE

The enactment of the Personal Responsibility and Work Opportunity Reconciliation Act (PRWORA) of 1996 prompted the then Immigration and Naturalization Service (INS) to issue guidance defining *public charge* and describing the application of the public charge grounds.[35] PRWORA is best known for generally barring noncitizens who are not "qualifying aliens" from receiving federal, state, and local "public benefits," and significantly restricting the receipt of "federal means-tested public benefits" by "qualified aliens." However, even with these restrictions, noncitizens may receive certain public benefits under PRWORA. For example, PRWORA expressly exempts specified benefits—including emergency medical assistance and certain disaster relief—from its general prohibition upon the provision of federal, state, and local public benefits to aliens who are not qualified aliens.[36] PRWORA also exempts specified categories of "qualified aliens"—including refugees, asylees, and certain victims of domestic violence—from the five-year bar upon their receipt of federal means-tested public benefits.[37] Because PRWORA permits noncitizens to receive some public benefits, aliens and commentators raised questions about whether aliens who took advantage of such benefits could potentially be found to be removable as a result of doing so.[38] In 1999, the INS responded to these questions by proposing regulations and issuing a field guide defining *public charge*, and describing how immigration officials viewed receipt of public benefits when making public charge determinations.[39]

The proposed regulations would have defined *public charge*, for purposes of both the grounds of inadmissibility and the grounds of deportability, to mean the following:

> an alien who has become primarily dependent on the Government for subsistence as demonstrated by either: (i) [t]he receipt of public cash assistance for income maintenance purposes, or (ii) [i]nstitutionalization for long-term care at Government expense (other than imprisonment for conviction of a crime).[40]

Government would have referred to any federal, state, or local entity.[41] Public cash assistance for income maintenance, in turn, would have been defined to include, but not be limited to, Supplemental Security Income (SSI) and, with certain exceptions, Temporary Assistance for Needy Families (TANF).[42] Forms of cash benefits "not intended for income maintenance" would have been expressly excluded from consideration in public charge determinations (e.g., the Low Income Home Energy Assistance Program (LIHEAP), Child Care and Development Block Grant Program (CCDBGP), food stamp benefits issued in cash).[43] Cash benefits that had been "earned" would also have been excluded, including benefits under Title II of the Social Security Act, government pension benefits, and veteran's benefits.[44]

The proposed regulation would also have spelled out the role that receipt of public cash assistance for income maintenance plays in determining whether an alien is inadmissible or deportable on public charge grounds. As to inadmissibility, the rule would have noted that Section 212 of the INA requires consular and immigration officers to consider, "'at a minimum, [the alien's] age, health, family status, assets, resources, financial status, education, and skills in making a decision on whether [the alien is] likely to become a public charge.'"[45] It would also have noted that public charge determinations are based on the "totality of the circumstances," and that "[n]o single factor," other than the lack of any required affidavit of support, is controlling, including past or current receipt of public cash assistance.[46] As to deportability, the rule would have specified that aliens are generally not deportable on public charge grounds unless the INS shows that

1) the government entity that provided, or is providing, public cash assistance for income maintenance, or the costs of institutionalization for long-term care, has a legal right to seek repayment of those benefits;
2) that entity demanded repayment of the benefit within five years of the alien's entry to the United States;
3) the alien or any other party obligated to repay the benefit failed to do so;
4) there is a final administrative or court judgment requiring the alien or another party to repay the benefit; and
5) the benefit-granting agency, or other applicable government entity, has taken "all actions necessary to enforce the judgment," including "all collections actions."[47]

The INS never finalized these regulations.[48] However, at the same time it issued the proposed regulations, the INS also issued a field guide on inadmissibility and deportability on public charge grounds that incorporated the definition of *public charge* and other guidance provided in the proposed regulations.[49] Commonly referred to as the "Pearson memorandum," after its author, this field guidance is still cited as an authoritative source on the public charge grounds of inadmissibility and deportability,[50] and similar guidance appears in other sources, most notably the State Department's *Foreign Affairs Manual*, discussed below.

CURRENT REGULATIONS AND OTHER GUIDANCE

The public charge grounds are currently discussed in the regulations of both the Departments of Homeland Security (DHS) and State (DOS), as well as in DOS's *Foreign Affairs Manual*. The DOS regulations address only the grounds of inadmissibility, since consular officers are responsible for the issuance of visas to aliens outside the United States, but play no role in determining whether aliens within the United States are deportable. DHS officials, in contrast, determine whether aliens arriving at U.S. ports of entry are to be admitted; whether applications for adjustment of status are to be granted; and whether aliens within the United States are to be removed. Thus, the DHS regulations address both inadmissibility and deportability.

DHS Regulations and Guidance

The INS never finalized the proposed regulations regarding the public charge grounds, discussed above, and DHS has not proposed or promulgated similar regulations. Instead, the INS and, later, DHS promulgated specific regulations regarding the "special rules" used in determining whether certain applicants for adjustment of status are public charges. For example, DHS regulations currently provide that "special agricultural workers" who meet certain requirements are subject to the public charge grounds, but may not be excluded if they have a "consistent employment history" which shows the aliens' ability to support themselves and their families.[51] The regulations further provide that "[p]ast acceptance of public cash assistance within a history of consistent employment will enter into" public charge determinations for special agricultural workers, with "the length of time an applicant has received [such] assistance" being viewed as a "significant factor."[52] However, the weight given to the acceptance of public cash assistance is expressly said to "depend on many factors,"[53] and the overall analysis is "prospective in that [immigration officials] shall determine, based on the applicant's history, whether he or she is likely to become a public charge."[54] In other words, pursuant to these regulations, *prior* receipt of public cash assistance would not necessarily result in an alien being found ineligible for adjustment of status if other factors suggest that the alien is unlikely to become a public charge *in the future*. There are similar "special rules" for other aliens seeking adjustment of status.[55]

DHS regulations are currently silent as to the public charge grounds of deportability.

The Pearson memorandum apparently still guides DHS's consideration of public charge determinations. The U.S. Citizenship and Immigration Service's (USCIS's) 2011 "fact sheet" on the public charge grounds, for example, defines *public charge* in the same way as the Pearson memorandum and expressly references the memorandum.[56]

State Department Regulations and Guidance

The current DOS regulations, in contrast, address the public charge grounds of inadmissibility more broadly than the DHS regulations do. The DOS regulations emphasize the role that the alien's "circumstances" play in determining whether an alien is inadmissible, in part, by specifying that

> [a]ny determination that an alien is ineligible [on public charge] grounds must be predicated upon circumstances indicating that, notwithstanding any affidavit of support that may have been filed on the alien's behalf, the alien is likely to become a public charge after admission, or, if applicable, that the alien has failed to fulfill the affidavit of support requirement.[57]

Consular officers are expressly authorized to issue visas to aliens subject to the affidavit of support requirement, noted above, who "giv[e] ... a bond or undertaking in accordance with INA 213 and INA 221(g)," provided that the officer is satisfied that the giving of such bond or undertaking removes the likelihood that the alien will become a public charge, and the alien is otherwise eligible for a visa.[58] However, consular officers are also required to presume that aliens not subject to the affidavit of support requirement who are relying solely on personal income to establish that they are not likely to become a public charge are ineligible for a visa if they do not demonstrate "an annual income above the federal poverty line," and are without "other adequate financial resources."[59]

The DOS guidance in the *Foreign Affairs Manual* (FAM) largely parallels that in the 1999 INS proposed regulations and the Pearson memorandum.[60] However, the FAM expressly characterizes the types of public cash assistance for income maintenance considered in public charge determinations as "means tested benefits."[61] The FAM also defines *institutionalization for longterm care*, which is not defined in the Pearson memorandum, as "care for an indefinite period of time for mental or other health reasons, rather than temporary rehabilitative or recuperative care even if such rehabilitation or recuperation may last weeks or months."[62] Overall, though, like the Pearson memorandum, the FAM emphasizes that public charge determinations are to be made based upon the "totality of the circumstances," considering the factors specified in the INA (e.g., age, health), as well as "any other factors thought relevant by an officer in a specific case."[63] Past or current receipt of cash benefits for income maintenance or institutionalization at public expense "may be factored into" the determination when it constituted the alien's primary means of subsistence. However, under the FAM, "[a] finding of inadmissibility [on public charge grounds] cannot be based solely on the prior receipt of public benefits," or on institutionalization at public expense.[64]

PUBLIC BENEFITS AND THE PUBLIC CHARGE GROUNDS

Collectively, the various sources addressing the meaning of *public charge* suggest that an alien's receipt of public benefits, per se, is unlikely to result in the alien being deemed removable on public charge grounds. As previously noted, the INA does not define *public charge*, or link the public charge grounds of inadmissibility and deportability with the receipt of public benefits. DHS and DOS regulations are also silent as to the definition of *public charge* and the role that receipt of public benefits may play in public charge determinations. Other guidance from DHS and DOS does link the INA's public charge grounds with public benefits, in part, by defining public charge in such a way as potentially to encompass aliens who receive certain public benefits (i.e., SSI; certain TANF assistance; state and local cash assistance for income maintenance). However, this guidance also indicates that prior or current receipt of public benefits, in itself, would generally not suffice for an alien to be found removable on public charge grounds. This guidance emphasizes that determinations as to *admissibility* involve projections regarding whether the alien is "likely to become a public charge" in the future that are based on the totality of the circumstances. This includes, but is not limited to, prior receipt of benefits. The guidance similarly emphasizes that determinations as to *deportability* are made by applying a three-part test, previously discussed, which considers whether payment for any government-provided assistance was legally required, was demanded, and could be made.

The case law interpreting and applying the public charge grounds also suggests that receipt of certain public benefits could potentially result in a determination that an alien is inadmissible or deportable on public charge grounds, if certain other conditions are met.[65] However, these cases also illustrate that prior receipt of public benefits, in itself, would not necessarily result in a determination that an alien is a public charge. For example, in *Matter of A—*, the BIA sustained an alien's appeal of a decision finding her ineligible for adjustment of status on public charge grounds. The INS district director had determined that the alien was ineligible because the alien's family had received "public cash assistance" for nearly four years, and neither the alien nor her spouse had worked for four years prior to filing the application for adjustment of status. The district director thus viewed the alien as "unable to support herself and her family without public assistance."[66] The Board, however, disagreed, noting that the alien was "young" and had no "physical or mental defect which might affect her earning capacity."[67] It also noted that the alien had recently begun working, and that during the time when she was absent from the workforce, she had been caring for her children.[68]

Likewise, in *Matter of T—*, the BIA sustained the appeal of a mother and child who had been excluded on public charge grounds after their husband/father was excluded for having committed a crime involving moral turpitude.[69] The mother and son sought permanent residence in the United States independent of the father, but were denied. In reversing this denial, the BIA noted that the mother was "quite capable of earning her own livelihood independent of her husband," and that the child had training in a field which represented "a wide field of employment for this country."[70] Prior or current receipt of public benefits was not at issue in this case. However, the Board's focus on the aliens' ability to earn a living, even without the contributions of the husband/father, is illustrative, and recurs in cases where aliens did receive public benefits (e.g., "welfare services," food stamps, "public assistance," Aid to Families with Dependent Children (AFDC), Medi-Cal).[71]

Similar conclusions have been reached in the cases construing and applying the public charge grounds of deportability. As *Matter of B—* illustrates, receipt of public assistance is merely one factor in determining deportability. There must also be (1) a legal obligation to repay that assistance; (2) a demand for repayment; and (3) a failure to repay the assistance. Where there is no legal obligation to repay the assistance, the alien cannot be found deportable on public charge grounds. This was the case in *Matter of B—*, where Illinois law provided that residents at the state hospital were entitled to receive free maintenance, care, and treatment.[72] In other cases, the government authorities did not request repayment,[73] or the alien (or another responsible party) had the ability to pay. Thus, in *Matter of P—*, the BIA terminated removal proceedings against an alien, in part, because no demand for payment was made upon the alien or his relatives, and "it appears that the respondent had property" which could have been used for making payment had payment been demanded.[74] The situation was the same in *Matter of C—*, because no demand for repayment of the assistance provided was made by the state within five years of the alien's last entry, and her husband had "some ability to pay."[75] It should also be noted that, in making determinations regarding aliens' deportability on public charge grounds, only causes that pre-date their entry are considered.[76] Causes which the alien can "affirmatively show" developed subsequent to entry do not factor into public charge determinations.[77]

CONCLUSION

Congressional interest in the public charge grounds of inadmissibility and deportability seems likely to persist, in part, because of the interplay between the provisions of the INA providing for aliens' removability on public charge grounds and other provisions of immigration law that permit noncitizens to receive certain benefits. On the one hand, Congress has provided that aliens may be excluded or deported if they are likely to become, or have become, *public charges*, which the executive branch has construed to mean that they are primarily dependent on the government for subsistence. On the other hand, Congress has also provided that certain public benefits (e.g., certain disaster relief) are exempt from PRWORA's restrictions upon the provision of federal, state, or local public benefits to aliens who are not qualified aliens. These two provisions are arguably reconcilable, especially if one focuses upon whether specific programs "count" as public benefits, or for purposes of public charge determinations. However, the overall picture can raise questions about how and why noncitizens may receive benefits without being subject to removal.

Relatedly, the 113th Congress is considering various proposals regarding the public charge grounds. The comprehensive immigration reform measure passed by the Senate (S. 744) would generally exempt aliens adjusting to registered provisional immigrant (RPI) status from the public charge ground of inadmissibility.[78] Other legislative proposals, in contrast, have sought to strengthen the public charge grounds of inadmissibility and deportability.[79]

End Notes

[1] Act of Aug. 3, 1882, 22 Stat. 58.

[2] Act of Mar. 3, 1903, 32 Stat. 1213.

[3] 8 U.S.C. §1601(2)(A).

[4] P.L. 104-193, tit. IV, §§401-435, 110 Stat. 2261-2276 (Aug. 22, 1996) (generally codified, as amended, in 8 U.S.C. §§1601-1646). PRWORA did not amend the INA, so citations to it reference only Title 8 of the *United States Code*.

[5] *See, e.g.*, Sessions To Vilsack: More Detail Needed On Food Stamp Partnership With Mexico; Controversial Promotions Must Cease, Oct. 10, 2012, *available at* http://www.budget.senate.gov/republican/public/index.cfm/pressreleases?ID=7e6dbe72-c2f9-431c-bea7-1a2ac7d8798f.

[6] INA §212(a)(4), 8 U.S.C. §1182(a)(4). The INA lists the grounds of inadmissibility separately from the grounds of deportability. *See* INA §212, 8 U.S.C. §1182 (inadmissibility); INA §237, 8 U.S.C. §1227 (deportability). The different grounds apply to different categories of aliens, as noted in the text. However, removal proceedings apply to all aliens, regardless of whether they are subject to the grounds of inadmissibility or deportability. INA §240, 8 U.S.C. §1229a.

[7] Certain aliens are, however, not subject to the public charge grounds when seeking admission or adjustment of status, including refugees and asylees seeking admission or adjustment to LPR status; Amerasian immigrants seeking admission pursuant to the Foreign Operations, Export Financing, and Related Programs Appropriations Act of 1988; Cuban and Haitian entrants seeking admission or adjustment of status as described in the Immigration Reform and Control Act; Nicaraguans and other Central Americans adjusting status as described in the Nicaraguan Adjustment and Central American Relief Act; Haitians adjusting status as described in the Haitian Refugee Immigration Fairness Act of 1998; aliens who entered the United States prior to January 1, 1972, and who meet other conditions for being granted LPR status under Section 249 of the INA; and Syrian asylees adjusting status pursuant to P.L. 106-378. *See* INA §207(c)(3), 8 U.S.C. §1157(c)(3) (asylees and refugees); *id.* §209(c), 8 U.S.C. 1159(c) (same); P.L. 100-202, §584(a)(2), 101 Stat. 1329-183 (Dec. 22, 1987) (Amerasian immigrants); P.L. 99-603, §202(a)(2), 100 Stat. 3404 (Nov. 6, 1986) (Cuban and Haitian entrants); P.L. 105-100, §202(a)(1)(B), 111 Stat. 2193 (Nov. 19, 1997) (Nicaraguans and other Central Americans); P.L. 105-277, §902(a)(1)(B), 112 Stat. 2681-538 (Oct. 21, 1988) (Haitians); INA §249, 8 U.S.C. §1259 (aliens who entered prior to January 1, 1972); and 8 C.F.R. §1245.20(c) (Syrian asylees). In addition, the public charge

grounds of inadmissibility may be waived for certain "aged, blind, or disabled" applicants for adjustment of status under Section 245A of the INA. *See* 8 C.F.R. §245a.3(g)(3)(ii).

[8] INA §237(a)(5), 8 U.S.C. §1227(a)(5).

[9] *See* INA §101(a)(13)(A), 8 U.S.C. §1101(a)(13)(A) ("The terms 'admission' and 'admitted' mean, with respect to an alien, the lawful entry of the alien into the United States after inspection and authorization by an immigration officer.").

[10] Illegal Immigration Reform and Immigrant Responsibility Act (IIRIRA), P.L. 104-208, §531, 110 Stat. 3009-674 to 3009-675 (Sept. 30, 1996) (codified at INA §212(a)(4)(B), 8 U.S.C. §1182(a)(4)(B)). As is discussed further below, consular officers of the Department of State (DOS) are responsible for the issuance of visas to aliens outside the United States. Department of Homeland Security (DHS) officials, in turn, determine whether aliens arriving at ports of entry are to be admitted, whether applications for adjustment of status are to be granted, and whether aliens within the United States are to be removed.

[11] INA §212(a)(4)(B)(i)(I)-(V), 8 U.S.C. §1182(a)(4)(B)(i)(I)-(V).

[12] INA §212(a)(4)(B)(ii), 8 U.S.C. §1182(a)(4)(B)(ii). Section 213a of the INA requires that sponsors of certain immigrants agree to "provide support to maintain" the immigrant at an annual income that is not less than 125% of the federal poverty line, and reimburse government entities for any means-tested public benefits that they provide to the immigrant, until specified conditions are met (e.g., the immigrant naturalizes or works for a certain period of time). INA §213a, 8 U.S.C. §1183a. Sponsors may also submit affidavits of support on behalf of other aliens. The affidavits of support required under Section 213a are submitted on Form I-864 and are generally legally binding. Other affidavits of support are submitted on Form I-134 and are not legally binding. *Compare* Wood-Schultz v. Schultz, No. 11-C-975, 2011 U.S. Dist. LEXIS 150119 (E.D. Wis. Dec. 30, 2011) ("The law provides that the [Form I-864] affidavit is a binding contract.") *with* Cheshire v. Cheshire, No. 3:05-cv-00453-TJC-MCR, 2006 U.S. Dist. LEXIS 26602 (M.D. Fla. May 4, 2006) (Form I-134 affidavit of support "is not a legally enforceable contract").

[13] INA §212(a)(4)(C)-(D), 8 U.S.C. §1182(a)(4)(C)-(D). *See, e.g., Matter of* Williams, No. A099 255 983, 2012 Immig. Rptr. LEXIS 4647 (BIA 2012) (alien's spouse failed to file an affidavit of support); *Matter of—*, No.—-Buffalo, NY, 2010 Immig. Rptr. LEXIS 7879 (BIA 2010) (spouse's income inadequate); *Matter of—*, No. A078-535-634, 2008 Immig. Rptr. LEXIS 5899 (BIA 2008) (affidavit of support was over four years old and reflected that respondent's wife has no income or assets).

[14] *Matter of Harutunian*, 14 I. & N. Dec. 583 (BIA 1974).

[15] *See* The Japanese Immigrant Case, 189 U.S. 86 (1903) (affirming a lower court decision remanding an alien for deportation on public charge grounds, in part, because the decisions of administrative or executive officers acting under their delegated powers constitute due process of law and are not subject to judicial review). *See also* Gegiow v. Uhl, 239 U.S. 3, 9-10 (1915) (reversing an order of deportation on public charge grounds that had been issued on the basis that the "labor market in the city of the [alien's] immediate destination is overstocked").

[16] 3 I. & N. Dec. 323 (BIA 1948). Two members of the Board dissented, which, pursuant to regulations in effect at that time, resulted in the case being certified to the Attorney General for review. The Acting Attorney General approved the majority's decision and order without discussion.

[17] *Id.* at 323.

[18] *Id.* at 325-26 (citing, among other things, *Nocchi v. Johnson*, 6 F.2d 1 (1st Cir. 1925); *Ex parte Kichmiriantz*, 283 F. 697 (N.D. Cal. 1922); and Solicitor of Labor opinions of January 22,

1929, file 55616/275 (case of B—D—), and Aug. 2, 1929, file 55612/741 (case of N—M—)).

19 *Id.* at 326.

20 *Id.* at 327. In particular, the Board noted that, under state law, the hospital could not bring suit against the alien or "any other person" to collect for these services, and any money received from the alien or another person on her behalf because of her care could only be treated as a donation, and not as a discharge of any liability she had incurred. *Id.*

21 *Id.*

22 *Id.* at 325.

23 14 I. & N. Dec. 583 (BIA 1974).

24 *Id.* at 590.

25 *Id.* at 584-85.

26 *Id.* at 586-89.

27 *Id.* at 588-89.

28 14 I. & N. Dec. at 588-89. Removable aliens within the United States do not have a constitutional right to remain in the United States. However, they are generally entitled to certain constitutional protections in the removal process and in other contexts. *See, e.g.*, Mathews v. Diaz, 426 U.S. 67, 77 (1972) ("There are literally millions of aliens within the jurisdiction of the United States. The Fifth Amendment, as well as the Fourteenth Amendment, protects every one of these persons from deprivation of life, liberty, or property without due process of law.").

29 14 I. & N. Dec. at 587-88 (discussing, among other things, provisions in S. RPRT. 1515, 81st Cong., 2d Sess., Apr. 20, 1950, pp. 346-50).

30 *Id.* at 588 (citing *Matter of Martinez-Lopez*, 10 I. & N. Dec. 409, 421-23 (AG 1964) and *Foreign Affairs Manual*).

31 *Id.* at 589.

32 *Id.* at 584.

33 *Id.* at 590.

34 *Id.*

35 When the INA was enacted, and for some time thereafter, the primary authority to interpret, implement, and enforce its provisions was vested with the Attorney General, who delegated authority over immigration enforcement and benefits to the INS, a component of DOJ. The INS was dissolved and many (although not all) of its functions were transferred to the Department of Homeland Security (DHS) when DHS was created in 2002.

36 8 U.S.C. §1611(b)(1)(A)-(B) (federal benefits); 8 U.S.C. §1621(b)(1)-(2) (state and local public benefits).

37 8 U.S.C. §1612(a)(2)(A) & (M).

38 *See, e.g.*, Stanley Mailman & Stephen Yale-Loehrn, *An Immigration Price for Receiving Public Benefits?*, 11-22 BENDER'S IMMIGR. BULL. 1 (2006); Charles Wheeler, *Public Charge and the Consequences of Receiving Public Benefits*, 3 BENDER'S IMMIGR. BULL. 278 (Apr. 1, 1998).

39 *See* Dep't of Justice, Immigration & Naturalization Serv., Inadmissibility and Deportability on Public Charge Grounds: Proposed Rule, 64 Fed. Reg. 28676 (May 26, 1999).

40 *Id.* at 28681, 28684.

41 *Id.*

42 *Id.* at 28682, 28684. For more information on these programs, see CRS Report 94-486, *Supplemental Security Income (SSI)*, by Umar Moulta-Ali, and CRS Report R42767,

Temporary Assistance for Needy Families (TANF): Welfare-to-Work Revisited, by Shannon Bopp and Gene Falk.

[43] 64 Fed. Reg. at 28682, 28684.

[44] *Id.* at 28682, 28684-85.

[45] *Id.* at 28682.

[46] *Id.*

[47] *Id.* at 28685.

[48] In part because the proposed regulations were never finalized, this guidance has generally been viewed as nonbinding. *See, e.g.*, Hernandez v. Gonzalez, 195 Fed. App'x 439 (6th Cir. 2006) (unpublished).

[49] *See* Dep't of Justice, Immigration & Naturalization Serv., Field Guidance on Deportability and Inadmissibility on Public Charge Grounds, 64 Fed. Reg. 28689 (May 26, 1999).

[50] *See, e.g.*, 6-71 IMMIGR. L. & PROC. § 71.07[3] (deportability).

[51] 8 U.S.C. §210.1(e)(4).

[52] *Id.* These regulations further define *public cash assistance* as "income or needs-based monetary assistance," including "supplemental security income received by the alien or his immediate family members through federal, state, or local programs designed to meet subsistence levels," but excluding "assistance in kind" (e.g., food stamps, public housing), work-related compensation, and "certain types of medical assistance (Medicare, Medicaid, emergency treatment, services to pregnant women or children under 18 years of age ..."). *See* 8 C.F.R. §210.1(n).

[53] 8 C.F.R. §210.1(e)(4).

[54] *Id.*

[55] *See* 8 C.F.R. §§245a.2(k)(4), 245a.3(g)(4) (applicants for adjustment of status under Section 245A of the INA); 8 C.F.R. §245a.4(b)(11)(iv) (applicants for adjustment of status from certain countries for which extended voluntary departure has been made available); 8 C.F.R. §245a.18(d)(1)-(3) (applicants for adjustment of status under the Legal Immigration Family Equity (LIFE) Act). Extended voluntary departure (EVD) is relief from removal that may be granted to nationals of specific countries.

[56] *See* USCIS, Public Charge: Fact Sheet, Apr. 29, 2011, *available at* http://www.uscis.gov/portal /site/uscis/ menuitem.5af9bb95919f35e66f614176543f6d1a/?vgnextoid=775d23cbea6bf210 VgnVCM100000082ca60aRCRD& vgnextchannel=8a2f6d26d17df110 VgnVCM100000 4718190aRCRD.

[57] 22 C.F.R. §40.41(a).

[58] 22 C.F.R. §40.41(d).

[59] 22 C.F.R. §40.41(f).

[60] Dep't of State, 9 FAM §40.41. DOS does, however, define *public charge* in terms of dependency on the "U.S. Government for subsistence," while the INS field guidance treated dependency on the government more broadly, defining "government" to include any federal, state, or local government entities. *Compare* 9 FAM §40.41 n.2(a) *with* 64 Fed. Reg. at 28681.

[61] 9 FAM §40.41 n.2.1(b). In addition to generally prohibiting aliens who are not "qualified aliens" (e.g., LPRs, asylees, refugees) from receiving public benefits, PRWORA also generally precludes qualified aliens from receiving means-tested public benefits for five years after obtaining a status within the meaning of the term *qualified alien*. 8 U.S.C. §1613(a) (general limitations upon receipt of means-tested public benefits); 8 U.S.C. §1641 (definition of *qualified alien*). The *Foreign Affairs Manual* is a DOS publication containing

the functional statements, organizational responsibilities, and authorities of each of the major components of the Department.

[62] 9 FAM §40.41 n.2.3(a). The FAM further notes that "public assistance" used to support aliens who reside in an institution for long-term care, including Medicaid, may be considered an "adverse factor" in the totality of the circumstances. However, short-term institutionalization for rehabilitation is "not subject to public charge consideration." 9 FAM §40.41 n.2.3(b).

[63] 9 FAM §40.41 n.4(a)-(b).

[64] 9 FAM §40.41 n.4.1(a).

[65] These cases focus exclusively upon applications of the public charge grounds by immigration officers, as opposed to consular officers, since consular officers' determinations about whether to grant visas are broadly shielded from judicial review by the doctrine of consular nonreviewability. *Compare* Saavedra v. Albright, 197 F.3d 1153, 1158-64 (D.C. Cir. 1999) (consular officials decisions to issue or withhold a visa are generally beyond judicial review) *with* Lisotta v. United States, 3 F.2d 108 (5th Cir. 1924) (rejecting the view that determinations as to whether aliens may be excluded on public charge grounds are committed to the unreviewable discretion of immigration officials). In addition, because of amendments made to the INA in 1996, some cases use the term *excludability*, while others use *inadmissibility*. Prior to 1996, arriving aliens seeking admission were subject to grounds of excludability, while aliens physically present within the United States were subject to the grounds of deportability. However, after the 1996 amendments, aliens physically present in the United States without having been admitted (i.e., those who entered unlawfully) were subject to the grounds of inadmissibility, along with aliens seeking admission to the United States.

[66] 19 I. & N. Dec. 867, 867 (BIA 1988).

[67] *Id.* at 870.

[68] *Id.* at 867, 870.

[69] 3 I. & N. Dec. 641 (BIA 1949).

[70] *Id.* at 644.

[71] *See, e.g., Ex Parte* Nunez, 93 F.2d 41 (9th Cir. 1937) (directing that an alien who had received monthly "grocery orders" and clothes from the government be discharged from immigration custody and not deported); *Matter of* X—, No. MSC-05-313-12160-Los Angeles, 2008 Immig. Rptr. LEXIS 17965 (AAO 2008) (alien who had received "welfare services" and food stamps for 18 years was eligible for adjustment of status under the special rule because she was employed); *Matter of*—, No. 02 143 63322-Los Angeles, 2007 Immig. Rptr. LEXIS 17474 (AAO 2007) (alien who had received "public assistance" for herself and her daughter was eligible for adjustment of status under the special rule because she had a consistent employment history); *Matter of*—, No. MSC 01 335 60316-Los Angeles, 2007 Immig. Rptr. LEXIS 17438 (AAO 2007) (same); *Matter of*—, No. MSC 02 058 61384-Los Angeles, 2006 Immig. Rptr. LEXIS 20378 (AAO 2006) (alien who received AFDC, food stamps and Medi-Cal for 22 years for herself and her three children eligible for adjustment of status under the special rule because she had a consistent employment history); *Matter of* X, No. A 34 199 222 New York, 6 Immig. Rptr. B2-48 (AAO 1988) (alien presently employed, and "the only occasion she received welfare payments was when she was pregnant and immediately after the birth of her child").

[72] 3 I. & N. Dec. at 327 ("State authorities could not and did not demand payment for these services and could not bring suit against respondent or any other person to collect for

[them].”). *But see Matter of* M—, 2 I. & N. Dec. 694 (BIA 1946) (New York state law making those treated liable for the costs of institutionalization at hospitals for the “insane”).

[73] Similarly, an alien is not subject to deportability on public charge grounds where any requisite payment is declined. *See, e.g., Matter of* V—, 2 I. & N. Dec. 78 (BIA 1944) (government entity refused payment). However, payment need not be demanded if a demand for payment would be futile. *See, e.g., Harutunian*, 14 I. & N. Dec. at 583.

[74] 4 I. & N. Dec. 565 (BIA 1951). The BIA found, in the alternative, that the alien was not subject to deportation on public charge grounds because he was confined to a penal institution and, thus, not subject to deportability on public charge grounds. *See also Matter of* V—, 5 I. & N. Dec. 725 (BIA 1954) (alien confined in penal institution does not constitute a public charge).

[75] 2 I. & N. Dec. 538 (BIA 1946). Actual payment is not necessarily required, so long as the alien or the alien’s sponsor had the ability to pay. *See, e.g.*, Nocchi v. Johnson, 6 F.2d 1 (1st Cir. 1925) (parents able and willing to pay, but did not understand that they should do so); *Ex parte* Orzechowska, 23 F. Supp. 428 (D. Or. 1938) (parents’ failure to pay was due to a misunderstanding); *Matter of* V—, 2 I. & N. Dec. 78 (BIA 1944) (mother had resources to pay).

[76] As used here, “entry” can mean the date of the most recent entry, not the initial entry. *See, e.g.*, Canciamilla v. Haff, 64 F.2d 875 (9th Cir. 1933) (relevant date of entry); *Ex parte* Kichmiriantz, 283 F. 697 (N.D. Cal. 1922) (date of last entry); *Matter of* L.—, 6 I. & N. Dec. 349 (BIA 1954).

[77] *See, e.g., Ex parte* Orzechowska, 23 F. Supp. at 429 (no proof that alleged reasons for alien’s institutionalization predated her entry); United States *ex rel.* Mandel v. Day, 19 F.2d 520 (E.D. N.Y. 1927) (“After careful perusal ..., the court finds no evidence to sustain the contention that [the] alien suffered from some mental defect at the time of entry.”); United States *ex rel.* Romanow v. Flynn, 17 F.2d 378 (W.D. N.Y. 1927); *Matter of* B—, 9 I. & N. Dec. 57 (BIA 1960); *Matter of* S.—, 5 I. & N. Dec. 21 (BIA 1954); *Matter of* F—, 5 I. & N. Dec. 209 (BIA 1953).

[78] Border Security, Economic Opportunity, and Immigration Modernization Act, S. 744, §2101 (generally barring aliens who are inadmissible under Section 212(a) of the INA from obtaining registered provisional immigrant status, but providing that the public charge grounds of inadmissibility do not apply in determining the alien’s admissibility).

[79] *See, e.g.*, “Sessions10-(MRW13340),” *available at* http://www.judiciary.senate.gov /legislation/immigration/ amendments.cfm (proposing to amend S. 744 to provide that “an alien shall be considered to be a public charge if the alien receives benefits under” the Medicaid program or the Supplemental Nutrition Assistance Program (SNAP)).

In: Law and Legal Issues in the United States ISBN: 978-1-63117-827-6
Editor: Laurent B. Landers

Chapter 3

AN OVERVIEW OF JUDICIAL REVIEW OF IMMIGRATION MATTERS*

Margaret Mikyung Lee

SUMMARY

Congress has plenary or sovereign power over the conditions for admitting aliens into the United States and permitting them to remain. This power is so completely entrusted to the political branch to legislate and implement as to be largely free from judicial review. However, this power is still subject to constitutional limitations, including substantive and procedural due process protections. In immigration cases, due process may be a flexible concept and the particular procedures that may be constitutionally required depend on the relative interests involved.

Historically, immigration policy has sought to encourage and enable the admission and integration of desirable immigrants (workers, family, refugees/asylees), while discouraging and preventing the entry of undesirable aliens (national security risks/terrorists, criminals, public charges). Accordingly, in deciding what degree of judicial review is appropriate in immigration matters, Congress has sought a balance between a system that is fair to desired immigrants, yet facilitates the removal of undesired aliens. Initially, a *habeas corpus* proceeding provided the primary avenue of judicial review of various immigration determinations. In the wake of Supreme Court decisions construing the

---

* This is an edited, reformatted and augmented version of Congressional Research Service Publication, No. R43226, dated September 11, 2013.

Administrative Procedure Act as applying to and providing an avenue for judicial review of immigration adjudications, Congress amended the Immigration and Nationality Act (INA) of 1952 by adding a judicial review provision in 1961 that provided for review by federal courts of appeal for deportation orders, but only for habeas corpus review of exclusion orders by federal district courts.

Beginning with the Antiterrorism and Effective Death Penalty Act of 1996 (AEDPA) and the Illegal Immigration Reform and Immigrant Responsibility Act of 1996 (IIRIRA), legislation and administrative actions have focused on reducing immigration litigation by limiting and streamlining both administrative appeal and judicial review procedures regarding removal of aliens and by rendering aliens in certain categories ineligible for certain types of relief from removal. Even when an alien may be considered for discretionary relief, judicial review of denials of relief from removal is restricted, as is review of removal orders issued to criminal aliens or national security risks. Also, the REAL ID Act restricted habeas review and certain other non-direct judicial review in response to U.S. Supreme Court holdings that such review was still available after the 1996 acts. In the 113th Congress, S. 744 and H.R. 2278, among other bills, would generally continue the trend of limiting judicial review; however, S. 744 provides for judicial review of its legalization programs.

This report will summarize judicial review for immigration matters, including visa denials and revocations; removal orders and detention; naturalization delays, denials, and revocations; expatriation; and legalization denials. Administrative adjudications such as removal proceedings or determination of immigration benefits such as naturalization are beyond the scope of this report.

INTRODUCTION

The power of Congress and the executive branch to legislate and implement the conditions for admitting aliens into the United States and permitting them to remain is so broad as to be virtually immune from judicial control.[1] However, this power is still subject to constitutional limitations, including substantive and procedural due process protections. In immigration cases, the degree of judicial review of administrative decisions and actions that may be constitutionally required depends on the relative interests involved.[2]

In deciding what degree of judicial review is appropriate in immigration matters, Congress has sought to balance judicial review between fairness to desired immigrants (workers, family, refugees/asylees) and facilitation of the removal of detrimental aliens (national security risks/terrorists, criminals, public charges). Initially, a *habeas corpus* proceeding provided the primary avenue of judicial review of various immigration determinations. However, in the wake of U.S. Supreme Court decisions construing the Administrative Procedure Act (APA) as applying to and providing an avenue for judicial review of immigration adjudications,[3] Congress amended the Immigration and Nationality Act (INA) of 1952[4] by adding a judicial review provision in 1961[5] that provided for review of deportation orders by federal courts of appeals, but only for *habeas corpus* review of exclusion orders by federal district courts.[6]

Concerns about the growing population of undocumented aliens, fraudulent asylum claims, terrorism threats, and crimes of drug, human, and arms trafficking, led to legislation in 1996[7] and 2005[8] that limited judicial review, including the availability of *habeas corpus* proceedings. In the 113th Congress, H.R. 2278 would generally continue the trend of limiting judicial review; S. 744 would more narrowly limit judicial review in certain instances of employer noncompliance with foreign worker visa programs. On the other hand, S. 744 also provides for judicial review for legalization programs.

VISA DENIAL AND REVOCATION

An "unadmitted and nonresident alien" has no constitutional right to be admitted into the United States.[9] Accordingly, consular officers within the U.S. Department of State (DOS) generally have nonreviewable authority to deny visas. Therefore, the DOS regulations only provide for administrative, supervisory review of visa denials.[10] This doctrine of consular non-reviewability has long been recognized by the courts and has rarely been challenged.[11] However, there is some case law supporting limited judicial review of a visa denial with regard to the First Amendment rights of U.S. citizens to hear and debate the religious and political views of aliens. In *Kleindienst v. Mandel*,[12] the U.S. Supreme Court held that, when an executive branch officer/agency exercised discretion to not waive the exclusion of an alien as an anarchist and communist advocate for a facially legitimate and bona fide reason, the courts will not look behind the exercise of discretion nor test it by balancing the reason against the First Amendment interests of U.S. citizens who desire to hear the political views of and debate the alien. Some later federal appellate decisions have followed *Mandel* and extended its holding to visa denials by consular officers[13] or to the assertion of other constitutional rights by U.S. citizens.[14] Although they cannot order a consular officer to grant or deny a visa, courts have differed about whether they have jurisdiction to review consular failure to perform the nondiscretionary duty of deciding to grant or deny a visa and to require a consular officer to make a decision.[15]

For a visa revocation, there is no judicial review[16] (including review pursuant to 28 U.S.C. §2241, or any other habeas corpus provision, and 28 U.S.C. §§1361 and 1651), except in the context of a removal proceeding if such revocation provides the sole ground for removal.[17] It appears that courts have generally held that the doctrine of consular nonreviewability applies to revocation of visas issued to aliens who are outside the United States,[18] but that revocation of a visa issued to an alien who is already in the United States is subject to judicial review.[19] Furthermore, federal courts have differed about whether the doctrine of nonreviewability extends to nonconsular officials, including officers of the former Immigration and Naturalization Service and the U.S. Department of Homeland Security (DHS).[20]

REMOVAL AND DETENTION

Judicial Review of Removal Orders under INA §242[21]

Judicial review does not provide a broad panacea to aliens subject to removal orders. First, appealing a removal order does not serve to stay the removal order absent a court order.[22] Second, there is no judicial review of removal determinations based on particular grounds of inadmissibility or deportability, including a public health ground certified by a medical officer and certain criminal grounds such as aggravated felonies, drug offenses, and firearm offenses.[23] Finally, a court cannot review the denial of most types of relief from removal that are granted at the discretion of the immigration officer or immigration judge, including a waiver of inadmissibility, cancellation of removal, voluntary departure, and adjustment of status to lawful permanent resident.[24] These bars to judicial review of removal determinations do not preclude a federal appellate court from reviewing constitutional claims or questions of law raised in matters that are otherwise nonreviewable.[25]

In the exception to the bar on judicial review of denials of discretionary administrative relief from removal, federal appellate courts can review an asylum determination, when an alien faces persecution or a well-founded fear of persecution on account of race, religion, nationality, membership in a particular social group, or political opinion,[26] which serves a humanitarian objective, except for determinations for aliens arriving without proper travel documents who may potentially be subject to expedited removal under INA §235.[27] However, there are restrictions on the scope and standards of judicial review of asylum determinations: (1)the administrative denial of relief is conclusive unless manifestly contrary to law; and (2) a court cannot reverse an administrative determination about the availability of evidence corroborating eligibility for removal relief. On the other hand, relief from removal is *mandatory* if the alien meets the eligibility requirements for either (1) withholding of removal under INA§241(b)(3),[28] when the alien's life or freedom would be threatened in the alien's country because of the alien's race, religion, nationality, membership in a particular social group, or political opinion, or (2) protection under the U.N. Convention Against Torture when there are substantial grounds for believing the alien would be in danger of being subjected to torture.[29] Therefore, a federal appellate court may review denials of these types of relief. Generally, judicial review of removal orders is available in the federal appellate court for the judicial circuit in which the removal proceedings were completed.[30] Judicial review of all questions of law and fact, including interpretation of constitutional and statutory provisions, that arise from a removal action or proceeding must be consolidated in a direct appeal of a final removal order to a federal circuit court of appeals; no *habeas corpus* review is permitted by any federal court.[31] The U.S. Supreme Court called this jurisdictional consolidation provision the "zipper" clause for judicial review of removals.[32] Except as explicitly provided in the INA judicial review provisions, courts may not review claims arising from Attorney General (or the Secretary of Homeland Security) decisions or actions to initiate removal proceedings, adjudicate cases, or execute removal orders against any alien.[33]

Federal district courts have a limited role in the judicial review of removal orders. With regard to U.S. nationality claims, if there is a genuine issue of material fact concerning whether the person appealing the removal order is a U.S. national, the federal appellate court will transfer the proceeding to the federal district court in whose jurisdiction the appellant resides for a new hearing and a declaratory judgment on that issue as if brought under 28 U.S.C. §2201, establishing federal court jurisdiction to declare the rights of the plaintiff.[34] In addition, the District Court for the District of Columbia has jurisdiction to review challenges to the constitutionality of the statute and/or implementing regulations for expedited removal[35] of certain inadmissible aliens or to the legality under other laws of the regulations and other administrative guidelines.[36] An appeal from the decisions described above would be made to the federal appellate court for the circuit in which the district court issuing the decision is located.[37]

Expedited Removal of Inadmissible Arriving Aliens

In contrast to aliens in the United States, aliens outside the United States (or at its borders or ports of entry) are generally not due any procedural rights with respect to their ability to enter the United States. With a limited exception for certain permanent resident aliens who are returning to the United States, aliens whom the government is seeking to exclude from entry are not guaranteed an expulsion process that comports with constitutional standards. The governing principle generally remains that due process for aliens seeking admission to the United States at a port of entry and for aliens who entered illegally without inspection consists of "[w]hatever the procedure authorized by Congress is."[38]

Generally, if an immigration officer determines that an arriving alien is inadmissible, that alien is removable without further hearing or review.[39] The exception occurs when an arriving alien asserts an asylum claim, in which case, the alien will be referred to an asylum officer who determines whether the alien has a credible fear of persecution for race, religion, nationality, membership in a particular social group, or political opinion.[40] If the asylum officer decides that an alien has a credible fear of persecution, the alien is placed into regular removal proceedings[41] where asylum claims will be given full consideration. If the asylum officer decides that an alien does not have a credible fear of persecution, the officer may order removal without further review unless the alien requests review by an immigration judge of the credible fear determination.

A credible fear review by an immigration judge must take place no later than 7 days after the initial negative credible fear determination.[42] The immigration judge may place the alien into regular removal proceedings if the immigration judge reverses the negative determination of the asylum officer.

Similarly if an alien makes a claim under oath, subject to the penalty of perjury, to already being a lawful permanent resident, refugee, or asylee, and if an immigration officer verifies such a claim, the alien will be not be placed in expedited removal but may be placed in regular removal proceedings. If the immigration officer cannot verify the claim, the case will be referred to an immigration judge who may determine the claim not to be valid and affirm expedited removal. If the immigration judge determines that it is valid, DHS may place the alien in regular removal proceedings.

For those who are not placed in regular removal proceedings, there is judicial review in *habeas corpus* proceedings under INA §242, but this is limited to determinations of whether the petitioner is an alien, was ordered removed under the expedited removal provisions of INA §235(b)(1), and can prove by a preponderance of evidence that the alien is a lawful permanent resident or currently in refugee/asylee status in the United States.[43]

Additionally, an immigration officer or judge may order the removal of an arriving alien suspected of being inadmissible for certain national security grounds.

Under such circumstances, the Attorney General can affirm the removal without any further review or hearing after the Attorney General reviews the case and consults with federal security agencies.[44]

Expedited Removal of Aliens Convicted of Committing Aggravated Felonies

In addition to expedited removal of certain arriving aliens, the immigration laws provide for expedited removal of aliens convicted of committing aggravated felonies,[45] criminal offenses that are grounds for deportation and also result in various other immigration consequences, including the expedited removal process.[46] A removal proceeding can be held while an alien convicted of an aggravated felony is incarcerated to enable expeditious removal upon the completion of the alien's sentence of imprisonment.[47]

A removal order against an alien who is not a lawful permanent resident and is convicted of an aggravated felony cannot be executed until 14 calendar days after the date of the removal order in order to allow the alien an opportunity to apply for judicial review under INA §242.[48] At the time of imposing a criminal sentence against an alien who is deportable, a federal district court has jurisdiction to enter a judicial removal order simultaneously; the issuance or denial of a judicial removal order may be appealed by the defendant deportable alien or the Attorney General to the federal court of appeals.[49]

Detention

The INA has two different detention provisions, one for the arrest and detention of removable aliens generally, with special provisions for criminal aliens, and another for the mandatory detention of suspected terrorists. Judicial review in both instances is very limited. Under the general arrest and detention provision, discretionary determinations regarding release on bond or parole is not reviewable.[50] Under the provision for mandatory detention of suspected terrorists, judicial review of actions and determinations, regarding certification as a terrorist and continued detention with periodic review, is exclusively available through *habeas corpus* proceedings pursuant to the specific guidelines of that provision, notwithstanding the guidelines of 28 U.S.C. §2241, the main *habeas corpus* provision.[51] The final order shall be subject to review, on appeal, by the United States Court of Appeals for the District of Columbia Circuit, and no other court of appeals.[52]

Habeas Corpus

In *INS v. St. Cyr*[53] and *Calcano-Martinez v. INS*,[54] concerning the removal requirements and restrictions on judicial review enacted in IIRIRA, the Supreme Court held that there is a strong presumption in favor of judicial review of administrative actions; therefore, in the absence of a clear statement of congressional intent to repeal habeas corpus jurisdiction over removal-related matters, such review was still available after the 1996 changes. Furthermore, the Court also found that eliminating any judicial review, including habeas review, without any substitute for review of questions of law including constitutional issues, would raise serious constitutional questions.[55] Therefore, it chose a statutory construction (habeas review was not eliminated) which would not raise serious constitutional questions.

Subsequent to these decisions, §106 of the REAL ID Act[56] expressly limited the use of *habeas corpus* petitions in removal matters, while providing for federal appellate court consideration of constitutional claims or other legal issues that formerly may have been raised in a habeas corpus petition in cases where direct review was unavailable. Section 106 further provided that, for INA purposes, any elimination of judicial review by other INA provisions included the elimination of habeas corpus petitions.[57]

Section 242(e) of the INA expressly allows habeas review for very limited purposes for expedited removal determinations made pursuant to INA §235(b), which was discussed above in "Expedited Removal of Inadmissible Arriving Aliens." Any review beyond the immigration judge's decisions under INA §235(b)(1), including administrative review by the Board of Immigration Appeals, is limited to *habeas corpus* review in the federal courts under INA §242(e).[58] This permits habeas review only with regard to (1) whether the petitioner is an alien; (2) whether the petitioner was ordered removed under INA §235(b); and (3) whether the petitioner can prove by a preponderance of the evidence that he or she is a lawful permanent resident or currently has refugee/asylee status in the United States and is thus entitled to further review. Under 28 U.S.C. §2241, habeas petitions may be filed initially in a district court, a circuit court of appeals, or in the U.S. Supreme Court, but they are generally filed in a district court because court rules and policy restrict initiation in the appellate courts. District court decisions may then be appealed to the circuit courts of appeals and the U.S. Supreme Court.

Citizenship-Related Determinations

Naturalization Denial or Delay

In 1990, amendments to the INA established an administrative process for naturalization that previously had been adjudicated by federal courts. While these amendments retained judicial review for naturalization denials and delays in the administrative process,[59] they require a denied applicant to request an administrative hearing.[60] Once the administrative process has been exhausted, the applicant may appeal the denial to the federal district court in whose jurisdiction he or she resides for a *de novo* review.[61] Applicants may also request federal district court hearings regarding delays in naturalization determinations if more than 120 days have elapsed after the U.S. Citizenship and Immigration Services (USCIS) has conducted a naturalization examination; depending on its findings, the court may remand the case to the agency, with instructions, for a determination or the court may adjudicate the naturalization case itself.[62]

Naturalization Revocation

Upon an affidavit showing good cause to revoke a naturalization because it was procured illegally, by concealment of a material fact, or by willful misrepresentation, a U.S. attorney is required to initiate denaturalization proceedings in any federal district court in whose jurisdiction the naturalized citizen resides.[63] However, the provision for judicial denaturalization proceedings does not restrict in any way the power of DHS to reopen or vacate a naturalization order administratively.[64]

Expatriation

Expatriation is the loss of nationality by a U.S. citizen regardless of whether the citizenship was acquired by birth or naturalization. Unlike denaturalization/revocation, expatriation does not involve fraudulent or illegal procurement of citizenship. Rather, expatriation results when a U.S. citizen voluntarily commits certain acts, enumerated in the expatriation statute, with the specific intent of relinquishing U.S. citizenship.[65] Expatriation does not necessarily entail administrative adjudication or determination.[66] However, unless there is an explicit, written renunciation of citizenship, expatriation is typically determined and disputed when a U.S. citizen is denied rights and privileges of a U.S. citizen such as a U.S. passport. Such a denial may be reviewed in an action for declaratory judgment brought by the nationality claimant under INA §360[67] and 28 U.S.C. §2201. As noted above, genuine issues of U.S. nationality that arise in removal proceedings are transferred to a federal district court for resolution.

LEGALIZATION UNDER IRCA

The judicial review provisions and related litigation for the legalization program under the Immigration Reform and Control Act of 1986 (IRCA)[68] remain relevant in light of the legalization provisions of S. 744, the Senate-passed bill known as the Border Security, Economic Opportunity, and Immigration Modernization Act. Under INA §245A(f)(3)[69] and pertinent regulations, there is a single level of administrative appellate review via the Administrative Appeals Unit of the USCIS. Pursuant to INA §245A(f)(4),[70] judicial review of IRCA legalization denials is only available as review of a deportation order under former INA §106,[71] since denial of legalization would generally lead to the initiation of deportation proceedings against the unauthorized alien. The statutory standard of review requires that judicial review can only be based on the administrative record established by the administrative appellate review and that the determinations and fact findings of this administrative record are conclusive unless the legalization applicant can show that there was abuse of discretion or that the administrative findings were directly contrary to clear and convincing facts in the record as a whole.

In 1996, the IIRIRA amended the IRCA judicial review provision to limit judicial review to cases where a person had actually filed a legalization application within the period defined by IRCA or had attempted to file a complete application and fee with a legalization officer but the officer refused to accept them.[72] Aside from such cases, there is no judicial or administrative review of a denial of legalization based on the late filing of an application.[73]

It is worth noting that the IRCA legalization program had led to a spate of litigation challenging different aspects of the program's implementation.[74] The U.S. Supreme Court interpreted the statute and implementing regulations for the IRCA legalization program as not precluding judicial review of the legalization process, given the strong presumption that Congress intends judicial review.[75]

LEGISLATION IN THE 113TH CONGRESS

H.R. 2278, as reported by the Senate Judiciary Committee, would further limit judicial review of visa denial or revocation by the DHS, as opposed to the DOS; voluntary departure, a form of removal relief; reinstatement of previously issued removal orders for aliens who illegally reenter the United States after being removed or having departed pursuant to a removal order; and naturalization delays or denials.[76] Section 405 of the bill would bar judicial review of a visa denial or revocation by DHS for security purposes and apply to denials and revocations before, on, and after the effective date of the bill's enactment. Although the INA already bars judicial review of post-removal denials of voluntary departure and court-ordered stays of removal pending consideration of a voluntary removal claim, §601 of the bill would further restrict courts from tolling the period permitted for voluntary departure. Section 603 of the bill would increase limits on judicial review of removal order reinstatements, already barred in general, by explicitly barring review of reinstated orders because of constitutional claims or questions of law raised in an appeal. Section 203 of the bill would revise judicial review of naturalization delays by restricting courts to reviewing the reason for the delay and eliminating current jurisdiction to take and decide a naturalization case on its merits. This provision would also eliminate the current *de novo* standard for judicial review of naturalization denials and limit judicial review of the DHS determination regarding certain naturalization requirements, including good moral character, understanding of and attachment to the Constitution, and disposition to the good order and happiness of the United States. Section 204 of the bill would authorize administrative denaturalization by the Attorney General of persons engaged in certain terrorism-related activities. Although the bill does not bar judicial review of such denaturalization, currently and historically, denaturalization has solely been a function of the federal courts.

In contrast, S. 744, as passed by the Senate, provides for judicial review of the various legalization avenues that the bill would establish; it does not include new restrictions on judicial review regarding removal/detention or visa denial or revocation, although it does include limits on judicial review in other contexts, such as penalties for employer noncompliance with various requirements for employing foreign workers. During the Senate Judiciary mark-up of the bill, some amendments to limit judicial review of legalization denials were rejected, as well as one to limit judicial review of DHS visa denial or revocation for security purposes.[77] In the Senate report accompanying the bill, the Committee noted that a number of advocacy groups warned that restricting judicial review of legalization programs would eliminate "the important backstop of the Federal court system to determine whether the executive branch properly implemented the bill."[78] During the mark-up, some Senators "voiced concern that the amendment would undermine the Constitutional system of checks and balances by eliminating independent oversight of a significant administrative program that will affect millions of people. They also emphasized the risk of error in the program, and the resulting need for judicial review."[79]

Minority views in the bill's report expressed concern about the "unnecessarily broad judicial review of the denial of any application, which would necessarily create a litany of litigation and undermine the enforcement of our immigration laws,"[80] and the "unlimited judicial review the bill creates for the new legalization and other visa programs."[81]

S. 744 contains some provisions restricting judicial review in the contexts other than the removal/detention and immigration benefits such as visa issuance and naturalization. For example, §4306 of the bill would bar judicial review of the finding of a violation of the L-visa nonimmigrant program for intracompany transferee executives or managers by L-visa employers. Although it does not bar judicial review, §3101 of the bill would revise the judicial review provision of INA §274A, concerning the unlawful employment of aliens, by specifying certain deadlines and standards for judicial review of determinations of violations and penalties against non-compliant employers. Finally, §4506 of the bill would bar judicial review of determinations related to the visa waiver program, including visa refusals, a decision to designate or not designate a country as a visa waiver program country, and DOS computation of visa refusal rates or DHS computation of visa overstay rates on which a designation is based.

End Notes

[1] *See* Harisiades v. Shaughnessy, 342 U.S. 580, 588-589 (1952); the Japanese Immigrant Case (Yamataya v. Fisher), 189 U.S. 86 (1903); Fong Yue Ting v. United States, 149 U.S. 698, 705 (1893); the Chinese Exclusion Case (Chae Chan Ping v. United States), 130 U.S. 581, 603, 604 (1889).

[2] Landon v. Plasencia, 459 U.S. 21, 34 (1982); *see also* Mathews v. Eldridge, 424 U.S. 319, 334-335 (1976).

[3] See Robbie Clarke, *Student Note: Reaffirming the Role of the Federal Courts: How the Sixties Provide Guidance for Immigration Reform*, 17 Wash. & Lee J. Civil Rts. & Soc. Just. 463, 472-476 (2011), discussing Shaughnessy v. Pedreiro, 349 U.S. 48, 52-53 (1955), as holding that the APA provides another avenue of judicial review for immigration adjudications conducted under the INA, in addition to the existing habeas review, and Wong Yang Sung v. McGrath, 339 U.S. 33, 51 (1950), as holding that immigration adjudications were required by the INA and Due Process requirements, and therefore the APA's formal adjudication procedures applied.

[4] P.L. 82-414, 66 Stat. 163 (1952), codified as amended at 8 U.S.C. §§1101 *et seq.*

[5] Former INA §106, added by P.L. 87-301, §5(a), 75 Stat. 651 (1961). This was subsequently repealed by the Illegal Immigration Reform and Immigrant Responsibility Act of 1996 (IIRIRA), P.L. 104-208, Div. C, §306(b), 110 Stat. 3009-612, which replaced it with current INA §242, codified as amended at 8 U.S.C. §1252.

[6] Before the IIRIRA, P.L. 104-208, Div. C, §§301-309, 110 Stat. 3009-546, 3009-579 to 3009-627, aliens were subject to two processes, *exclusion* when seeking to enter the United States and *deportation* when they were deemed to have entered the United States and were being expelled. The IIRIRA reformed the process so that those seeking entry but deemed *inadmissible* and those in the United States but deemed *deportable* are both subject to *removal*. Certain inadmissible aliens may be subject to *expedited removal*, under which there is limited administrative and judicial review. Due process analyses remain subject to the same considerations.

[7] Antiterrorism and Effective Death Penalty Act of 1996 (AEDPA), 110 Stat. 1214, and the Illegal Immigration Reform and Immigrant Responsibility Act of 1996 (IIRIRA), 110 Stat. 3009-546. These acts focused on reducing immigration litigation by limiting and streamlining both administrative appeal and judicial review procedures regarding removal of aliens and by rendering aliens in certain categories ineligible for certain types of relief from removal. Even when an alien may be considered for discretionary relief, judicial review of denials of relief from removal is restricted, as is review of removal orders issued to criminal aliens.

[8] Section 106 of the REAL ID Act, P.L. 109-13, Division B, 119 Stat. 302 (2005), restricted *habeas* review and certain other non-direct judicial review in response to U.S. Supreme Court holdings that such review was still available after the 1996 acts. In INS v. St. Cyr, 533 U.S. 289 (2001), and Calcano-Martinez v. INS, 533 U.S. 348 (2001), which concerned the IIRIRA restrictions on judicial review, the Supreme Court held that there is a strong presumption in favor of judicial review of administrative actions; therefore, in the absence of a clear statement of congressional intent to repeal habeas corpus jurisdiction over removal-related matters, such review was still available after the 1996 changes. Furthermore, the Court also found that eliminating any judicial review, including habeas review, without any substitute for review of questions of law including constitutional issues, would raise serious constitutional questions. 533 U.S. at 305. Therefore, it chose a statutory construction (habeas review was not eliminated) which would not raise serious constitutional questions.

[9] Kleindienst v. Mandel, 408 U.S. 753, 762 (1972).

[10] 22 C.F.R. §§41.121 and 42.81.

[11] James Lockhart, *Construction and Application of Doctrine of Consular Nonreviewability*, 42 A.L.R. Fed. 2d 1 (citing Kleindienst v. Mandel and other cases).

[12] 408 U.S. 753.

[13] *See* Margaret Laufman, Comment: American Academy of Religion v. Napolitano, 55 N.Y.L. Sch. L. Rev. 1173 (2010 / 2011), discussing cases including *American Academy of Religion v. Napolitano*, 573 F.3d 115, 119, 124-25 (2d Cir. 2009*); Bustamante v. Mukasey*,531 F.3d 1059 (9th Cir. 2008); *Adams v. Baker*, 909 F.2d 643 (1st Cir. 1990); *Allende v. Shultz*, 845 F.2d 1111 (1st Cir. 1988); *Abourezk v. Reagan*, 785 F.2d 1043 (D.C. Cir. 1986).

[14] *E.g., Bustamante v. Mukasey*,531 F.3d 1059 (9th Cir. 2008) (U.S. citizen had a protected liberty interest in her marriage to an alien and a procedural due process claim regarding his visa denial.

[15] Lockhart, *supra* note 12, at §II.4 to II.6.

[16] This includes review pursuant to the habeas corpus provisions at 28 U.S.C. §2241, or any other habeas corpus provision in the federal statutes, or pursuant to the provisions at 28 U.S.C. §§1361(actions in federal district court to compel a federal officer or employee to perform a duty owed to the plaintiff) and 1651 (federal court authority to issue writs, typically for injunctive relief).

[17] INA §221(i), codified as amended at 8 U.S.C. §1201(i).

[18] *See, e.g., Castellanos v. Pfizer, Inc.*, 555 F. Supp. 2d 1343 (S.D. Fla. 2008).

[19] *See, e.g., Knoetze v. United States, Dep't of State*, 634 F.2d 207 (5th Cir. 1981) (reviewing revocation of a visa issued to an alien within the United States under the APA, 5 U.S.C. §706).

[20] Lockhart, *supra* note 12, at §III.27 to III.28.

[21] Codified as amended at 8 U.S.C. §1252.

[22] INA §242(b)(3)(B); codified as amended at 8 U.S.C. §1252(b)(3)(B).

[23] INA §242(a)(2)(C), codified as amended at 8 U.S.C. §1252(a)(2)(C).

[24] INA §242(a)(2); codified as amended at 8 U.S.C. §1252(a)(2).

[25] INA §242(a)(2)(D), codified as amended at 8 U.S.C. §1252(a)(2)(D).

[26] INA §§101(a)(42) and 208, codified as amended at 8 U.S.C. §§1101(a)(42) and 1158.

[27] Codified as amended at 8 U.S.C. §1225.

[28] Codified as amended at 8 U.S.C. §1241(b)(3).

[29] This protection was implemented by section 2242 of the Foreign Affairs Reform and Restructuring Act of 1998, P.L. 105-277, 112 Stat. 2681, 2681-821.

[30] INA §§242(a)(1) and (b)(2); codified as amended at 8 U.S.C. §§1252(a)(1) and (b)(2). Also, if a district court finds that a removal order is invalid in a separate hearing before a criminal trial for refusal/failure to depart pursuant to a removal order, it shall dismiss the criminal indictment and the Federal Government may appeal the dismissal to the court of appeals for the appropriate circuit within 30 days (INA §242(b)(7)(C); 8 U.S.C. §1252(b)(7)(C)).

[31] INA §242(b)(9), codified as amended at 8 U.S.C. §1252(b)(9).

[32] Reno v. American-Arab Anti-Discrimination Committee (AADC), 525 U.S. 471 (1999), described this provision as an "unmistakable 'zipper' clause" that says "no judicial review in [removal] cases unless [section 1252] provides judicial review." *Id.* at 482-3.

[33] INA §242(g), codified as amended at 8 U.S.C. §1252(g).

[34] INA §242(b)(5)(B), codified as amended at 8 U.S.C. §1252(b)(5)(B).

[35] INA §235(b)(1), codified as amended at 8 U.S.C. §1225(b)(1).

[36] INA §242(e)(3), codified as amended at 8 U.S.C. §1252(e)(3).

[37] 28 U.S.C. §§1294, 1295, 2106, 2107.

[38] Shaughnessy v. United States *ex rel.* Mezei, 345 U.S. 206, 212 (1953); United States *ex rel.* Knauff v. Shaughnessy, 338 U.S. 537, 544 (1950).

[39] INA §235, codified as amended at 8 U.S.C. §1225.

[40] INA §235(b)(1), codified as amended at 8 U.S.C. §1225(b)(1). This subsection provides for the expedited removal (except for Cubans) of (1) an alien arriving in the United States without proper documents or with fraudulent documents and of (2) an alien who arrives in or has entered the United States without having been formally admitted or paroled into the United States after inspection and who has not established to the satisfaction of the immigration officer that he/she has been physically present in the United States continuously for the two-year period immediately before the officer determines that the alien is inadmissible. The immigration officer may order the removal of such an alien without any further hearing unless the alien makes a claim (1) to asylum, (2) to be a lawful permanent resident, or (3) to have previously been admitted as a refugee or been granted asylum (such status not having terminated). *Id.*

[41] INA §240, codified as amended at 8 U.S.C. §1229a.

[42] INA §235(b)(1)(B)(iii)(IV), codified as amended at 8 U.S.C. §1225(b)(1)(B)(iii)(IV).

[43] INA §242(e)(2), codified as amended at 8 U.S.C. §1252(e)(2).

[44] INA §242(a)(2); codified as amended at 8 U.S.C. §1252(a)(2).

[45] Aggravated felonies are defined at INA §101(a)(43), codified as amended at 8 U.S.C. §1101(a)(43). *See* CRS Report WSLG454, *Will Immigration Reform Legislation Revisit the Definition of "Aggravated Felony"?*, by Michael John Garcia.

[46] *See* CRS Report RL32480, *Immigration Consequences of Criminal Activity*, by Michael John Garcia.

[47] INA §238(a); codified as amended at 8 U.S.C. §1228(a).

[48] INA §238(b)(3); codified as amended at 8 U.S.C. §1228(b)(3).

[49] INA §238(c); codified as amended at 8 U.S.C. §1228(c).

[50] INA §236(e); codified as amended at 8 U.S.C. §1226(e).

[51] INA §236A(b); codified as amended at 8 U.S.C. §1226a(b).

[52] *Id.*

[53] 533 U.S. 289 (2001).

[54] 533 U.S. 348 (2001).

[55] INS v. St. Cyr, 533 U.S. 289 (2001). According to the Court, the Suspension Clause, Article I, §9, cl. 2, of the Constitution, requires some judicial intervention in removal/deportation cases and at least protects the writ of habeas corpus as it existed in 1789. 533 U.S. at 300-

301. In light of ambiguities in the scope of the writ of habeas corpus at common law and Supreme Court decisions suggesting that judicial intervention can only be restricted to the extent consistent with the Constitution, the Court found that a serious Suspension Clause issue would arise if it were to accept the INS position that the 1996 acts eliminated habeas review without any substitute. 533 U.S. at 305. To preclude review of a pure question of law by any court would give rise to substantial constitutional questions. The Court observed that traditionally the courts distinguished between ruling on eligibility for relief (a question of law) and ruling on the favorable exercise of discretion (a question of fact). 533 U.S. at 307-308. Although a court could not rule on the validity of the actual granting of discretionary relief, which is not a matter of right, it could rule on the legality of an erroneous failure to exercise discretion at all. *Id.*

56 P.L. 109-13, Division B, 119 Stat. 302 (2005).

57 *Id.*

58 As noted above, INA §242(e) also provides for challenges to the validity of the statutory scheme and its implementation through an action initiated in the U.S. District Court for the District of Columbia.

59 Nancy Morawetz, *Immigration Law and Policy: Article: Citizenship and the Courts*, 2007 U Chi Legal F 447, 454- 456 (2007), discussing the Immigration Act of 1990, P.L. 101-649, 104 Stat. 3978, and changes made to the naturalization system.

60 INA §336(a), codified as amended at 8 U.S.C. §1447(a).

61 INA §310(c), codified as amended at 8 U.S.C. §1421(c); 8 C.F.R. §336.9.

62 INA §336(b), codified as amended at 8 U.S.C. §1447(b).

63 INA §340(a), codified as amended at 8 U.S.C. §1451(a).

64 INA §340(h), codified as amended at 8 U.S.C. §1451(h).

65 INA §349, codified as amended at 8 U.S.C. §1481.

66 However, the cancellation of a passport or issuance of a certificate of loss of nationality may be appealed administratively and judicially. *See* INA §§358, 361, codified as amended at 8 U.S.C. §§1501, 1504.

67 Codified as amended at 8 U.S.C. §1503.

68 P.L. 99-603, 100 Stat. 3359.

69 Codified as amended at 8 U.S.C. §1255a(f)(3); *see also* regulations at 8 C.F.R. §245a.2(p), for the lawful temporary resident status, and §245a.3(j), for the lawful permanent resident status. The IRCA legalization process was two stages, the first resulting in a temporary resident status and the second resulting in a lawful permanent resident status, with appeals from denials available at each stage.

70 Codified as amended at 8 U.S.C. §1255a(f)(4).

71 Formerly codified as amended at 8 U.S.C. §1105a and repealed by the Illegal Immigration Reform and Immigrant Responsibility Act of 1996 (IIRIRA), P.L. 104-208, div. C, §306(b) and (c), 309, 110 Stat. 3009–612, 3009–625.

72 Codified as amended at 8 U.S.C. §1255a(f)(4)(C).

73 INA §245A(f)(2), codified as amended at 8 U.S.C. §1255a(f)(2).

74 Lucas Guttentag, Symposium: Immigrant's Rights & Critical Perspectives On Immigration Reform, February 10, 2007: Introduction: Immigration Reform: A Civil Rights Issue, 3 Stan. J.C.R. & C.L. 157, 162 (2007) (citing various cases, noting the role of judicial review in ensuring the fairness and integrity of the IRCA legalization program, and advocating effective judicial review for any future legalization program).

[75] *See* Immigration and Naturalization Service v. Zambrano, 509 U.S. 918 (1993); Reno v. Catholic Social Services, Inc., 509 U.S. 43 (1993); McNary v. Haitian Refugee Center, Inc., 498 U.S. 479 (1991).

[76] For a discussion of judicial review provisions in H.R. 2278, *see* CRS Report R43192, *Immigration Enforcement: Major Provisions in H.R. 2278, the Strengthen and Fortify Enforcement Act (SAFE Act)*, by Michael John Garcia and Kate M. Manuel, at pp. 20, 23, 29.

[77] S.Rept. 113-40, at 48.

[78] *Id.* at 41.

[79] *Id.*

[80] *Id.* at 176.

[81] *Id.* at 186.

In: Law and Legal Issues in the United States ISBN: 978-1-63117-827-6
Editor: Laurent B. Landers

Chapter 4

CONGRESSIONAL AUTHORITY TO ENACT CRIMINAL LAW: AN EXAMINATION OF SELECTED RECENT CASES*

Charles Doyle

SUMMARY

The powers of Congress begin and end with the Constitution. The Constitution vests Congress with explicit authority to enact criminal laws relating to counterfeiting, piracy, crimes on the high seas, offenses against the law of nations, and treason. It grants Congress other broad powers, such as the power to regulate interstate commerce. The Constitution's Necessary and Proper Clause allows Congress to enact criminal laws when reasonably related to the regulation of commerce or to one of the other constitutionally enumerated powers. The Constitution also imposes limits on the powers of Congress, however. It places those limits in the terms it uses in its grants of authority, in explicit prohibitions, and in the Tenth Amendment reminder of the restrictions implicit in the federal union. Recently, the Supreme Court and the lower federal appellate courts have supplied several examples of the scope and limits of congressional authority.

In the case of the Commerce Clause, seven Justices of the Supreme Court endorsed separate opinions in *National Federation* explaining that

* This is an edited, reformatted and augmented version of Congressional Research Service Publication, No. R43023, dated March 27, 2013.

the power to regulate interstate commerce does not include the power to require participation in commerce. The Fifth Circuit held in *Kebodeaux* that the Commerce Clause does not embody the power to outlaw purely intrastate movement with only an attenuated nexus to commercial activity. As for foreign commerce, the circuits disagree on whether Congress's regulatory authority is subject to the same constraints that apply to its powers over domestic commerce. The Ninth Circuit (*Clark*) believes it is not. The Third Circuit (*Pendleton*) disagrees. (The Violence Against Women Reauthorization Act, P.L. 113-4 (S. 47), eliminates the need to prove a foreign commerce element in the law that gave rise to the circuit split.)

In the realm of the Necessary and Proper Clause, the Eleventh Circuit in *Belfast* observed that Congress may pass criminal legislation in order to implement a treaty obligation, and the Third Circuit in *Bond* held that it may do so without regard to federalism concerns. Moreover, the Ninth Circuit Court of Appeals concluded in *Elk Shoulder* that Congress may outlaw the unregistered movement within a state of a federally convicted sex offender who is on supervised release. The Fifth Circuit held in *Kebodeaux*, however, that the Clause does not permit enactment of a statute that outlaws such movement after the offender has been fully discharged.

Although they did not join in a single opinion, seven Justices in *National Federation* concluded that Congress's power under the Spending Clause may not be used to compel the states to accept expansion of a federal regulatory regime or to face draconian economic consequences. The case did not involve criminal penalties, but a limit on Congress's Spending Clause power is a limit on its authority to enact implementing necessary and proper criminal legislation.

Article I, Section 8, clause 10 grants Congress the power "to define and punish Piracies and Felonies committed on the high Seas, and Offenses against the Law of Nations." Federal appellate courts have looked to customary international law for explanations of the power over offenses against the law of nations (*Bellaizac-Hurtado*) and piracy (*Dire*). The High Seas cases (*Saac* and *Ibarguen-Mosquera*) continue to acknowledge congressional authority to outlaw drug trafficking in international waters subject only to an elusive due process limitation. The Constitution's Military Clauses permit Congress to criminalize overseas assaults by Defense Department foreign contractors (*Brehm*), but do not permit it to punish an individual's conduct based solely on his status as a former member of the Armed Forces even when supplemented by the Necessary and Proper Clause (*Kebodeaux*).

INTRODUCTION

The federal government is a creature of the Constitution.[1] It enjoys no authority that cannot be traced back to the Constitution. This is as true of Congress as of the other branches.[2] Although the Constitution grants Congress extensive legislative powers,[3] it vests Congress with explicit authority to enact criminal law in only three places. Article I, Section 8, clause 6 states that "Congress shall have Power ... To provide for the Punishment of counterfeiting the Securities and current Coin of the United States." A few lines later, the Constitution gives Congress authority over three additional classes of crime, when it declares that "Congress shall have Power ... To define and punish Piracies and Felonies committed on the high Seas, and Offenses against the Law of Nations."[4] Finally, the Constitution defines the crime of treason, but empowers Congress to set its punishment.[5]

A casual reader might conclude that Congress may enact no other class of criminal statutes. After all, the Tenth Amendment denies Congress any authority that the Constitution does not grant it.[6] Upon closer examination, however, it becomes clear that the Constitution elsewhere gives Congress, the President, and the federal courts sweeping powers. Moreover, the authority it places in the hands of Congress includes an implementing power, that is, the authority to enact laws necessary and proper to the implementation of those other powers—authority that by implication includes the authority to enact reasonably related criminal laws.[7]

Nevertheless, Congress's criminal law enacting powers are not boundless. Some limitations reside with the grant of authority. Article III, for example, allows Congress to set the punishment for treason, but denies it permission to punish treason with corruption of the blood.[8] The Constitution mentions other limitations in areas apart from its grants of authority, like the prohibition on ex post facto laws or abridgement of freedom of speech.[9] The third class of limitations is more difficult to discern. Whether understood as contextual, or structural, or implicit in the Tenth Amendment, they are the limitations of federalism, the limitations that flow from the fact the Constitution emerged as a compact between the sovereign it created and the sovereigns that created it.[10]

What follows is a discussion of selected recent cases that illustrate the scope and boundaries of Congress's power to enact criminal laws under the Constitution's necessary and proper, commerce, high seas, law of nations, spending, and military clauses.

NECESSARY AND PROPER CLAUSE

> The Congress shall have Power ... To make all Laws which shall be necessary and proper for carrying into Execution the foregoing Powers, all other Powers vested by this Constitution in the Government of the United State, or in any Department or Officer there.[11]

"[T]he Necessary and Proper Clause makes clear that the Constitution's grants of specific federal legislative authority are accompanied by broad power to enact laws that are 'convenient or useful' or 'conductive' to the authority's 'beneficial exercise.'"[12] The phrase "necessary and proper" does not demand absolute necessity.[13] It is enough that a statute is rationally related to the constitutional power it seeks to "carry into execution."[14]

The Supreme Court's *Comstock* decision offered an expansive view of the Necessary and Proper Clause, with caveats. Two Sex Offender Registration and Notification Act (SORNA) cases, *Kebodeaux* and *Elk Shoulder*,[15] treat the caveats and thus the scope of the Clause very differently. Two other recent appellate decisions, *Bond* and *Belfast*,[16] raise questions of the Tenth Amendment limits, if any, on congressional authority under the Clause. The Supreme Court has granted certiorari in *Bond* and *Kebodeaux*.

United States v. Comstock

The Supreme Court in *Comstock* stated that a statute that relies on the Necessary and Proper Clause need not always be but one step removed from the constitutional power it brings to life.[17] Comstock and his fellow petitioners challenged the constitutional underpinning of 18 U.S.C. 4248. Section 4248 authorizes federal courts to order the civil commitment of federal inmates whose release is imminent on the grounds that the prisoners are mentally ill and sexually dangerous.

The Court did not rule upon whether Section 4248 was a necessary and proper means of carrying into execution the Commerce Clause pursuant to which the statute of Comstock's conviction had been enacted. Instead of reference to the Commerce Clause, it began with the observation that, other than in the case of piracy and other constitutionally identified crimes, the enactment of criminal statutes generally occurs by operation of the Necessary and Proper Clause. It then identified the links in the chain that began with the constitutional authority to enact criminal laws and ended with Section 4248. Section 4248, it held, "is a 'necessary and proper' means of exercising the federal authority that permits Congress to create federal criminal laws, to punish their violation, to imprison violators, to provide appropriately for those imprisoned, and to maintain the security of those who are not imprisoned but who may be affected by the federal imprisonment of others."[18]

The *Comstock* Court confirmed, however, that a statute cannot be "proper" if it is constitutionally prohibited or inconsistent with the letter or spirit of the Constitution.[19] The Court listed five considerations upon which its decision was predicated. Although it did not say so, the implication is that without the five, the Court might have found Section 4248 inconsistent with the spirit of federalism that permeates the Constitution. The five were

> (1) the breadth of the Necessary and Proper Clause, (2) the long history of federal involvement in arena [of the mental health of federal prisoners], (3) the sound reasons for the statute's enactment in light of the Government's custodial interest in safeguarding the public from dangers posed by those in federal custody; (4) the statute's accommodation of state interests [e.g., the statute demands that federal custody of the committed inmate be surrendered when the appropriate state expresses a willingness to assume responsibility], and (5) the statute's narrow scope.[20]

SORNA Cases

The United States Court of Appeals for the Fifth Circuit and the United States Court of Appeals for the Ninth Circuit read the *Comstock* five considerations differently. The Fifth Circuit, sitting en banc in *United States v. Kebodeaux,*[21] applied the considerations and found the Necessary and Proper Clause insufficient to support the application of the Sex Offender Registration and Notification Act (SORNA) to a fully discharged federal sex offender. The Ninth Circuit, in *United States v. Elk Shoulder,*[22] applied the same considerations and came to opposite conclusions in the case of a federal sex offender still under supervised release.

While a 21-year-old soldier, Kebodeaux was court martialed for engaging in consensual sex with a 15-year-old.[23] Some years after his release and discharge, Congress enacted SORNA, which required federal sex offenders to register with state authorities and to maintain the currency of their registrations.[24] Shortly thereafter, the Attorney General exercised his statutory authority to impose the obligation upon those who had been convicted of federal offenses prior to SORNA's passage.[25] Then, Kebodeaux moved from El Paso to San Antonio within the state of Texas without reporting his relocation to state authorities.[26] He was convicted under 18 U.S.C. 2250(a) for the failure.[27]

Elk Shoulder was convicted of sexually abusing a six-year-old within the territorial jurisdiction of the United States in violation of 18 U.S.C. 2241(c).[28] He had been released from prison, but was on supervised release when SORNA was enacted.[29] He moved from place to place in Montana, but never registered and was subsequently convicted under 18 U.S.C. 2250(a) for the failure.[30]

Both Circuits agreed that the *Comstock* decision provides the proper mode of analysis for challenges grounded in the Necessary and Proper Clause.[31] Their respective views of the *Comstock* considerations differ dramatically thereafter. First, the Fifth Circuit conceded that the Necessary and Proper Clause vests Congress with broad authority.[32] The Ninth Circuit went a step further and concluded that "SORNA was rationally related to an enumerated power" (the power to enact legislation governing activities within the territorial jurisdiction of the United States).[33]

Second, the *Comstock* Court noted that the civil commitment statute at issue was "a modest addition to a set of federal prison-related mental-health statutes that have existed for many decades."[34] The Ninth Circuit stated that in like manner SORNA was a modest addition to the federal parole, probation, and supervised release laws that date back to 1910. SORNA and those provisions both deal with the post-incarceration supervision.[35] The Fifth Circuit found SORNA historically novel.[36] It found the probation-supervised release analogy wanting because, unlike SORNA, both probation and supervised release are part of the punishment for the original federal offense crime.[37] Although failure to comply is a crime, SORNA's registration demands are not considered punitive.[38] Moreover, SORNA did not exist until long after Kebodeaux had served his sentence.

In its third consideration, the *Comstock* Court highlighted the sound policy reasons for the statute's enactment (protection of the public from those in federal custody).[39] In the mind of the Ninth Circuit, the *Comstock* statute authorized civil commitment to protect the public from federal sex offenders, while SORNA required registration to protect the public from federal sex offenders. Both were reasonably adapted to a legitimate end.[40] The Fifth Circuit disagreed. It believed that custodial responsibility for those soon to be released differs from custodial responsibility for those released long ago. The difference prevented the

Fifth Circuit from classifying SORNA's application to Kebodeaux as reasonably related to a constitutional power.[41]

The Fourth *Comstock* consideration is the accommodation of state interest. The *Comstock* statute allowed the appropriate state to assume jurisdiction over soon-be-released prisoners whom federal authorities would otherwise subject to federal civil commitment.[42] The Ninth Circuit found at least equivalent accommodation in SORNA.[43] It does not supplant the state systems.[44] Its criminal penalties only apply with respect to state sex offenders who travel in interstate commerce or to federal sex offenders.[45] Its encouragement of state acceptance of federal standards is modest.[46] The Fifth Circuit, on the other hand, viewed SORNA as less accommodating than the *Comstock* statute. Unlike the *Comstock* statute, SORNA gives state authorities no option to substitute state discretion for that of federal authorities.[47]

Finally, the *Comstock* Court observed that the regulatory scheme under consideration was neither too remote from the enumerated power upon which it relied nor too sweeping in scope.[48] The same could be said of SORNA, the Ninth Circuit asserted.[49] Again, the Fifth Circuit took a different view: the government's rationale in defense of SORNA—that federal conviction vests Congress with boundless, timeless legislative authority over the individual—"is anything but narrow."[50]

The Fifth Circuit concluded that SORNA, as applied to Kebodeaux, failed to satisfy the *Comstock* considerations and consequently exceeded Congress's authority under the Necessary and Proper Clause.[51] The Ninth Circuit, writing after the Fifth Circuit's opinion had been announced, explicitly disagreed with it: "Because we reject the Fifth Circuit's conclusion that Congress cannot 'reassert jurisdiction over someone it had long ago unconditionally released from custody,' a proposition for which the Fifth Circuit provided no support, we disagree with its analysis of the *Comstock* considerations, which is based almost exclusively on that conclusion."[52]

United States v. Bond

The *Bond* decision addressed the question of whether structural, federalism concerns limit congressional authority under the Necessary and Proper Clause to enact treaty implementing legislation. Mrs. Bond sought revenge against her husband's paramour by coating the woman's car door handles and door knobs with toxic chemicals. Mrs. Bond was convicted of using a chemical weapon in violation of the Chemical Weapons

Implementation Act.[53] She argued on appeal that either the statute did not apply to her conduct or that Congress lacked the constitutional authority to enact legislation that swept into federal court a local "run of the mill" assault case, like her own. The Third Circuit Court of Appeals initially held that Mrs. Bond had no standing to challenge her conviction on federalism grounds, maintaining that only a state could object to intrusion upon its sovereign prerogatives.[54] The Supreme Court reversed. Mrs. Bond may claim the benefits of federalism, since it "secures to citizens the liberties that derive from the diffusion of sovereign power."[55]

When the case returned to the Third Circuit for a decision on the merits, the court was faced with the question of the extent to which principles of federalism limit congressional authority under the Necessary and Proper Clause to implement a United States treaty. The Supreme Court appeared to have provided the answer in *Missouri v. Holland*. There, in the face of a federalism objection, the Court declared that "[i]f the treaty is valid there can be no dispute about the validity of the statute under Article I, Section 8, as a necessary and proper means to execute the powers of the Government."[56]

In theory, a treaty may be invalid in three ways. First, it may exceed the authority granted in the Treaty Power. Second, it may exceed an express limitation that appears elsewhere in the Constitution. Finally, it may exceed an implicit constitutional limitation. As to the first, the *Holland* Court considered the Migratory Bird Treaty subject matter properly attributed to the Treaty Power: it constituted a matter of national concern that could "be protected only by national action in concert with that of another power."[57] Second, the Migratory Bird Treaty "[did] not contravene any prohibitory words to be found in the Constitution."[58] Therefore, "[t]he only question [was] whether [the Migratory Bird Treaty was] forbidden by some invisible radiation from the general terms of the Tenth Amendment."[59]

The *Holland* Court answered this last question by comparing the strength of the competing state and federal claims. Missouri's claim rested on a "slender reed. Wild birds are not in possession of anyone; and possession is the beginning of ownership. The whole foundation of the State's rights is the presence within [its] jurisdiction of birds that yesterday had not arrived; tomorrow may be in another State and in a week a thousand miles away."[60]

The federal interest, on the other hand, was substantial:

> Here a national interest of very nearly the first magnitude is involved. It can be protected only by national action in concert with that of another power. The subject-matter is only transitorily within

> the State and has no permanent habitat therein. But for the treaty and the statute there soon might be no birds for any powers to deal with. We see nothing in the Constitution that compels the Government to sit by while a food supply is cut off and the protectors of our forests and our crops are destroyed. It is not sufficient to rely upon the States. The reliance is vain, and were it otherwise, the question is whether the United States is forbidden to act. We are of [the] opinion that the treaty and statute must be upheld.[61]

In the Third Circuit upon return, Mrs. Bond conceded the validity of the Chemical Weapons Convention.[62] She argued instead that the Constitution imposes explicit and implicit limits on congressional authority under the Necessary and Proper Clause.[63] "The problem with [Mrs.] Bond's attack," in the eyes of the Third Circuit, was "that, with practically no qualifying language in *Holland* to turn to" the court was "bound to take at face value the Supreme Court's statement that '[i]f the treaty is valid there can be no dispute about the validity of the statute ... as a necessary and proper means to execute the powers of the Government.'"[64] Nor was the court convinced that the implementing statute "disrupts the balance of power between the federal government and the states,"[65] the argument at the heart of Mrs. Bond's challenge.

The court was not unsympathetic to Mrs. Bond's contention that her case did not belong in federal court: Mrs. "Bond's prosecution seems a questionable exercise of prosecutorial discretion, [The decision to use the Act—a statute designed to implement a chemical weapons treaty—to deal with a jilted spouse's revenge on her rival is, to be polite, a puzzling use of the federal government's power], and indeed appears to justify her assertion that this case 'trivializes the concept of chemical weapons.'"[66] A concurring member of the panel was even more critical and expressed the hope that the Supreme Court would accept the case for review.[67] The Court has done so.[68]

United States v. Belfast

The *Belfast* decision addressed the question of whether due process limits Congress's treaty implementing authority. The United States District Court for the Southern District of Florida convicted Belfast of overseas violations of the Torture Act, a statute enacted to implement the Convention Against Torture and Other Cruel, Inhuman or Degrading Treatment or Punishment (CAT).[69] Belfast argued that the Torture Act exceeded congressional authority under the

Treaty Power and Necessary and Proper Clauses, because it outlawed conspiracy when the Convention did not mention and because the statute included a more sweeping definition of torture.[70] On appeal, the Eleventh Circuit Court of Appeals concluded that "[a]pplying the [Necessary and Proper Clause's] rational relationship test in this case, we are satisfied that the Torture Act is a valid exercise of congressional power under the Necessary and Proper Clause, because the Torture Act tracks the provisions of CAT in all material respects."[71]

Since the violations occurred overseas, the threat to state law enforcement interests was minimal and posed no restriction on congressional authority. Nevertheless, the Constitution confines congressional authority both explicitly[72] and implicitly for the protection of the people of the United States.[73]

Belfast asserted that the absence of CAT ratification by the nation where the torture occurred denied him the notice of its application to him which due process required. The court was unconvinced. It reminded him that "[t]he Supreme Court made clear long ago that an absent United States citizen is nonetheless 'personally bound to take notice of the laws [of the United States] that are applicable to him and to obey them.'"[74] The issue of structural limitations did not arise.

COMMERCE CLAUSE

> The Congress shall have Power ... To regulate Commerce with foreign Nations, and among the several States, and with the Indian Tribes.[75]

Interstate Commerce

The classic statement of Congress's legislative power under the Interstate Commerce Clause appears in *United States v. Lopez*,[76] *United States v. Morrison*,[77] and *Gonzales v. Raich*.[78] There the Court points out that the Clause grants Congress authority to enact three classes of statutes. "First, Congress may regulate the use of the channels of interstate commerce,"[79] as it has done when it outlawed the interstate transportation of stolen property or the interstate transportation of kidnap victims.[80] "Second, Congress is empowered to regulate and protect the instrumentalities of interstate commerce, or persons or things in interstate commerce, even though the treat may come only from intrastate activities,"[81] as it has done when it outlawed the destruction of aircraft or the theft of property from interstate shipment.[82] "Finally, Congress' commerce authority includes the power to regulate those activities having a substantial relation to interstate commerce,"[83] as it has done when it outlaws cultivation and possession of controlled substances.[84]

In *New York v. United States*, the Court noted that Congress could not rely on the Commerce Clause to commandeer the legislative and regulatory processes of the states in order to enforce a federal program for the disposal of radioactive waste. This is no less true when a statute offers the states a choice of two unpalatable alternatives—federal commandeering or taking title to radioactive waste.[85] The Court explained in *Printz v. United States* that by the same token, Congress could claim no Commerce Clause or Necessary and Proper Clause authority to compel state law enforcement officials to conduct background checks on prospective handgun purchasers as part of a federal regulatory program.[86]

Moreover, the Court held in *Lopez* that the Commerce Clause did not empower Congress to enact statutes that outlawed possession of a firearm in a school yard and in *Morrison* that it does not permit creation of a federal cause of action for the victims of violent, gender-based animus. The Clause does not enable any such attempt to regulate activities without a more immediate relation to commerce, particularly if the activities are markedly local.[87] This is not to deny, as the Court acknowledged in *Raich*, that Congress may regulate intrastate activity such as the cultivation and possession of marijuana that has a substantial impact on a class of interstate commercial activity such as the interstate and international traffic in marijuana.

Seven *National Federation of Independent Business* justices found the Patient Protection and Affordable Care Act's individual mandate more than the Interstate Commerce Clause empowers. The *Kebodeaux* court found the outer reaches of the Sex Offender Registration and Notification Act (SORNA) beyond Congress's power under the Interstate Commerce Clause as well as the Necessary and Proper Clause.

National Federation of Independent Business v. Sebelius

A confluence of views, rather than a holding, in *National Federation of Independent Business v. Sebelius*,[88] appears to identify a previously unannounced limitation on the congressional power under the Interstate Commerce Clause: the Clause does not empower Congress to penalize the failure to engage in commerce.

The question involved the so-called individual mandate feature of the Patient Protection and Affordable Care Act. The individual mandate, with some exceptions, requires healthy individuals, who might otherwise forgo purchasing health insurance, to obtain insurance or to pay a penalty.[89] The provision is designed to compensate insurers for their required coverage of certain unhealthy individuals.[90] Although a majority of the Court found that the mandate is the valid exercise of Congress's constitutional taxing power,[91] seven Justices—three members of the majority and four dissenters—stated that the Commerce Clause afforded insufficient constitutional authority for its enactment. Chief Justice Roberts, joined by Justices Breyer and Kagan, observed that the power to regulate commerce does not include the power to require individuals to engage in commerce.[92] The four dissenters struck much the same cord when they noted: "The Individual Mandate in the Act commands that every individual shall ... ensure that the individual ... is covered under minimum essential coverage. If this provision 'regulates' anything, it is the *failure* to maintain minimum essential coverage.... But that failure—that abstention from commerce—is not 'Commerce.' To be sure, *purchasing* insurance is 'Commerce'; but one does not regulate commerce that does not exist by compelling its existence."[93] However, the dissenters' opinion was grounded also on the principle that "Whatever may be the conceptual limits upon the Commerce Clause ... [it] cannot be such as will enable the Federal Government to regulate all private conduct...."[94]

The case did not involve enactment of a criminal statute. However, the scope of the Commerce Clause defines the scope of congressional authority to enact implementing criminal legislation.

United States v. Kebodeaux

Having concluded that application of SORNA in the case before it exceeded Congress's Necessary and Proper powers, the Fifth Circuit in *Kebodeaux* also rejected the suggestion that SORNA, as applied, might be considered a valid exercise of Congress's Commerce Clause powers under the "channels of commerce," the "instrumentalities of commerce," or the "substantial effect on commerce" prong of the Clause.[95] It held that "Congress lacks the constitutional authority under the 'channels of interstate commerce' to require fully discharged former federal sex offenders to register whenever they relocate within a state, because it risks the use of interstate travel by sex offenders; nor under the protecting the instrumentalities of interstate commerce because sex offenders may pose a risk to interstate traffic if they travel interstate."[96] The Fifth Circuit concluded that the justifications were too sweeping and too intrusive upon state criminal law prerogatives.[97] As for the substantial impact on commerce prong, the Fifth Circuit thought SORNA, as applied, looked too much like the regulation of non-economic activity in *Lopez* and *Morrison* and too little like the regulation of "quintessentially economic activity" in *Raich*.[98]

Foreign Commerce

A disagreement has recently developed in the lower federal appellate courts over whether the *Lopez* Interstate Commerce Clause standards relating to commercial channels, instrumentalities, and effects apply with equal force to the Foreign Commerce Clause. A few years ago, the Ninth Circuit stated that congressional authority under the Foreign Commerce Clause could be defined without reference to the *Lopez* standards.[99] More recently, the Third Circuit expressly questioned that approach.[100] In between, the Second Circuit sidestepped the question with a statutory construction that avoided the constitutional issues,[101] a construction Congress may have had in mind when it expanded a related proscription in reauthorization of the Violence Against Women Act.[102]

United States v. Clark

Clark, an American expatriate, lived in Cambodia but about once a year returned to the United States for family and business reasons.[103] Clark was convicted under 18 U.S.C. 2423(c) for traveling in foreign commerce and engaging in commercial sexual activity with children under the age of 18 in Cambodia.[104] Clark appealed, arguing among other things, that his conduct rested beyond the outer limits of the Foreign Commerce Clause. The Ninth Circuit held that "[t]he combination of Clark's travel in foreign commerce and his conduct of an illicit commercial sex act in Cambodia shortly thereafter puts the statute squarely within Congress's Foreign Commerce Clause authority. In reaching this conclusion, we view the Foreign Commerce Clause independently from its domestic brethren."[105] A dissenting member of the panel objected that the Foreign Commerce Clause should not be read to permit Congress to regulate all commercial activities once an individual has engaged in international travel.[106]

United States v. Weingarten

Weingarten, another American expatriate, sexually abused his daughter for years.[107] He was eventually convicted for transportation of a child with intent to engage in unlawful sexual activity in violation of 18 U.S.C. 2423(a) and for travel in foreign commerce with the intent to engage in unlawful sexual activity with a child in violation of 18 U.S.C. 2423(b).[108] A flight between Belgium and Israel formed the basis of one of the foreign commerce counts.[109] On appeal, Weingarten argued alternatively that (1) travel between two foreign countries without a nexus to the United States could not meet the statutory requirement of "travel in foreign commerce," or (2) if the statute purported to do so, it exceeded congressional authority under the Foreign Commerce Clause.

The Second Circuit opted to construe the statute so that it did not apply to travel between foreign countries with no nexus to the United States.[110] Constitutional avoidance, however, seems to have played a role in the court's election.[111]

United States v. Pendleton

Pendleton flew from New York to Germany where he sexually assaulted a child.[112] He was convicted of traveling in foreign commerce and engaging in unlawful sexual activity with a child in violation of 18 U.S.C. 2423(c).[113] He challenged the constitutional authority of Congress to rely on the Foreign Commerce Clause to enact a statute that punishes noncommercial overseas sexual activity.[114]

The Third Circuit disagreed. Although it declined the government's invitation to endorse the Ninth Circuit's *Clark* decision, it found it need not resolve the issue. The facts before it satisfied *Lopez's* "channels of commerce," making it unnecessary to decide whether the Foreign Commerce Clause reaches areas not covered by the Interstate Commerce Clause's channels, instrumentalities, and affects standards. Congress enjoys constitutional authority to prevent the use of the channels of commerce for purposes of illicit sex tourism, the Third Circuit held.[115]

VAWA Reauthorization

The Violence Against Women Reauthorization Act of 2013 amends Section 2423(c) to permit prosecution of American expatriates who engage in unlawful sexual conduct overseas without the need to establish travel in foreign commerce: "Any United States citizen or alien admitted for permanent residence who travels in foreign commerce *or resides either temporarily or permanently in foreign country*, and engages in any illicit sexual conduct with another person shall be fined under this title or imprisoned not more than 30 years, or both."[116]

ARTICLE I, SECTION 8, CLAUSE 10

> The Congress shall have Power ... To define and punish Piracies and Felonies committed on the high Seas, and Offenses against the Law of Nations.

Clause 10 is said to contain three distinct components: one for piracy, one for felonies committed upon the high seas, and one for offenses against the law of nations.[117] The *Bellaizac-Hurtado* court's understanding of the Law of Nations Clause leaves Congress with little discretion to "define and punish." The *Dire* court's construction of the piracy statute leaves the scope of the Piracy Clause somewhat uncertain. On the other hand, once due process concerns are resolved, Congress seems to be thought to enjoy much greater legislative latitude under the High Seas Clause, as evidenced by cases decided under the Maritime Drug Law Enforcement Act (MDLEA) and the Drug Trafficking Vessel Interdiction Act (DTVIA).

Law of Nations

United States v. Bellaizac-Hurtado

Panamanian authorities arrested Bellaizac-Hurtado and his co-defendants after they abandoned in Panamanian waters an unflagged vessel containing 760 kilograms of cocaine.[118] A federal grand jury subsequently indicted them under the Maritime Drug Law Enforcement Act (MDLEA) for possession of cocaine, with intent to distribute, aboard a vessel subject to United States jurisdiction.[119] They pleaded guilty, but reserved the right to appeal the questions of congressional power to authorize their convictions under the Piracy, High Seas, and Law of Nations Clause.[120] The court determined that congressional authority under the Law of Nations Clause did not extend to a prohibition of drug trafficking within the territorial waters of another nation.[121]

The court's analysis began with the proposition that Congress's authority to "define and punish ... Offenses against the Law of Nations" does not include the authority to define what constitutes an offense under the law of nations.

"Whether the offense as defined is an offense against the law of nations depends on the thing done, not on any declaration to that effect by congress."[122] It then decided that an offense must be contrary to customary international law in order to constitute an offense against the law of nations.[123] Customary international law, the court said, is that law which is generally and consistently practiced by nations throughout the world out of a sense of legal obligation.[124]

Drug trafficking, the offense at issue, was not recognized as contrary to customary international law when the Law of Nations Clause was drafted nor has since acquired that status, the court stated.[125] Although most nations have endorsed treaties obligating them to suppress drug trafficking, the court cited evidence that the practice in many nations belies any assertion that they feel compelled to do so out of a sense of legal obligation.[126]

The *Bellaizac-Hurtado* court had little Supreme Court jurisprudence upon which to build. Although not relevant for the court's analysis, the only Supreme Court decision directly on point suggests that Congress's power under the Law of Nations Clause may be slightly more robust in other contexts: "The law of nations requires every national government to use 'due diligence' to prevent a wrong being done within its own dominion to another nation with which it is at peace, or to the people thereof."[127]

High Seas

The High Seas Clauses cases primarily arise out of the Maritime Drug Law Enforcement Act (MDLEA) and more recently out of the Drug Trafficking Vessel Interdiction Act (DTVIA). Early on, the lower federal appellate courts concluded that Congress's power "to define and punish Piracies and Felonies committed on the High Seas, and Offences against the Law of Nations" vested it with authority to enact MDLEA.[128] Some also recognized a due process limitation on the courts' ability to try and punish MDLEA defendants.[129] The DTVIA cases continue this line of reasoning.

The DTVIA Cases

United States v. Ibarguen-Mosquera

Ibarguen-Mosquera was convicted of operating an unflagged, semi-submersible vessel in international waters in violation of the Drug Trafficking Vessel Interdiction Act (DTVIA).[130] He argued unsuccessfully that DTVIA exceeded congressional authority under Article I, Section 8, and violated due process.[131]

The court dispensed with the first contention quickly by pointing to Congress's authority under the High Seas Clause.[132] Its sole remaining concern was any due process limitation on Congress's ability to reach foreign nationals traveling outside U.S. territorial waters.[133] The lower federal appellate courts generally conclude that the demands of due process have been satisfied, if the assertion of jurisdiction is consistent with international law.[134] For this, the court cited its precedents and those of some of the other circuits which have consistently held that unflagged, stateless vessels enjoy no right to freely travel the high seas.[135]

United States v. Saac

Saac was likewise convicted under DTVIA, and he too challenged its constitutionality.[136] The court referred to the High Seas Clause and noted that the Clause did not explicitly confine its scope to either U.S. territorial waters or U.S. citizens.[137] The court disposed of the due process argument with the observation that the DTVIA is consistent with the due process satisfying principles of international law that allow a country to enact laws against universally condemned misconduct (e.g., drug trafficking), and against threats to its national security (e.g., smuggling).[138]

United States v. Cardales-Luna

Cardales-Luna was convicted under MDLEA after U.S. Coast Guard officials interdicted his Bolivian-registered vessel on the high seas and discovered that it contained 400 kilograms of cocaine.[139] Bolivian authorities consented to the application of MDLEA aboard the vessel,[140] thereby satisfying MDLEA's "vessel within the jurisdiction of the United States" requirement.[141] The court did not address the issue of Congress's legislative authority, since neither CardalesLuna nor the government raised the issue.[142]

A dissenting member of the panel, however, would have done so. Judge Torruella contended that "the application to MDLEA to Appellant [constitutes an] ultra vires extension of [Congress'] Article I legislative powers to foreign territory, as applied to persons and/or activities that have no nexus with the United States." Moreover, he suggested that "the question of Congress exceeding its Article I power under the facts of this [MDLEA] case is structural in nature and [therefore] cannot be waived by the individual concerned or the nation of which he is a citizen or on whose vessel he is apprehended."[143]

In the course of his analysis, Judge Torruella examined and rejected several possible sources of congressional authority. He found power under the Piracy, High Seas, and Law of Nations Clause wanting because he understood the Clause confined to piracy, slave trading, and offenses contrary to customary international law.[144] Implementation of the maritime jurisdiction of the federal courts demands an American vessel.[145] Implementation of the Treaty Clause requires a treaty.[146] The Foreign Commerce Clause demands a "demonstrable and direct nexus to the United States."[147]

Piracy

United States v. Dire

Dire was convicted of piracy under 18 U.S.C. 1651 following his participation in an armed attack on a U.S. Navy frigate that he believed to be a merchant ship.[148] The Fourth Circuit acknowledged that Congress has the constitutional authority to define and punish piracy.[149]

Section 1651 outlaws piracy "as defined by the law of nations." This, the court concluded, means piracy as understood by customary international law at the time of the offense.[150]

SPENDING CLAUSE

> The Congress shall have Power To lay and collect Taxes ... to provide ... for the general Welfare of the United States.[151]

The Supreme Court has said in the past that Congress's exercise of the Spending Clause is subject to certain limitations: "[F]irst[,] ... the exercise of the spending power must be in pursuit of 'the general welfare.' ... Second, ... if Congress desires to condition the States' receipt of federal funds, it must do so unambiguously enabling the States to exercise their choice knowingly, cognizant of the consequences of their participation. Third, ... conditions on federal grants might be illegitimate if they are unrelated to the federal interest in particular national projects or programs.... Finally, ... other constitutional provisions may provide an independent bar to the conditional grant of federal funds."[152] *National Federation* brings home the point that Congress may not use its spending power to coerce state participation in a federal program.[153]

National Federation of Independent Business v. Sebelius

The Patient Protection and Affordable Care Act purported to condition the continued receipt of federal Medicaid funds upon a state's participation in an expanded Medicaid program. Seven Justices of the Court—three from the majority and four dissenters—felt that was more than the Spending Clause conveys.[154] Coercion doomed the effort. Congress may employ the power of the purse to encourage the states to participate in a federal program; it may not use it to compel them to do so. The dissenters pointed out that "'the legitimacy of Congress' power to legislate under the spending power ... rests on whether the State *voluntarily* and knowing accepts' [a condition].... Congress effectively engages in [] impermissible compulsion when state participation in a federal spending program is coerced, so that the States' choice whether to enact or administer a federal regulatory program is rendered illusory."[155]

Chief Justice Roberts, in the portion of his opinion joined by Justices Breyer and Kagan, made the same point.[156] Neither he nor the dissenters found it necessary to mark precisely where persuasion becomes coercion. Wherever the line, the Medicaid expansion was beyond it.[157]

Again, *National Federation* did not involve a criminal statute, but the scope of the power defines the scope of power to enact criminal laws in its implementation.

MILITARY CLAUSES

> The Congress shall have Power ... To declare War ... To raise and support Armies ... To provide and maintain a Navy; To make Rules for the Government and Regulation of the land and naval Forces ... To provide for organizing, arming, and disciplining the Militia....[158]

United States v. Brehm

Brehm, a foreign national and Department of Defense (DOD) contractor, assaulted another foreign DOD contractor at Kandahar Airfield in Afghanistan.[159] He was brought to the United States and convicted of assault resulting in serious bodily injury under the Military Extraterritorial Jurisdiction Act (MEJA).[160] Brehm argued that the Constitution gave Congress no authority to outlaw altercations between foreign nationals outside the United States and that due process precluded any effort to do so.[161] The Fourth Circuit concluded that the Military Clauses supplemented by the Necessary and Proper Clause supplies all the constitutional authority required.[162] As for due process limitations, the circumstances and the nature of his conduct afforded Brehm fair notice that his dangerous assault exposed him to prosecution.[163]

End Notes

[1] *Reid v. Covert*, 354 U.S. 1, 5-6 (1957)(Black, J. with Warrant, Ch.J., Douglas and Brennan, JJ.)(opinion and announcing the judgment of the court)("The United States is entirely a creature of the Constitution. Its power and authority have no other source. It can only act in accordance with all the limitations imposed by the Constitution").

[2] *United States v. Morrison*, 529 U.S. 598, 607 (2000)("Every law enacted by Congress must be based on one or more of its powers enumerated in the Constitution").

[3] U.S. Const. Art. I, §1 (All legislative Powers herein granted shall be vested in a Congress of the United States ...").

[4] U.S. Const. Art. I, §8, cl. 10.

[5] U.S. Const. Art. III, §3.

[6] U.S. Const. Amend. X ("The powers not delegated to the United States by the Constitution, nor prohibited by it to the States, are reserved to the States respectively, or to the people").

[7] U.S. Const. Art. I, §8, cl. 18.

[8] U.S. Const. Art. III, §3, cl. 2 ("The Congress shall have Power to declare the Punishment of Treason, but no Attainder of Treason shall work Corruption of Blood, or Forfeiture except during the Life of the Person attainted").

[9] U.S. Const. Art. I, §9, cl. 3; Amend. I.

[10] See generally CRS Report RL30315, *Federalism, State Sovereignty, and the Constitution: Basis and Limits of Congressional Power*, by Kenneth R. Thomas.

[11] U.S. Const. Art. I, §8, cl. 18.

[12] *United States v. Comstock*, 130 S.Ct. 1949, 1956 (2010), quoting, *McCulloch v. Maryland*, 4 Wheat. (17 U.S.) 316 (1819).

[13] *Jinks v. Richland County*, 538 U.S. 456, 462 (2003), citing, *McCulloch v. Maryland*, 4 Wheat. [(17 U.S.)] at 414-15.

[14] *United States v. Comstock*, 130 S.Ct. at 1956-957, citing inter alia, *Gonzales v. Raich*, 545 U.S. 1, 22 (2005).

[15] *United States v. Kebodeaux*, 687 F.3d 232 (5th Cir. 2012), cert. granted, 133 S.Ct. 928 (2013); and *United States v. Elk Shoulder*, 696 F.3d 922 (9th Cir. 2012).

[16] *United States v. Bond*, 681 F.3d 149, 159 (3d Cir. 2012), cert. granted 133 S.Ct. 978 (2013); and *United States v. Belfast*, 611 F.3d 783 (11th Cir. 2010).

[17] *United States v. Comstock*, 130 S.Ct. at 1964; see generally CRS Report R40958, *United States v. Comstock: Legislative Authority Under the Necessary and Proper Clause*, by Charles Doyle.

[18] *United States v. Comstock*, 130 S.Ct. at 1965.

[19] *Id.* at 1956, again quoting, *McCulloch v. Maryland*, 4 Wheat. (17 U.S.) at 316 (emphasis added)("Let the end be legitimate, let it be within the scope of the constitution, and all means are appropriate, which are plainly adapted to that end, *which are not prohibited, but consist with the letter and spirit of the constitution*, are constitutional").

[20] *United States v. Comstock*, 130 S.Ct. at 1965.

[21] *United States v. Kebodeaux*, 687 F.3d 232 (5th Cir. 2012), cert. granted, 133 S.Ct. 928 (2013); see also CRS Legal Sidebar WSLG198, *Fifth Circuit Overturns Federal Sex Offender Registration Conviction as Beyond Congress' Legislative Power.*

[22] *United States v. Elk Shoulder*, 696 F.3d 922 (9th Cir. 2012).

[23] *United States v. Kebodeaux*, 687 F.3d at 234.

[24] P.L. 109-248 (2006), codified at 42 U.S.C. 16901 to 16991 and 18 U.S.C. 2250.

[25] 28 C.F.R. pt. 72, pursuant to 42 U.S.C. 16913(d).

[26] *United States v. Kebodeaux*, 687 F.3d at 234.

[27] 18 U.S.C. 2250(a) provides in pertinent part: "Whoever ... (2)(A) is a sex offender as defined for the purposes of the Sex Offender Registration and Notification Act by reason of a conviction under ... the Uniform Code of Military Justice ... and (3) knowingly fails to ... update a registration as required by the ... Act; shall be fined under this title or imprisoned not more than 10 years, or both."

[28] *United States v. Elk Shoulder*, 696 F.3d at 924.

[29] *Id.* at 931 n.10.

[30] *Id.* at 925.

[31] *United States v. Kebodeaux*, 687 F.3d at 236 ("Kebodeaux argues that Congress has no authority under Article I to subject him to conviction pursuant to §2250(a)(2)(A).... The most analogous Supreme Court decision is *United States v. Comstock*"); *United States v. Elk Shoulder*, 696 F.3d at 928 ("The Supreme Court provided a framework for analyzing such arguments in *United States v. Comstock*").

[32] *United States v. Kebodeaux*, 687 F.3d at 236-37("First, the *Comstock* Court explained ... that Congress has broad authority to enact legislation under the Necessary and Proper Clause. Thus, to be constitutional under that clause, a statute must constitute a means that is 'rationally related' or 'reasonably adapted' to an enumerated power. Congress has 'a large discretion' as to the choice of means, and we apply a 'presumption of constitutionality' to its enactments. This first factor is not fact-specific; it suggests that the analysis always starts with a heavy thumb on the scale in favor of upholding government action").

[33] *United States v. Elk Shoulder*, 696 F.3d at 930.

[34] *United States v. Comstock*, 130 S.Ct. 1958; see also *id.* at 1961("Aside from its specific focus on sexually dangerous persons, §4248 is similar to the provisions first enacted in 1949. Cf. §4246 [relating to the pre-release civil commitment of federal prisoners for mental health reasons]. In that respect, it is a modest addition to a longstanding federal statutory framework, which has been in place since 1855").

[35] *United States v. Elk Shoulder*, 696 F.3d at 929("Requiring sex offenders to register and update their addresses is a 'modest' addition to the federal government's long history of regulating federal offenders after their release from incarceration through probation, parole and supervised release").

[36] *United States v. Kebodeaux*, 687 F.3d at 238 ("The Department of Justice cannot find a single authority, from more than two hundred years of precedent, for the proposition that it can reassert jurisdiction over someone it had long ago unconditionally released from custody just because he once committed a federal crime. Thus, SORNA's registration requirements for federal sex offenders are constitutionally novel").

[37] *Id.*("There is, however, a big difference between SORA's sex-offender-registration requirements and probation or supervised release—a distinction that goes to the heart of this case. Unlike the situation involving probation or supervised release, SORNA's ex-offender-registration requirements (and §2250(a)(2)(A)'s penalties) were not a condition of Kebodeaux's release from prison, let alone a punishment for his crime").

[38] *Id.*

[39] *United States v. Comstock*, 130 S.Ct. at 1961.

[40] *United States v. Elk Shoulder*, 696 F.3d at 929(internal citations omitted)("Comstock held that the civil commitment statute at issue was reasonably adapted to its ends. Among other things, Congress could have reasonably concluded that federal inmates who suffer from mental illness that causes them to have serious difficulty in refraining from sexually violent conduct, would pose an especially high danger to the public if released. Here, Congress's decision to enact SORNA to enhance public safety by imposing a registration requirement on convicted federal sex offenders and criminalizing the failure to register, is also reasonable adopted to the attainment of a legitimate end, namely to protect the public from sex offenders and offenders against children").

[41] *United States v. Kebodeaux*, 687 F.3d at 242-43("In sum, as applied to Kebodeaux, SORNA's registration requirements are not, and cannot be, an attempt to ... act as a responsible custodian of prisoners; they are merely an effort to protect the public from those who may be dangerous because they once were convicted of a sex offense. By that logic, Congress would have never ending jurisdiction to regulate anyone who was ever convicted of a federal crime of any sort, no matter how long ago, he served his sentence, because he may pose a risk of re-offending. Indeed, that logic could easily be extended beyond federal crimes: Congress could regulate a person who once engaged in interstate commerce (and was thereby subject to federal jurisdiction) on the grounds that he now poses a risk of engaging interstate commerce again. In short, the only 'rational relation' between §2250(a)(2)(A)'s application to Kebodeaux and an enumerated federal power is that Kebodeaux was once subject to federal jurisdiction—reasoning that is so expansive that it would put an end to meaningful limits on federal power").

[42] *United States v. Comstock*, 130 S.Ct. at 1962.

[43] *United States v. Elk Shoulder*, 696 F.3d at 930("SORNA likewise reasonably accommodates state interests").

[44] *Id.*

[45] *Id.*; 18 U.S.C. 2250(a).

[46] *United States v. Elk Shoulder*, 696 F.3d at 930 ("SORNA's requirement that states implement SORNA-compliant registration and notifications systems in order to receive certain funds, see 42 U.S.C. 16925, does not improperly invade state interests").

[47] *United States v. Kebodeaux*, 687 F.3d at 243-44("Here, [in contrast to the *Comstock* statute], there is no provision by which someone federally prosecuted under SORNA can be subjected to state penalties or transferred to state custody instead. Unless a former federal sex offender proves that a state has made it impossible for him to register, he is subject to federal prosecution and up to ten years of imprisonment for failing to update his state registration within three days of a change of address, employment, name, or student status, even if the state believes a more moderate response would be appropriate (which Texas and many other states apparently do). The state is thus forced into the binary choice of keeping a former federal sex offender off its own registry entirely or subjecting him to §2250(a)(2)(A)'s harsh penalties; it cannot control the punishment given to those who fail to update their registration").

[48] *United States v. Comstock*, 130 S.Ct. at 1963.

[49] *United States v. Elk Shoulder*, 696 F.3d at 930-31("Here, the links between Congress's enumerated powers and SORNA are no more attenuated than those in *Comstock*. It is a small step from Congress's power to enact laws, criminalize their violation, place the violators in custody, and protect the public from federal convicts even after release, see [*Comstock*] at 1964-65, to requiring federal convicts who may be dangerous to the public to provide information regarding their residence, and punishing those who fail to do so.... The SORNA registration requirements are likewise not 'too sweeping in scope.' Contrary to Elk Shoulder's assertion that authorization of lifelong registration requirements would grant a 'general police power' to Congress, the requirement to register is not nearly as significant a burden as the indefinite detention authorized in *Comstock*").

[50] *United States v. Kebodeaux*, 687 F.3d at 245(SORNA's "logic is expansive, because the only jurisdictional basis for §2250(a)(2)(A) is the fact that a person once committed a federal crime. That reasoning opens the door ... to congressional power over anyone who was ever convicted of a federal crime of any sort. That is anything but narrow").

[51] *Id.*("The statute's regulation of an individual, after he has served his sentence and is no longer subject to federal custody or supervision, solely because he once committed a federal crime, (1) is novel and unprecedented despite over 200 years of federal criminal law, (2) is not 'reasonably adapted' to the government's custodial interest in its prisoners or its interest in punishing federal criminals, (3) is unprotective of states' sovereign interest over what intrastate conduct to criminalize within its own borders, and (4) is sweeping in the scope of its reasoning").

[52] *United States v. Elk Shoulder*, 696 F.3d 922, 932 (9th Cir. 2012)(internal citations omitted).

[53] 18 U.S.C. 229.

[54] *United States v. Bond*, 581 F.3d 128 (3d Cir. 2009).

[55] *United States v. Bond*, 131 S.Ct. 2355, 2364 (2011), quoting, *New York v. United* States, 505 U.S. 144, 181 (1992).

[56] *Missouri v. Holland*, 252 U.S. 416, 432 (1920).

[57] *Id.* at 434.

[58] *Id.* at 433.

[59] *Id.* at 433-34.

[60] *Id.* at 434.

[61] *Id.* at 435.

[62] *United States v. Bond*, 681 F.3d 149, 159 (3d Cir. 2012), cert. granted 133 S.Ct. 978 (2013).

[63] *Id.* at 162.

[64] *Id.*

[65] *Id.* at 166.

[66] *Id.* at 165 (footnote 20 of the court's opinion in brackets).

[67] *Id.* at 170 (Ambro, J. concurring)(internal citations omitted)("Since *Holland*, Congress has largely resisted testing the outer bounds of its treaty-implementing authority. But if ever there were a statute that did test those limits, it would be Section 229. With its shockingly broad definitions, Section 229 federalizes purely local, run-of-the-mill criminal conduct. The statute is a troublesome example of the Federal Government's appetite for criminal lawmaking. Sweeping statutes like Section 229 are in deep tension with an important structural feature of our Government: 'The States possess primary authority for defining and enforcing the criminal law.' *Brecht v. Abrahamson*, 507 U.S. 619, 635 (1993); see also *Patterson v. New York*, 432 U.S. 197, 201 (1977) ('It goes without saying that preventing and dealing with crime is much more the business of the States than it is of the Federal

Government ... '). I hope that the Supreme Court will soon flesh out '[t]he most important sentence in the most important case about the constitutional law of foreign affairs,', and, doing so, clarify (indeed curtail) the contours of federal power to enact laws that intrude on matters so local that no drafter of the Convention contemplated their inclusion in it").

[68] *Bond v. United States*, 133 S.Ct. 978 (2013).

[69] *United States v. Belfast*, 611 F.3d 783, 793 (11th Cir. 2010).

[70] *Id.*

[71] *Id.* at 806.

[72] E.g., U.S. Const. Amend. V ("No person shall ... be deprived of life, liberty, or property, without due process of law ...").

[73] U.S. Const. Amend. X (emphasis added)("The powers not delegated to the United States by the Constitution, nor prohibited by it to the States, are reserved to the States respectively, *or to the people*"); cf., *United States v. Bond*, 131 S.Ct. 2355, 2364 (2011), quoting, *New York v. United* States, 505 U.S. 144, 181 (1992)("[F]ederalism secures to citizens the liberties that derive from the diffusion of sovereign power").

[74] *Id.* at 809, quoting, *Blackmer v. United States*, 284 U.S. 421, 438 (1932).

[75] U.S. Const. Art. I, §8, cl. 3.

[76] 514 U.S. 549 (1995).

[77] *United States v. Morrison*, 529 U.S. 598 (2000).

[78] *Gonzales v. Raich*, 545 U.S. 1 (2005).

[79] *United States v. Lopez*, 514 U.S. at 558; *United States v. Morrison*, 529 U.S. at 609; *Gonzales v. Raich*, 545 U.S. at 16.

[80] E.g., 18 U.S.C. 2314 (transportation of stolen property), 1201 (kidnaping).

[81] *United States v. Lopez*, at 558; *United States v. Morrison*, 529 U.S. at 609; *Gonzales v. Raich*, 545 U.S. at 16-7.

[82] 18 U.S.C. 32 (destruction of aircraft), 659 (theft from interstate shipments).

[83] *United States v. Lopez*, at 558-59; *United States v. Morrison*, 529 U.S. at 609; *Gonzales v. Raich*, 545 U.S. at 17.

[84] E.g., 21 U.S.C. 841, 844.

[85] *New York v. United States*, 505 U.S. 174-77 (1992).

[86] *Printz v. United States*, 521 U.S. 898, 935 (1997).

[87] *United States v. Morrison*, 529 U.S. at 617-18("We accordingly reject the argument that Congress may regulate noneconomic, violent criminal conduct based solely on that conduct's aggregate effect on interstate commerce. The Constitution requires a distinction between what is truly national and what is truly local. In recognizing this fact we preserve one of the few principles that has been consistent since the Clause was adopted. The regulation and punishment of intrastate violence that is not directed at the instrumentalities, channels, or goods involved in interstate commerce has always been the province of the States"); *United States v. Lopez*, 514 U.S. at 564 (The Government admits, under its 'cost of crime' reasoning, that Congress could regulate not only all violent crime, but all activities that might lead to violence crime, regardless of how tenuously they relate to interstate commerce. Similarly, under the Government's 'national productivity' reasoning, Congress could regulate any activity that it found was related to the economic productivity of individual citizens.... Under the theories that the Government presents ... it is difficult to perceive any limitation on federal power, even in areas such as criminal law enforcement or education where States historically have been sovereign").

[88] *National Federation of Independent Business v. Sebelius*, 132 S.Ct. 2566 (2012).

[89] 26 U.S.C. 5000A.

[90] *National Federation of Independent Business v. Sebelius*, 132 S.Ct. at 2585("By requiring that individuals purchase health insurance, the mandate prevents cost-shifting by those who would otherwise go without it. In addition, the mandate forces into the insurance risk pool more healthy individuals, whose premiums on average will be higher than their health care expenses. This allows insurers to subsidize the costs of covering the unhealthy individuals the reforms require them to accept").

[91] *Id.* at 2594-2601.

[92] *Id.* at 2586, 2591(Roberts, Ch.J., with Breyer and Kagan, JJ.)(emphasis in the original)("The power to *regulate* commerce presupposes the existence of commercial activity to be regulated.... The individual mandate forces individual into commerce precisely because they elected to refrain from commercial activity. Such a law cannot be sustained under a clause authorizing Congress to 'regulate Commerce'").

[93] *Id.* at 2644 (Scalia, Kennedy, Thomas, & Alito, JJ., dissenting) (internal citations omitted)(emphasis in the original) and later the four also declared, "It is true enough that Congress needs only a 'rational basis' for concluding that the *regulated activity* substantially affects interstate commerce. But it must be *activity* affecting commerce that is regulated, and not merely the failure to engage in commerce," *id.* at 2649.

[94] *Id.* at 2643. The dissenters reiterated the theme throughout: "If Congress can reach out and command even those furthest removed from an interstate market to participate in the market, then the Commerce Clause becomes a font of unlimited power, or in Hamilton's words, 'the hideous monster whose devouring jaws ... spare neither sex nor age, nor high no low, nor sacred nor profane.' ... The lesson of these cases [*New York*, *Printz*, *Lopez*, and *Morrison*] is that the Commerce Clause, even when supplemented by the Necessary and Proper Clause, is not *carte blanche* for doing whatever will help achieve the ends Congress seeks by the regulation of commerce. And the last two of these cases show that the scope of the Necessary and Proper Clause is exceeded not only when the congressional action directly violates the sovereignty of the States but also when it violates the background principle of enumerated (and hence limited) federal power.... [*Raich*'s] prohibition of growing and of possession did not represent the expansion of the federal power to direct into a broad new field. The mandating of economic activity does, and since it is a field so limitless that it converts the Commerce Clause into a general authority to direct the economy, that mandating is not 'consist[ent] with the letter and spirit of the constitution.' ... As we said at the outset, whereas the precise scope of the Commerce Clause and the Necessary and Proper Clause is uncertain, the proposition that the Federal Government cannot do everything is a fundamental precept. Section 5000A is defeated by the proposition," *id.* at 2646, 2646-647, 2647 (internal citations and parentheticals omitted).

[95] *United States v. Kebodeaux*, 687 F.3d at 245-253.

[96] *Id.* at 247.

[97] *Id.* at 249-50("The basic flaw [in the government's argument] is that it overlooks the role of the states in policing within their own borders, relying on the implicit premises that the federal government must regulate sex offenders' intrastate movements because the states will not do so.... To give ... to the federal government the overlapping power to do exactly what a state could already do itself, in an area completely unrelated to commerce, just because criminals, like all human beings, can potentially cross state lines, would violate basic tenets of federalism").

[98] *Id.* at 687 F.3d at 252 ("In contrast to the statute in *Raich*, and like the statutes in *Lopez* and *Morrison*, the statute here regulates non-economic, intrastate conduct that is not 'an essential part of a larger regulation of economic activity.' *Lopez*, 514 U.S. at 561. It is a

criminal statute that 'by its terms has nothing to do with 'commerce' or any sort of economic enterprise, however broadly one might define those terms.' *Morrison*, 529 U.S. at 610(quoting *Lopez*, 514 U.S. at 561). It would thus fail the *Lopez/Morrison/Raich* test under the third Commerce Clause category as it should. To hold a non-commercial statute regulating purely intrastate conduct constitutional would read the word 'commerce' out of the Commerce Clause").

[99] *United States v. Clark*, 435 F.3d 1100, 1116 (9th Cir. 2006).

[100] *United States v. Pendleton*, 658 F.3d 299, 307-308 (3d Cir. 2011)("The Government urges us to adopt the Ninth Circuit's approach to the Foreign Commerce Clause. Although we agree with *Clark* that the Interstate Commerce Clause developed to address 'unique federalism concerns' that are absent in the foreign commerce context, we are hesitant to dispose of *Lopez's* 'time-tested framework' without further guidance from the Supreme Court").

[101] *United States v. Weingarten*, 632 F.3d 60, 71 (2d Cir. 2011).

[102] Section 1211(b), P.L. 113-4, 127 Stat.142 (2013), amending 18 U.S.C. 2433(c).

[103] *United States v. Clark*, 435 F.3d 1100, 1103 (9th Cir. 2006).

[104] *Id.*

[105] *Id.* at 1116. The court also explained that "forcing foreign commerce cases into the domestic commerce rubric is a bit like one of the stepsisters trying to don Cinderella's glass slipper; nonetheless, there is a good argument that, as found by the district court, §2423(c) can also be viewed as a valid regulation of the 'channels of commerce,'" *id.*

[106] *Id.* at 1119-120 (Ferguson, J., dissenting)(" ... §2423(c) neither punishes the act of traveling in foreign commerce, or the wrongful use or impediment of use of the channels of foreign commerce. Rather, it punishes future conduct in a foreign country entirely divorced from the act of traveling except for the fact the travel occurs at some point prior to the regulated conduct.... The mere act of boarding an international flight, without more, is insufficient to bring all of the Clark's downstream activities that involve an exchange of value within the ambit of Congress's Foreign Commerce power. On some level, every act by a U.S. citizen abroad takes place subsequent to an international flight or some form of travel in foreign commerce. 18 U.S.C. 2423(c). This cannot mean that every act with a bare economic component that occurs downstream from travel is subject to regulation by the United States under its Foreign Commerce power, or the Commerce Clause will have been converted into a general grant of police power").

[107] *United States v. Weingarten*, 632 F.3d 60, 62-3 (2d Cir. 2011).

[108] *Id.* at 61.

[109] *Id.*

[110] *Id.* at 61-2. The court also noted that the statute does apply to travel beginning in the United States, but involving multiple overseas stops and that its analysis would be different had the statute prohibited travel *affecting* foreign commerce rather than *in* foreign commerce, *id.* at 71.

[111] *Id.* at 70-1("We note, finally, that our determination that §2423(b) does not extend to travel occurring wholly between foreign nations and without any territorial nexus to the United States appropriately avoids the necessity of addressing whether such an exercise of congressional power would comport with the Constitution").

[112] *United States v. Pendleton*, 658 F.3d 299, 301 (3d Cir. 2011).

[113] *Id.* at 301-302.

[114] *Id.* at 302.

[115] *Id.* at 311(internal citations omitted)("And just as Congress may cast a wide net to stop sex offenders from traveling in interstate commerce to evade state registration requirements, so

too may it attempt to prevent sex tourists form using the channels of foreign commerce to abuse children.... In sum, because the jurisdictional element in §2423(c) has an 'express connection' to the channels of foreign commerce, we hold that it is a valid exercise of Congress's power under the Foreign Commerce Clause").

[116] Section 1211(b), P.L. 113-4, 127 Stat.142 (2013), amending 18 U.S.C. 2433(c)(language of the amendment in italics).

[117] United States v. Smith, 18 U.S. (5 Wheat.) 153, 158-59 (1820); see also United States v. Bellaizac-Hurtado, 700 F.3d 1245, 1248 (11th Cir. 2011)("The Supreme Court has interpreted that Clause to contain three distinct grants of power").

[118] *United States v. Bellaizac-Hurtado*, 700 F.3d 1245, 1247-248 (11th Cir. 2012).

[119] *Id.* at 1248.

[120] *Id.*

[121] *Id.* at 1258 ("Because drug trafficking is not a violation of customary international law, we held that Congress exceeded it power under the Offenses Clause, when it proscribed the defendants' conduct in the territorial waters of Panama"). See also *United States v. Carvajal*, ___ F.Supp.2d, ___ *24 (D.D.C. Feb. 20, 2013)("The United States has argued in its petition for rehearing en banc in *Bellaizac-Hurtado* in the Eleventh Circuit that Congress had the power to criminalize MDLEA offenses charged in that case under the Treaty Power").

[122] *Id.* at 1249, quoting, *United States v. Arjona*, 120 U.S. 479, 488 (1887).

[123] *Id.* at 1251(some internal citations omitted)("We and our sister circuits agree that the eighteenth-century phrase, the 'law of nations' is contemporary terms, means customary international law. And although the Supreme Court has never held that the 'law of nations' is synonymous with 'customary international law,' its decision *Sosa v. Alvarez-Machain*, 542 U.S. 692 (2004), confirms that it is. *See id.* at 735 (evaluating whether the 'prohibition of arbitrary arrest has attained the status of binding customary law' to determine whether Alvarez could bring a claim under the Alien Tort Statute")(The Alien Tort Statute was enacted relatively soon after ratification of the Constitution).

[124] *Id.* at 1252("We agree with our sister circuits that customary international law is determined by examining state practice and opinio juris: 'Customary international law ... consists of two components. First, there must be a general and consistent practice of states.... Second , there must be a sentence of legal obligation, or opinio juris sive necessitatis").

[125] *Id.* at 1254-257.

[126] *Id.* at 1255("The 2011 Report of the [International Narcotic Control] Board found that '[c]orruption and limited law enforcement capacity in Central America and the Caribbean have facilitated the use of smuggling channels and drug trafficking activities. The Board also has expressed concern about corruption and lack of progress in reducing illicit opium poppy cultivation in Afghanistan. The practice of these specially affected States evidences that drug trafficking is not yet considered a violation of customary international law").

[127] *United States v. Arjona*, 120 U.S. 479, 484 (1887)(upholding congressional authority to outlaw counterfeiting foreign securities in the United States, under the Law of Nations Clause, inter alia).

[128] E.g., *United States v. Davis*, 905 F.3d 245, 248 (9th Cir. 1990).

[129] E.g., *United States v. Klimavicius-Viloria*, 144 F.3d 1249, 1256 (9th Cir. 1998)("Before a United States court may entertain a prosecution for violation of the Act, there must be a sufficient nexus between the defendant and the United States so that such application would not be arbitrary and fundamentally unfair").

[130] *United States v. Ibarguen-Mosquera*, 634 F.3d 1370, 1376-377 (11th Cir. 2011).

[131] *Id.* at 1377-378.
[132] *Id.* at 1378.
[133] *Id.*
[134] *Id.* at 1378-379.
[135] *Id.* at 1379.
[136] *United States v. Saac*, 632 F.3d 1203, 1206-207 (11th Cir. 2011).
[137] *Id.* at 1209.
[138] *Id.* at 1211.
[139] *United States v. Cardales-Luna*, 632 F.3d 731, 732 (1st Cir. 2011).
[140] *Id.* at 736.
[141] 46 U.S.C. 70503(a)("An individual may not knowingly ... possess with intent to ... distribute, a controlled substance on board ... a vessel subject to the jurisdiction of the United States"); 70502(c)(1)("In this chapter, the term 'vessel subject to the jurisdiction of the United States' includes ... (C) a vessel registered in a foreign nation if that nation has consented or waived objection to enforcement of United States law by the United States ...").
[142] *Id.* at 737-38.
[143] *Id.* at 742-43.
[144] *Id.* at 743-47.
[145] *Id.* at 747-48.
[146] *Id.* at 748-49 ("No court decision dealing with MDLEA refers to any treaty obligation as the source of Congress's Article I authority").
[147] *Id.* at 750.
[148] *United States v. Dire*, 680 F.3d 446, 449 (4th Cir. 2012).
[149] *Id.* at 452.
[150] *Id.* at 469.
[151] U.S. Const. Art. I, §8, cl. 1.
[152] *South Dakota v. Dole*, 483 U.S. 203, 207-208 (1987)(upholding a statute which permitted withholding a percentage of the otherwise available federal highway funds from a state that allowed the possession of alcoholic beverages by individuals under 21 years of age).
[153] *National Federation of Independent Business v. Sebelius*, 132 S.Ct. 2566 (2012).
[154] *Id.* at 2601-607 (2012)(Roberts, Ch.J., with Breyer and Kagan, JJ); *id.* at 2666-667 (Scalia, Kennedy, Thomas, Alito, JJ., dissenting)("Seven Members of the Court agree that the Medicaid Expansion, as enacted by Congress, is unconstitutional"). Other than the dissenters, the Members of the Court determined that the appropriate remedy was to bar withholding funds for non-participation, *id.* at 2607 (Roberts, Ch.J., with Breyer and Kagan, JJ.); *id.* at 2630-631 (Ginsburg with Sotomayor, JJ. concurring in the judgment).
[155] *Id.* at 2660 (Scalia, Kennedy, Thomas, Alito, JJ., dissenting), quoting, *Pennhurst State School and Hospital v. Halderman*, 451 U.S. 1, 17 (1981).
[156] *Id.* at 2602 (Roberts, Ch.J., with Breyer and Kagan, JJ.)(internal citations and quotation marks omitted)("Congress may use its spending power to create incentives for States to act in accordance with federal policies. But when pressure turns into compulsion, the legislation runs contrary to our system of federalism. The Constitution simply does not give Congress the authority to require the States to regulate").
[157] *Id.* at 2606 ("The Court in *Steward Machine* did not attempt to fix the outermost line where persuasion gives way to coercion.... We have no need to fix a line either. It is enough for today that wherever that line may be, this statute is surely beyond it"); *id.* at 2660 (Scalia, Kennedy, Thomas, Alito, JJ., dissenting)("Whether federal spending legislation crosses the line from enticement to coercion is often difficult to determine, and court should not

conclude that legislation is unconstitutional on this ground unless the coercive nature of an offer is unmistakably clear. In this case, however, there can be no doubt. In structuring the ACA, Congress unambiguously signaled its belief that every State would have no real choice but to go along with the Medicaid Expansion. If the anticoercion rule does not apply in this case, then there is no such rule").

[158] U.S. Const. Art. I, §8, cls. 11, 12, 13, 14, 16.

[159] *United States v. Brehm*, 691 F.3d 547, 549 (4th Cir. 2012).

[160] *Id.* MEJA, 18 U.S.C. 3261-3267, treats certain offenses committed overseas by certain members of the Armed Forces or DOD contractors as if they were committed within the special maritime and territorial jurisdiction of the United States, 18 U.S.C. 3261.

[161] *United States v. Brehm*, 691 F.3d at 550.

[162] *Id.* at 551(some internal citations omitted)("The enumerated powers granted Congress by Article I, Section 8 of the Constitution are of sufficient reach to encompass any of the scenarios articulated about, including Brehm's. Of particular relevance here is Congress's express authority to 'raise and support Armies.' More generally, Congress is entitled 'make all Laws which shall be necessary and proper' to adequately support our armed forces").

[163] *Id.* at 552-54.

In: Law and Legal Issues in the United States ISBN: 978-1-63117-827-6
Editor: Laurent B. Landers

Chapter 5

JUDICIAL ACTIVITY CONCERNING ENEMY COMBATANT DETAINEES: MAJOR COURT RULINGS*

Jennifer K. Elsea and Michael John Garcia

SUMMARY

As part of the conflict with Al Qaeda and the Taliban, the United States has captured and detained numerous persons believed to have been part of or associated with enemy forces. Over the years, federal courts have considered a multitude of petitions by or on behalf of suspected belligerents challenging aspects of U.S. detention policy. Although the Supreme Court has issued definitive rulings concerning several legal issues raised in the conflict with Al Qaeda and the Taliban, many others remain unresolved, with some the subject of ongoing litigation.

This report discusses major judicial opinions concerning suspected enemy belligerents detained in the conflict with Al Qaeda and the Taliban. The report addresses all Supreme Court decisions concerning enemy combatants. It also discusses notable circuit court opinions addressing issues of ongoing relevance. In particular, it summarizes notable decisions which have (1) addressed whether the Executive may lawfully detain only persons who are "part of" Al Qaeda, the Taliban, and

---

* This is an edited, reformatted and augmented version of a Congressional Research Service publication, CRS Report for Congress R41156, prepared for Members and Committees of Congress, from www.crs.gov, dated December 11, 2012.

affiliated groups, or also those who provide support to such entities in their hostilities against the United States and its allies; (2) adopted a functional approach for assessing whether a person is "part of" Al Qaeda; (3) decided that a preponderance of evidence standard is appropriate for detainee habeas cases, but suggested that a lower standard might be constitutionally permissible, and instructed courts to assess the cumulative weight of evidence rather than each piece of evidence in isolation; (4) determined that Guantanamo detainees have a limited right to challenge their proposed transfer to foreign custody, but denied courts the authority to order detainees released into the United States; and (5) held that the constitutional writ of habeas does not presently extend to noncitizen detainees held at U.S.-operated facilities in Afghanistan. Finally, the report discusses a few criminal cases involving persons who were either involved in the 9/11 attacks (Zacarias Moussaoui) or were captured abroad by U.S. forces or allies during operations against Al Qaeda, the Taliban, and associated entities (John Walker Lindh and Ahmed Ghailani).

For over a decade, the primary legal authority governing the detention of enemy belligerents in the conflict with Al Qaeda was the 2001 Authorization for Use of Military Force ("AUMF," P.L. 107-40. In December 2011, Congress passed the National Defense Authorization Act for FY2012 ("2012 NDAA," P.L. 112-81), which contains a provision that is largely intended to codify the current understanding of the detention authority conferred by the AUMF, as has been interpreted and applied by the Executive and the D.C. Circuit. The full implications of the 2012 NDAA upon wartime detention jurisprudence remain to be seen. In any event, the act does not address many of the legal issues involving wartime detention that have not been squarely resolved by the Supreme Court. Among other things, these unresolved issues include the precise scope of the Executive's wartime detention authority, including the circumstances in which U.S. citizens may be detained; the degree to which noncitizens (or in one case, U.S. citizens) held abroad are entitled to protections under the Constitution; the authority of federal habeas courts to compel the release into the United States of detainees determined to be unlawfully held; and the ability of detainees to receive advance notice and to challenge their proposed transfer to foreign custody.

INTRODUCTION

As part of the conflict with the Taliban and Al Qaeda, the United States has captured and detained numerous persons believed to have been part of or associated with enemy forces. Over the years, federal courts have considered a multitude of petitions by or on behalf of suspected belligerents challenging aspects of U.S. detention policy. The Supreme Court has issued definitive rulings concerning several legal issues raised in the conflict with Al Qaeda and the Taliban, including executive authority under the 2001 Authorization for Use of Military Force ("AUMF," P.L. 107-40) to detain properly designated enemy belligerents captured on the Afghan battlefield; the application of at least some provisions of the 1949 Geneva Conventions to the conflict with Al Qaeda; and the ability of detainees held in the United States or at the U.S. Naval Station in Guantanamo Bay, Cuba, to challenge the legality of their detention in habeas corpus proceedings.

In December 2011, Congress passed the National Defense Authorization Act for FY2012 ("2012 NDAA," P.L. 112-81), which contains a provision largely intended to codify the present understanding of the detention authority conferred by the AUMF, as interpreted and applied by the Executive and the D.C. Circuit.[1] The full implications of the 2012 NDAA upon judicial activity concerning wartime detention remains to be seen. In any event, the act does not address many of the legal issues involving wartime detention which, while occasioning significant political debate, have not been squarely resolved by the Supreme Court. These issues include the full scope of the Executive's detention authority, including the circumstances in which U.S. citizens may be detained as enemy belligerents; the degree to which noncitizens held at Guantanamo and other locations outside the United States are entitled to protections under the Constitution; the authority of federal habeas courts to compel the release of detainees determined to be unlawfully held into the United States if the Executive cannot effectuate their release to another country; and the ability of detainees to receive advance notice and challenge their proposed transfer to a foreign country. Additionally, the Supreme Court may be called upon to determine the nature of procedural rules to be applied in habeas cases and the proper standard of evidence to be applied. To the extent that these rules are found to differ from the Federal Rules of Civil Procedure and other court rules, it may be necessary to determine whether the same procedural rules apply to both U.S. citizens and foreign nationals who may be detained under the AUMF authority.

This report briefly summarizes major judicial opinions concerning suspected enemy belligerents[2] detained in the conflict with Al Qaeda and the Taliban. It discusses all Supreme Court decisions concerning enemy combatants. It also addresses notable circuit court opinions addressing issues of ongoing relevance to U.S. detention policy. The report also discusses a few notable decisions by federal district courts, including criminal cases involving persons who were either involved in the 9/11 attacks or were captured abroad by U.S. forces or allies during operations against Al Qaeda and the Taliban.

SUPREME COURT DECISIONS

Since 2004, the Supreme Court has made several rulings concerning enemy combatants. These have addressed, *inter alia*, the Executive's authority to detain enemy belligerents under the 2001 AUMF; the legality of military commissions established by presidential order to try suspected belligerents for violations of the law of war; and detainees' access to federal courts.

Hamdi v. Rumsfeld, 542 U.S. 507 (2004)[3]

The *Hamdi* case addressed the President's authority to detain "enemy combatants" as part of the conflict authorized by the AUMF, and whether a detained individual could seek independent review of the legality of his detention. Four separate opinions were written, with none receiving support of a majority of the justices. However, a majority of the Court recognized that, as a necessary incident to the 2001 AUMF, the President is authorized to detain persons captured while fighting U.S. forces in Afghanistan (including U.S. citizens), and potentially hold such persons for the duration of the conflict to prevent their return to hostilities.[4] A divided Court found that persons deemed "enemy combatants" have the right to challenge the legality of their detention before a judge or other "neutral decision-maker," with a majority of the Justices clearly recognizing the existence of such a right in the case of a detained U.S. citizen.[5]

In a plurality opinion joined by three other Justices, Justice O'Connor wrote that a citizen detained as an enemy combatant must receive notice of the factual basis for his classification and a fair opportunity to rebut the government's factual assertions before a neutral decision-maker, and has a right to counsel in connection with such a hearing. The plurality suggested, however, that the exigencies of the circumstances of a detainee's capture may allow for a tailoring of enemy combatant proceedings "to alleviate their uncommon potential to burden the Executive at a time of ongoing military conflict," possibly allowing hearsay evidence and "a presumption in favor of the Government's evidence," as long as a fair opportunity to rebut such evidence is provided.[6]

***Rumsfeld v. Padilla*, 542 U.S. 426 (2004)**[7]

The *Padilla* case, decided on the same day as *Hamdi*, concerned a habeas challenge by Jose Padilla, a U.S. citizen who was designated as an "enemy combatant" and militarily detained in the United States for his alleged involvement in an Al Qaeda plot to detonate a "dirty bomb." Unlike the petitioner in *Hamdi*, who was captured in the Afghan zone of combat, Padilla was captured on U.S. soil. In a 5-4 ruling, the Court remanded the case without deciding the merits on the ground that Padilla's habeas petition had not been filed in the proper venue. In doing so, the majority did not reach the merits of Padilla's claim that any authority the President might have under the AUMF to detain "enemy combatants" did not extend to persons captured on American soil and away from the Afghan battlefield. Four Justices would have found jurisdiction based on the "exceptional circumstances" of the case and affirmed the holding below that detention is prohibited under the Non-Detention Act, 18 U.S.C. §4001(a) (prohibiting the detention of U.S. citizens unless authorized by an act of Congress). Padilla filed a new petition in the Fourth Circuit, and the appellate court considered the legality of his detention in *Padilla v. Haft*, discussed *infra*.

***Rasul v. Bush*, 542 U.S. 466 (2004)**[8]

In *Rasul v. Bush*, the Court held in a 6-3 ruling that the federal habeas corpus statute, 28 U.S.C. §2241, provided federal courts with jurisdiction to consider habeas corpus petitions by or on behalf of persons detained at the U.S. Naval Station in Guantanamo Bay, Cuba. Having found that Guantanamo detainees were entitled by statute to seek habeas review of their detention, the Court did not reach the issue of whether the constitutional writ of habeas also extended to noncitizens held at Guantanamo. The Court also did not address whether a less rigorous burden of proof or relaxed evidentiary procedures would be appropriate in comparison to ordinary habeas cases. Congress subsequently attempted to limit the reach of the federal habeas statute to Guantanamo detainees through the enactment of the Detainee Treatment Act of 2005 (DTA)[9] and the Military Commissions Act of 2006 (MCA).[10]

Hamdan v. Rumsfeld, 548 U.S. 557 (2006)[11]

In *Hamdan v. Rumsfeld*, the Supreme Court reviewed the validity of military tribunals established pursuant to presidential order to try suspected terrorists for violations of the law of war. The petitioner Hamdan was charged with conspiracy to commit a violation of the law of war. Prior to reaching the merits of the case, the *Hamdan* Court first had to determine whether the DTA stripped it of jurisdiction to review habeas corpus challenges by or on behalf of Guantanamo detainees whose petitions had already been filed prior to enactment of the DTA. In a 5-3 opinion, the Court held that the DTA did not apply to such petitions. Turning to the merits of the case, the majority held that the convened tribunals did not comply with the Uniform Code of Military Justice (UCMJ) or the law of war, as incorporated in the UCMJ and embodied in the 1949 Geneva Conventions, which the Court held applicable to the armed conflict with Al Qaeda. The Court concluded that, at a minimum, Common Article 3 of the Geneva Conventions applies to persons captured in the conflict with Al Qaeda, according to them a minimum baseline of protections, including protection from the "passing of sentences and the carrying out of executions without previous judgment pronounced by a regularly constituted court, affording all the judicial guarantees which are recognized as indispensable by civilized peoples." The Court held that military commissions were not "regularly constituted" because they deviated too far from the rules that apply to courts-martial, without a satisfactory explanation of the need for departing from such rules. In particular, the Court noted that the commission rules allowing the exclusion of the defendant from attending portions of his trial or hearing some of the evidence against him deviated substantially from court-martial procedures.

A four-justice plurality of the Court also recognized that for an act to be triable under the common law of war, the precedent for it being treated as an offense must be "plain and unambiguous."[12] After examining the history of military commission practice in the United States and internationally, the plurality further concluded that conspiracy to violate the law of war was not in itself a crime under the common law of war or the UCMJ.

Boumediene v. Bush, 553 U.S. 723 (2008)[13]

In the aftermath of the *Hamdan* decision, Congress enacted the MCA, which, *inter alia*, expressly eliminated court jurisdiction over all pending and future causes of action other than via the limited review permitted under the DTA. In the 2008 case of *Boumediene v. Bush*, the Court ruled in a 5-4 opinion that the constitutional privilege of habeas extends to Guantanamo detainees. In doing so, the Court stated that the Constitution's extraterritorial application turns on "objective factors and practical concerns."[14] The Court deemed at least three factors to be relevant in assessing the extraterritorial scope of the constitutional writ of habeas: (1) the citizenship and status of the detainee and the adequacy of the status determination process; (2) the nature of the site where the person is seized and detained; and (3) practical obstacles inherent in resolving the prisoner's entitlement to the writ.

The Court also found that MCA §7, which limited judicial review of executive determinations of the *Boumediene* petitioners' enemy combatant status to that authorized by the DTA, did not provide an adequate habeas substitute and therefore acted as an unconstitutional suspension of the writ of habeas corpus. The majority listed a number of potential constitutional infirmities in the DTA review process, including the absence of provisions (1) empowering a reviewing court to order the release of a detainee found to be unlawfully held; (2) permitting petitioners to challenge the President's authority to detain them indefinitely; (3) enabling a presiding court to review or correct administrative findings of fact which formed the legal basis for an individual's detention; and (4) permitting the detainee to present exculpatory evidence discovered after the conclusion of administrative proceedings.

Although the *Boumediene* Court held that the constitutional writ of habeas extends to noncitizens held at Guantanamo, it did not opine as to the scope of habeas review available to detainees, the remedy available for those persons found to be unlawfully held by the United States, or the extent to which other constitutional provisions extend to noncitizens held at Guantanamo and elsewhere.

Gates v. Bismullah, 554 U.S. 913 (2008)

Prior to the Supreme Court's decision in *Boumediene*, the D.C. Circuit Court of Appeals considered a number of challenges brought under the DTA in which detainees contested determinations by Combatant Status Review Tribunals (CSRTs) that they were properly detained as enemy combatants. In 2008, the government petitioned the Supreme Court to review two rulings by the D.C. Circuit regarding the scope of judicial review of CSRT determinations.[15] The Supreme Court granted certiorari and vacated the appellate court's decisions, remanding for reconsideration in light of the Supreme Court's decision in *Boumediene*. Upon remand, the D.C. Circuit reinstated without explanation its decisions, presumably because it did not find the *Boumediene* ruling to conflict with its decisions in these cases.

al-Marri v. Spagone, 555 U.S. 1220 (2009)

In December 2008, the Supreme Court granted certiorari to review an *en banc* ruling by the Fourth Circuit Court of Appeals regarding petitioner al-Marri, an alien lawfully admitted into the United States on a student visa who had been arrested by civilian law enforcement and thereafter transferred to military custody for detention as an enemy combatant. At the time, the Court's decision to review the Fourth Circuit's ruling was thought to have potentially set the stage for a definitive pronouncement regarding the President's authority to militarily detain terrorist suspects apprehended away from the Afghan battlefield. However, before the Court could consider the merits of the case, the government requested that the Court authorize al-Marri's release from military custody and transfer to civilian authorities to face criminal charges. The Court granted the government's request, vacated the appellate court's earlier judgment, and transferred the case back to the lower court with orders to dismiss it as moot. The appellate court's ruling is discussed in more detail below.

Kiyemba v. Obama, 130 S.Ct. 1235 (2010)

In October 2009, the Supreme Court agreed to review a ruling by a three-judge panel of the D.C. Circuit Court of Appeals in the case of *Kiyemba v. Obama*, discussed *infra*. The *Kiyemba* case involved several Guantanamo detainees who, despite no longer being considered enemy combatants and having been cleared for release, had not been transferred from Guantanamo on account of the government being unable to effectuate their release to a foreign country. The *Kiyemba* petitioners sought reversal of a D.C. Circuit ruling finding that a federal habeas court lacked the authority to compel the executive to release the detainees into the United States. Following the Supreme Court's grant of certiorari, however, several *Kiyemba* petitioners were resettled in foreign countries, and the United States was able to find countries willing to settle the remaining petitioners, although five petitioners rejected these countries' offers for resettlement. On March 1, 2010, the Supreme Court vacated the appellate court's opinion and remanded the case in light of these developments. Because the Supreme Court had granted certiorari on the understanding that no remedy was available for the petitioners other than release into the United States, it returned the case to the D.C. Circuit to review the ramifications of the new circumstances. Discussion of subsequent action taken by the D.C. Circuit, as well as by the Supreme Court with respect to another petition for certiorari by the *Kiyemba* petitioners, is found below.

Kiyemba v. Obama, 131 S. Ct. 1631 (2011)

Following the Supreme Court's remand of the *Kiyemba* case back to the D.C. Circuit, the circuit panel reinstated its opinion with slight modifications. The *Kiyemba* petitioners once again sought Supreme Court review of the circuit court's ruling that federal habeas courts lacked authority to compel the petitioners' release into the United States. On April 18, 2011, the Supreme Court denied their request for review. Eight Supreme Court Justices took part in the decision, with Justice Kagan recusing herself. In joining the opinion, Justice Breyer issued a statement joined by Justices Kennedy, Ginsburg, and Sotomayor, which emphasized that the issue that had initially been presented when the *Kiyemba* petitioners first sought review by the Supreme Court was "whether a district court may order the release of an unlawfully held prisoner into the United States *where no other remedy is available*." Because the government had received offers of resettlement for the petitioners, the petitioners had not proffered or alleged evidence that they would face torture or other harm, and the government continued to seek plaintiffs' resettlement, Justice Breyer found "no Government-imposed obstacle to petitioners' timely release and appropriate resettlement." However, Justice Breyer stated that should these circumstances materially change, the petitioners "may of course raise their original issue (or related issues) again in the lower courts and in this Court."

RULINGS BY THE D.C. CIRCUIT COURT OF APPEALS

Most judicial activity concerning U.S. detention policy in the conflict with Al Qaeda has occurred within the D.C. Circuit. Following the Supreme Court's ruling in *Boumediene* that the constitutional writ of habeas corpus extends to detainees held at Guantanamo, over 200 habeas petitions were filed by detainees in the U.S. District Court for the District of Columbia. Courts considering habeas claims have sometimes reached differing conclusions regarding the scope of the Executive's detention authority; the admissibility of hearsay evidence and involuntary statements made by detainees; the appropriate methodology for assessing the sufficiency and reliability of evidence proffered by the government to justify the legality of a habeas petitioner's detention; and the remedy available for those persons whom a habeas court determines to have been unlawfully detained.[16] Decisions by the U.S. Court of Appeals for the D.C. Circuit have generally been favorable to the legal positions advanced by the government. Since 2009, the appellate court has issued rulings concluding, among other things, that:

- the Executive may lawfully detain persons who are "part of" Al Qaeda, the Taliban, and affiliated groups, and possibly also persons who provide a sufficient degree of support to such entities in their hostilities against the United States and its allies (*Al-Bihani v. Obama*);
- a functional approach is appropriate when assessing whether a person is "part of" Al Qaeda, meaning that judges should consider the significance of a person's activities in relation to the organization, rather than requiring formal proof of membership, such as evidence the petitioner received orders from the organization's hierarchy (*Awad v. Obama*, *Bensayah v. Obama*, *Salahi v. Obama*);
- the government may satisfy its evidentiary burden in support of a person's detention when its factual claims are supported by a preponderance of evidence (*Al-Bihani v. Obama*, *Al Odah v. United States*), but a lower standard might be constitutionally permissible (*Al-Adahi v. Obama, Almerfedi v. Obama*);
- it is proper for a habeas court to assess the cumulative weight and effect of proffered evidence according to a "conditional probability analysis" when determining whether the government has demonstrated factual grounds for detaining a habeas petitioner (*Al-Adahi v. Obama*, *Salahi v. Obama*);
- consideration of hearsay evidence in habeas cases is not determined by the Federal Rules of Evidence (*Al Odah v. United States*, *Al-Madhwani v. Obama*);

- official government records, including government intelligence reports, are entitled to a presumption of regularity in Guantanamo habeas litigation (*Latif v. Obama*);
- the writ of habeas affords Guantanamo detainees with a limited right to challenge their proposed transfer to the custody of a foreign government (*Kiyemba II*);
- habeas courts lack authority, absent an authorizing statute, to compel the Executive to release non-citizen detainees into the United States, even if such persons have been determined by the court to be unlawfully detained (*Kiyemba I* and *III*);
- it is unlikely that noncitizens who have been transferred to foreign custody may seek judicial review of their designation as enemy combatants by the U.S. government (*Gul v. Obama*); and
- the constitutional writ of habeas does not presently extend to noncitizen detainees held at U.S.-operated facilities in Afghanistan (*Maqaleh v. Gates*).

In some of these cases, affected detainees have requested Supreme Court review. Several of these requests have been denied. It remains to be seen whether the Supreme Court will ultimately agree to review any of the D.C. Circuit's decisions, or whether the appellate court's rulings will remain controlling for the foreseeable future.

The following section discusses major rulings made by the D.C. Circuit Court of Appeals regarding persons designated as enemy combatants that involve matters of continuing relevance to U.S. detention policy. It does not discuss those rulings that were subsequently overruled by the Supreme Court on the merits.

Scope of Executive's Detention Authority and Related Evidentiary Burdens

The D.C. Circuit has issued several opinions relating to the scope of the Executive's authority to detain persons as part of the conflict with Al Qaeda, the Taliban, and associated forces. These opinions have also addressed the issues related to the sufficiency and reliability of evidence proffered by the government in support of its factual claims.

Al-Bihani v. Obama, 590 F.3d 866, En Banc Rehearing Denied, 619 F.3d 1 (D.C. Cir. 2010), Cert. Denied, 131 S. Ct. 1814 (2011)

In January 2010, a three-judge panel of the D.C. Circuit Court of Appeals issued a ruling concerning the scope of the government's detention authority under the AUMF in the case of *AlBihani v. Obama*. In an opinion supported in full by two members of the panel,[17] the appellate court recognized that, at a minimum, the President was authorized to detain persons who were subject to the jurisdiction of military commissions established pursuant to the Military Commissions Acts of 2006 and 2009; namely, any person who was "part of forces associated with Al Qaeda or the Taliban," along with "those who purposefully and materially support such forces in hostilities against U.S. Coalition partners."[18] While the panel concluded that either purposeful and material support for an AUMF-targeted organization in hostilities against the United States or membership in such an organization may be independently sufficient to justify detention, the court declined "to explore the outer bounds of what constitutes sufficient support or indicia of membership to meet the detention standard." It did, however, note that this standard would permit the detention of a "civilian contractor" who "purposefully and materially supported" an AUMFtargeted organization through "traditional food operations essential to a fighting force and the carrying of arms."[19] Notwithstanding the government's reliance on the law of war to interpret the scope of the AUMF and arguably in conflict with Supreme Court discussion of the issue in *Hamdi*, the panel rejected the idea that the international law of war has any relevance to the courts' interpretation of the scope of the detention power conferred by the AUMF.

The panel also held that the procedural protections afforded in habeas cases involving wartime detainees do not need to mirror those provided to persons in the traditional criminal law context, where evidence must demonstrate guilt beyond reasonable doubt, or the lesser procedures courts have used in any specific habeas context. The panel stated:

> [C]ourts are neither bound by the procedural limits created for other detention contexts nor obliged to use them as baselines from which any departures must be justified. Detention of aliens outside the sovereign territory of the United States during wartime is a different and peculiar circumstance, and the appropriate habeas procedures cannot be conceived of as mere extensions of an existing doctrine. Rather, those procedures are a whole new branch of the tree.[20]

In the context of military detention of enemy belligerents, the court found, the government need only support its authority to detain using a "preponderance of evidence" standard.[21] The court rejected the petitioner's argument, based on his reading of *Hamdi*,[22] that any relaxation of procedural standards must be justified by the particular exigencies of the case. The court established the hearsay rule for detainee habeas cases, at least those brought by aliens abroad[23]:

> [T]he question a habeas court must ask when presented with hearsay is not whether it is admissible—it is always admissible—but what probative weight to ascribe to whatever indicia of reliability it exhibits.[24]

The D.C. Circuit Court of Appeals thereafter denied a petition for an *en banc* rehearing of the *AlBihani* case. However, a concurring opinion joined by a majority of the active appellate court judges characterized certain aspects of the panel's decision, concerning the application of international law of war principles in interpreting the AUMF, to be non-binding dicta.[25] It did not address whether any portions of the *Al-Bihani* ruling concerning the lawfulness of detaining persons on account of membership or support for Al Qaeda, the Taliban, or associated forces also constituted non-binding dicta. However, circuit court decisions since *Al-Bihani* have appeared to construe the AUMF as authorizing the Executive to detain persons who are "part of" organizations targeted by the AUMF as well as those who provide support to such entities.[26]

Moreover, the 2012 NDAA expressly authorizes the detention of persons who have "substantially supported al-Qaeda, the Taliban, or associated forces that are engaged in hostilities against the United States or its coalition partners, including any person who has...directly supported such hostilities in aid of such enemy forces."[27]

In any event, in litigation following *Al-Bihani* involving Guantanamo detainees, the Obama Administration has not justified its detention claims solely on the grounds that a particular detainee provided support to Al Qaeda or the Taliban. Instead, its legal justification for holding persons on account of wartime activity has been that they were at least functionally "part of" Al Qaeda, the Taliban, or an associated force at the time of capture.

On April 4, 2011, the Supreme Court denied a petition to review the *Al-Bihani* decision. The case should not be confused with ongoing litigation in a similarly-named case involving the petitioner's brother.[28] The habeas petitioner in that case sought Supreme Court review of the denial of his habeas petition, but the Court declined to hear the case.

Al-Adahi v. Obama, 613 F.3d 1102 (D.C. Cir. 2010), Cert. Denied, 131 S. Ct. 1001 (2011)

In *Al-Adahi*, a three-judge panel of the D.C. Circuit endorsed the use of "conditional probability analysis" by habeas courts when considering the sufficiency and reliability of evidence proffered by the government in support of its claim that a person is lawfully detained under the AUMF. The case involved review of a district court decision granting a habeas petition by a Guantanamo detainee who the government claimed was "part of" Al Qaeda, following its determination that the government had failed to demonstrate its claim by a preponderance of evidence.

On appeal, the D.C. Circuit panel assumed *arguendo* that the government was required to show by a preponderance of evidence that the petitioner was lawfully detained under the AUMF, but suggested that reliance on this standard may not be constitutionally required. It next turned to the district court's analysis of evidence proffered by the government in support of its detention of petitioner, and concluded that the lower court "clearly erred in its treatment of the evidence" and its application of the preponderance of evidence standard.

Examining the record, the circuit panel held that the lower court erred by separately considering the sufficiency of each item of evidence proffered by the government, and finding that the government failed to meet its evidentiary burden because no individual piece of evidence provided sufficient grounds to justify the petitioner's detention. The circuit panel was also critical of the lower court for failing to make any findings regarding the petitioner's "implausible" and inconsistent explanations for some of his activities, stating that it is a "well-settled principle that false exculpatory statements are evidence—often strong evidence—of guilt."

According to the circuit panel, "conditional probability analysis" is appropriate for assessing whether a person's detention under the AUMF is supported by the preponderance of the evidence. Using this framework, a habeas court must consider the cumulative weight and effect of proffered evidence when assessing whether the government has satisfied its evidentiary burden. In describing "conditional probability analysis" and its implications for the assessment of the evidence in the case before it, the *Al-Adahi* panel wrote:

"Many mundane mistakes in reasoning can be traced to a shaky grasp of the notion of conditional probability." JOHN ALLEN PAULOS, INNUMERACY: MATHEMATICAL ILLITERACY AND ITS CONSEQUENCES 63 (1988). The key consideration is that although some events are independent (coin flips, for example), other events are dependent: "the occurrence of one of them makes the occurrence of the other more or less likely.... " JOHN ALLEN PAULOS, BEYOND NUMERACY: RUMINATIONS OF A NUMBERS MAN 189 (1991). Dr. Paulos gives this example: "the probability that a person chosen at random from the phone book is over 250 pounds is quite small. However, if it's known that the person chosen is over six feet four inches tall, then the conditional probability that he or she also weighs more than 250 pounds is considerably higher." INNUMERACY [63].

Those who do not take into account conditional probability are prone to making mistakes in judging evidence. They may think that if a particular fact does not itself prove the ultimate proposition (e.g., whether the detainee was part of al-Qaida), the fact may be tossed aside and the next fact may be evaluated as if the first did not exist. This is precisely how the district court proceeded in this case: Al-Adahi's ties to bin Laden "cannot prove" he was part of Al-Qaida and this evidence therefore "must not distract the Court." ... The fact that AlAdahi stayed in an al-Qaida guesthouse "is not in itself sufficient to justify detention." AlAdahi's attendance at an al-Qaida training camp "is not sufficient to carry the Government's burden of showing that he was a part" of al-Qaida. And so on. The government is right: the district court wrongly "required each piece of the government's evidence to bear weight without regard to all (or indeed any) other evidence in the case. This was a fundamental mistake that infected the court's entire analysis."[29]

Employing this standard, the circuit panel examined the evidentiary record (including false exculpatory statements made by the petitioner during interrogation),[30] and concluded that the government had satisfied its evidentiary burden of proving that the petitioner was subject to detention on account of membership in Al Qaeda. The circuit panel also concluded that some of the individual pieces of evidence proffered by the government—including evidence showing that the petitioner had voluntarily stayed at an Al Qaeda guesthouse and had received and executed orders from Al Qaeda members while at a weapons training camp—constituted sufficient grounds to justify his detention.

On January 18, 2011, the Supreme Court denied a petition of certiorari to review the *Al-Adahi* ruling.

Awad v. Obama, 608 F.3d 1 (D.C. Cir. 2010), Cert. Denied, 131 S. Ct. 1814 (2011)

This case involved the review of a district court's denial of habeas relief to a Guantanamo detainee whom the government alleged to have been "part of" Al Qaeda at the time of capture. The petitioner, a Yemeni national, admitted to U.S. interrogators that he had travelled to Afghanistan to receive weapons training and fight U.S. forces. He was subsequently injured in an air raid, which resulted in the amputation of one of his legs. When Al Qaeda took over a portion of a hospital where petitioner was being treated, he allegedly joined Al Qaeda fighters barricaded there when coalition forces attempted to re-take the hospital, but he was surrendered by Al Qaeda fighters due to his injury.

In upholding the district court's denial of habeas relief, the circuit panel rejected several legal and factual challenges raised by petitioner. As an initial matter, the *Awad* panel reaffirmed the propriety of using conditional probability analysis, previously relied upon by the D.C. Circuit in *Al-Adahi*, to assess petitioner's evidentiary challenges; accordingly, it would not "weigh each piece of evidence in isolation, but [would] consider all of the evidence taken as a whole." The circuit panel then proceeded to consider petitioner's argument that some of the evidence that had been proffered against him, including Al Qaeda documents and out-of-court statements by another detainee who was present at the hospital where petitioner was apprehended, were unreliable hearsay. The panel noted past jurisprudence recognizing that "hearsay evidence is admissible in this type of habeas proceeding if the hearsay is reliable," and concluded that the proffered evidence was sufficiently reliable to have been considered by the lower court.

The court then turned to petitioner's legal challenges. The panel rejected petitioner's argument the government was required to justify its claims that he was lawfully detainable through clear and convincing evidence, and found that the less rigorous "preponderance of evidence" standard that had been relied upon by the district court was constitutionally permissible. The circuit panel also dismissed petitioner's argument that his habeas petition could only be denied if a specific finding of fact was made that petitioner would pose a threat to the United States and its allies if released. The panel characterized the circuit court's prior decision in *Al-Bihani* as foreclosing this argument, and it went on to state that

> the United States's authority to detain an enemy combatant is not dependent on whether an individual would pose a threat ... if released but rather upon the continuation of hostilities.... Whether a

> detainee would pose a threat to U.S. interests if released is not at issue in habeas corpus proceedings in federal courts concerning aliens detained under the authority conferred by the AUMF.

Finally, the panel rejected petitioner's argument that, in order for the government to justify his detention under the AUMF, it would have to demonstrate that he was part of Al Qaeda's "command structure." The panel held that petitioner's actions in joining Al Qaeda fighters behind a barricade were sufficient grounds to conclude he was "part of" Al Qaeda. It also suggested other situations where the government would not need to prove that a detainee was subject to Al Qaeda's "command structure" in order to justify its conclusion that he was "part of" Al Qaeda, such as when a person was captured in Afghanistan as part of a group that was shooting at U.S. forces and identified himself upon capture as an Al Qaeda member.

The Supreme Court denied a petition to review the *Awad* decision on April 4, 2011.

Al Odah v. United States, 611 F.3d 8 (D.C. Cir. 2010), Cert. Denied, 131 S. Ct. 1812 (2011)

In June 2010, a three-judge panel of the D.C. Circuit Court of Appeals upheld a district court's denial of a habeas petition brought on behalf of a person who had been detained at Guantanamo since 2002 due to his allegedly being part of Al Qaeda and Taliban forces. The petitioner challenged the procedures used by the district court when admitting evidence, and also the sufficiency of the evidence upon which its judgment on the merits was based. The circuit panel rejected these challenges as being foreclosed by controlling legal precedent. Specifically, the panel rejected the petitioner's argument that the government was required to support its factual claims in support of the legality of the petitioner's detention through "clear and convincing evidence." The panel recognized that based on binding precedent within the circuit, it is "well-settled law that a preponderance of the evidence standard is constitutional in considering a habeas petition from an individual detained pursuant to authority granted by the AUMF."[31]

The panel further rejected petitioner's argument that the admission of hearsay was statutorily restricted by the Federal Rules of Evidence and federal habeas statute. The court found this argument unpersuasive, citing both to the Supreme Court's ruling in *Hamdi* and the appellate court's prior jurisprudence as recognizing that district courts may admit reliable hearsay evidence when considering a habeas petition by an individual detained under the AUMF. In this case, the court agreed with the lower court that the hearsay evidence demonstrated sufficient indicia of reliability to be accorded weight:

> For example, in considering interrogation reports of a third party concerning al Qaeda and Taliban travel routes into Afghanistan, the [district] court noted that this hearsay was corroborated by "multiple other examples of individuals who used this route to travel to Afghanistan for the purpose of jihad." The court indicated that it was aware of the limitations of this evidence when it concluded that "[although far from conclusive, the Government's evidence suggests that an individual using this travel route to reach Kandahar may have done so because it was a route used by some individuals seeking to enter Afghanistan for the purpose of jihad."[32]

The court approved this analysis of hearsay and declined to find an abuse of discretion on the part of the district court. The panel also rejected the petitioner's challenges to the individual pieces of evidence proffered by the government in support of his detention.

On April 4, 2011, the Supreme Court denied a petition to review the *Al-Odah* decision. The *AlOdah* ruling has been relied upon by the D.C. Circuit in other cases, including in one case where which a petition for certiorari was denied by the Supreme Court.[33]

Bensayah v. Obama, 610 F.3d 718 (D.C. Cir. 2010)

This case involved the review of a district court denial of habeas relief to an Algerian citizen who had been arrested by Bosnian authorities in 2001 and was subsequently transferred to U.S. custody for detention at Guantanamo. The government claimed that although the petitioner had not directly taken part in combat activities against the United States, he had intended to travel to Afghanistan to fight U.S. forces and had facilitated the travel of others to do the same. The executive branch initially argued that it had legal authority to hold the detainee, pursuant to the authority vested by the AUMF and the President's "inherent authority" as Commander-in-Chief, on account of the detainee's alleged membership in and support for Al Qaeda. In 2008, a federal district court judge denied the detainee's habeas petition.[34] The court found that the government had sufficient grounds to detain the petitioner for providing support to Al Qaeda, but declined to decide whether there were also sufficient grounds to detain the petitioner for being "part of" the organization.

On appeal, the executive eschewed reliance on certain evidence that it earlier relied upon to demonstrate that petitioner acted as a travel facilitator for

Al Qaeda, and also modified its argument in support of petitioner's detention—abandoning its argument that the petitioner was subject to detention on account of providing support to Al Qaeda, and instead arguing that he was subject to detention on account of being "part of" the organization. The government also relied solely on the authority granted by the AUMF to justify its detention authority, rather than any independent authority deriving from the Commander-in-Chief Clause. The reviewing circuit panel reversed and remanded the case back to the district court, finding that evidence relied upon by the lower court to conclude that the petitioner had supported Al Qaeda was insufficient to show that he was "part of" the organization.

Portions of the appellate panel's opinion discussing the sufficiency and reliability of the evidence proffered by the government were largely redacted. However, the published opinion provided further clarification regarding the D.C. Circuit's view of the detention authority conferred by the AUMF. The *Bensayah* panel recognized that the D.C. Circuit had previously made clear that "the AUMF authorizes the Executive to detain, at the least, any individual who is functionally part of al Qaeda." According to the panel, because Al Qaeda's organizational structure is generally unknown and thought to be amorphous, a determination as to whether an individual is "part of" the organization "must be made on a case-by-case basis by using a functional rather than a formal approach and by focusing upon the actions of the individual in relation to the organization." Although the panel concluded that evidence demonstrating that a person operated within Al Qaeda's command structure was sufficient to show that he was "part of" the organization, it suggested that there "may be other indicia that a particular individual is sufficiently involved with the organization to be deemed part of it." Nonetheless, the panel indicated that the "purely independent conduct of a freelancer" is not sufficient grounds to deem him to be functionally part of Al Qaeda.

Salahi v. Obama, 625 F.3d 745 (D.C. Cir. 2010)

This case involved review of a district court order granting habeas relief to a Guantanamo detainee captured in 2001 in Mauritania. Although the petitioner had not fought against the United States, the government alleged that he was lawfully detained on the grounds that he was "part of" Al Qaeda. Most of the evidence proffered by the government in support of its allegations concerned activities by the petitioner which occurred years before the 9/11 attacks. In habeas proceedings before the lower court, the government presented evidence that petitioner swore an oath of loyalty to Al Qaeda in

1991 and provided support to the organization at various points thereafter, including by recruiting members, hosting organization leaders, and providing the organization with financial support. For his part, the petitioner claimed that he severed ties with Al Qaeda in the early 1990s. The district court ruled that the government failed to satisfy its evidentiary burden in proving that the petitioner was "part of" Al Qaeda at the time of capture, and ordered the detainee to be released. In doing so, it rejected the government's argument that once the petitioner swore an oath of allegiance to Al Qaeda, he bore the burden of demonstrating that he had later withdrawn from the organization.

On appeal, a three-judge panel vacated the lower court's decision, finding that intervening case law—namely, the circuit court's opinions in the *Al-Adahi*, *Awad*, and *Bensayah* cases discussed above—cast doubt on the lower court's approach to determining whether petitioner was "part of" Al Qaeda. In particular, the *Salahi* panel found that the lower court had improperly required the government to prove that the petitioner had received and executed orders from Al Qaeda in order to demonstrate his membership in the organization. Subsequent circuit jurisprudence established that membership could be demonstrated not only from evidence that a person was part of Al Qaeda's "command structure," but also from activities which revealed a person to be functionally part of the organization. The panel recognized, however, that in cases like the one involving petitioner, who had not engaged in combat activities against the United States, "the government's failure to prove that an individual was acting under orders from al-Qaida may be *relevant* to the question of whether the individual was 'part of' the organization when captured."[35]

Although the government requested that the *Salahi* panel direct the district court to deny the habeas petition, it declined to do so, finding that it was appropriate to remand the case so the lower court could conduct further proceedings consistent with circuit jurisprudence that developed after its initial ruling. The panel found that because the lower court lacked guidance from subsequent circuit jurisprudence, it had primarily looked for evidence as to whether petitioner participated in Al Qaeda's command structure, but "did not make definitive findings regarding certain key facts necessary for us to determine as a matter of law whether Salahi was in fact 'part of' al-Qaida when captured."

In remanding the case to the lower court for further factual findings, the *Salahi* panel reiterated the admonition made by the circuit court in *Al-Adahi* that courts considering habeas petitions by Guantanamo detainees must consider the assorted evidence relating to the government's claims collectively rather than in isolation. While the panel stated that the lower court appeared to have generally followed this approach, it suggested that its consideration of certain evidence "may have been unduly atomized." Notably, the panel suggested that when the lower court determined that the petitioner's limited relationships with Al Qaeda operatives might have been too insubstantial to independently serve as a basis for deeming the petitioner "part of" Al Qaeda, those connections made it more probable that the petitioner was a member of the organization and were thus relevant to an assessment as to whether he had been lawfully detained. The panel also suggested that examining the petitioner's oath to Al Qaeda in isolation from his subsequent "sporadic support" may have resulted in the lower court failing to consider the possibility that this support demonstrated the petitioner's continued adherence to his oath of loyalty.

In reaching its ruling, the appellate court did not squarely address the government's argument that the petitioner's oath to Al Qaeda in the early 1990s established an evidentiary burden upon him to demonstrate that he had subsequently withdrawn from the organization. The appellate court also declined to consider the government's argument that the district court had accorded insufficient weight to certain inculpatory statements that were made by petitioner in interrogations subsequent to a period of time when he had been, by the government's admission, subject to mistreatment, because the panel viewed this issue to be irrelevant to the legal questions addressed by its opinion conditional probability analysis.

Uthman v. Obama, 637 F.3d 400 (D.C. Cir. 2011), Cert. Denied, 132 S. Ct. 2739 (2012)

In *Uthman*, a three-judge circuit panel reversed and remanded a district court decision that had granted habeas relief to a Yemeni national who had been captured in Afghanistan and detained by U.S. forces since December 2001. In prior cases, including the *Bensayah* and *Salahi* decisions discussed *supra*, the D.C. Circuit had recognized that the determination of whether a person was "part of" Al Qaeda was based on a functional, case-by-case assessment which focused on the individual's actions in relation to the organization. The *Uthman* decision provided further clarification as to the kind of circumstantial evidence that could potentially provide sufficient grounds to support the detention of a person under the AUMF.

The government made several claims regarding Uthman's activities in relation to Al Qaeda – including that he attended an Al Qaeda training camp, fought against the Northern Alliance in Afghanistan, and served as a bodyguard to Osama Bin Laden – which were contested. Nonetheless, the D.C. Circuit panel found that the following facts, which were either found by the district court or which were uncontested by Uthman, were sufficient to demonstrate that Uthman was "more likely than not" part of Al Qaeda and therefore subject to detention: (1)he was captured in December of 2001 in the vicinity of Tora Bora, where Al Qaeda forces had gathered to fight United States and its allies; (2) at the time of capture, Uthman was travelling with a small group including two Al Qaeda members who were bodyguards for Osama Bin Laden and a Taliban fighter; (3) he had previously studied at a religious school in Yemen which was known as "a fruitful al Qaeda recruiting ground," and which had also been attended by the Al Qaeda and Taliban fighters with whom Uthman had been captured; (4) Uthman's travel route to Afghanistan resembled that commonly used by Al Qaeda recruits; (5) his explanation for how he raised funds to travel to Afghanistan was not viewed as credible by the district court, and constituted a "false exculpatory" statement lending credence to the government's claims of wrongdoing; (6) Uthman was seen at an al Qaeda guesthouse; and (7) Uthman's exculpatory explanation of his activities in Pakistan and Afghanistan involved "many coincidences that are perhaps possible, but not likely." Although the panel recognized that at least some of these findings, when viewed in isolation, would not necessarily be sufficient to find that Uthman was functionally part of Al Qaeda, it ruled that when the evidence proffered by the government was considered in totality, "Uthman's actions and recurrent entanglement with al Qaeda show that he more likely than not was part of al Qaeda."

The Supreme Court declined to review the decision.

Al-Madhwani v. Obama, 642 F.3d 1071 (D.C. Cir. 2011), Cert. Denied, 132 S. Ct. 2739 (2012)

In *Al-Madhwani*, a three-judge appellate panel reviewed and affirmed a lower court dismissal of a habeas petition by a Guantanamo detainee. Madhwani argued that the government provided insufficient evidence to demonstrate that he was subject to detention under the AUMF, and also alleged that the district court had improperly considered evidence outside the record and had committed procedural errors. The petitioner also claimed that he had been tortured by U.S. authorities prior to his transfer to Guantanamo, and argued that statements he made to military authorities at Guantanamo were tainted by his earlier coercion.

In upholding the district court's denial of habeas, the circuit panel found it unnecessary to reach Madhwani's challenge that certain evidence had been tainted by undue coercion, as there was sufficient evidence untainted by these claims to support the district court's decision. The panel noted that the district court had considered 260 exhibits and held a four-day merits hearing during which petitioner himself testified for over one day, and discounted "a substantial portion" of the government's evidence based on a finding that it was tainted by mistreatment suffered by petitioner prior to his transfer to Guantanamo. The panel found the evidence considered by the lower court, including incriminating testimony by Madhwani in testimony, provided sufficient grounds to support the government's determination that he was "part of" Al Qaeda. This evidence included admissions by Madhwani of his stay at an Al Qaeda-affiliated guest house and military training camp; his admission to carrying a rifle at the behest of camp superiors, his "suspicious" travel after departing the camp with recruits and "implausible" explanation for his travel; and the circumstances of his final capture in the company of at least one known Al Qaeda operative.

The panel also rejected several other legal and evidentiary arguments made by Madhwani, including certain arguments that had been previously rejected by the D.C. Circuit, including his claim that hearsay evidence could only be admitted in wartime detention cases if it fell within an exception recognized under the Federal Rules of Evidence.

The Supreme Court declined to review the case.

Almerfedi v. Obama, 654 F.3d 1 (D.C. Cir. 2011), Cert. Denied, 132 S. Ct. 2739 (2012)

In *Almerfedi*, a three-judge panel of the D.C. Circuit considered the government's appeal of a district court ruling granting habeas relief to a Guantanamo detainee whom the government claimed had acted as a facilitator for Al Qaeda. The government based its claim primarily upon admissions made by habeas petitioner Almerfedi himself, as well as statements made by another Guantanamo detainee. The district court concluded, however, that Almerfedi's statements did not demonstrate by a preponderance of the evidence that Almerfedi was "part of" Al Qaeda. It also declined to consider the testimony of the fellow Guantanamo detainee, concluding that it was unreliable. The circuit panel reversed and remanded with instructions to the lower court to deny Almerfedi's habeas petition.

The circuit court's ruling did not clearly pronounce any new legal standards governing consideration of detainees' habeas claims (though the majority opinion reiterated the suggestion made in *Al-Adahi* that the government might be able to support the detention of a person using a lower standard than one based on the preponderance of evidence).[36] However, some have viewed the decision as significant because the court implied that the government's evidence was not as compelling as evidence proffered in prior cases reviewed by the D.C. Circuit, and might signify "the minimum amount of evidence" necessary to demonstrate under a preponderance of evidence standard that an individual was lawfully detained.[37]

The government's contention that Almerfedi served as a facilitator for Al Qaeda was based on several factors. By Almerfedi's own admission, he had travelled from Yemen to Pakistan in 2001, where he stayed for more than two months at the headquarters of Jama'at Tablighi, an Islamic missionary organization designated by U.S. intelligence as a Terrorist Support Entity closely aligned with Al Qaeda. He subsequently travelled to Iran, where he admitted staying for over a month before being arrested by Iranian authorities with at least $2,000 cash in his possession. The government further claimed, based on statements Almerfedi allegedly made to another Guantanamo detainee named al-Jadani, that while Almerfedi was in Iran he stayed at an Al Qaeda guest house in Tehran. Al-Jadani also claimed that other, unnamed Guantanamo detainees had informed him that a "Hussain al-Aden" acted as an Al Qaeda facilitator at the Tehran guesthouse, and the government believed that "Hussain al-Adeni was the same person as Almerfedi because the *nisha* 'al-Adeni' means 'from Aden,' which is [the Yemeni city] where Almerfedi is from."[38]

For his part, Almerfedi denied that he had ever stayed at an Al Qaeda guesthouse or served as a facilitator, and noted that the dates when al-Jadani claimed he stayed at the guesthouse were obviously incorrect, because it was undisputed that Almerfedi had been arrested by Iranian authorities at least a year earlier. Almerfedi alleged that he had left Yemen in order to seek a better life in Europe. He claimed to have travelled to Pakistan because it would be easier to obtain a visa there, and that he stayed with Jama'at Tablighi in the hope that he could take advantage of the travel discounts they offered members (even though he denied ever being a member of the organization). He further alleged that his subsequent travel to and stay in Iran were part of a failed attempt to be smuggled into Europe.

Examining the record, the circuit court concluded that "the government's evidence, combined with Almerfedi's incredible explanations" provided sufficient grounds to detain Almerfedi even without consideration of al-Jadani's statements. The court noted that Almerfedi's stay at the headquarters of Jama'at Tablighi was "probative, by itself it presumably would not be sufficient to carry the government's burden because there are surely some persons associated with Jama'at Tablighi who are not affiliated with al-Qaeda."[39] However, when this fact was considered along with Almerfedi's travel route, which the court described as being "quite at odds with his professed desire to travel to Europe," in addition to the circumstances of Almerfedi's capture with at least $2,000 of unexplained cash in his possession, the government's case that Almerfedi acted as an Al Qaeda facilitator "was on firmer ground." Further, the circuit panel found that although the lower court had recognized Almerfedi's explanation of his activities as "perplexing" and unconvincing, it erred by failing to assess these "false exculpatory statements" as amounting to evidence in favor of the government's position, as the D.C. Circuit had held in *Al-Adahi*.

While finding that the admission of al-Jadani's statements was unnecessary for the government to satisfy the evidentiary burden justifying Almerfedi's detention, two panel members nonetheless concluded that the lower court clearly erred in ruling these statements as unreliable "jail house gossip." The district court had rejected al-Jadani's statements at least in part because al-Jadani alleged that Almerfedi told him that he was at an Al Qaeda guesthouse in 2002 or 2003, though Almerfedi had already been taken into custody by that time. The majority of the circuit panel believed, however, that al-Jadani's "timing confusions were inconsequential," because the correct date of Almerfedi's capture had been given in some reports of al-Jadani's interrogations by U.S. authorities, and al-Jadani's reliability had been established via a classified government declaration which buttressed many of his statements regarding Al Qaeda guesthouses in Iran. The majority of the panel also believed that the district court erred when it failed to assess al-Jadani's recounting of conversations with unnamed detainees that implicated Almerfedi. The panel majority viewed it as "quite understandable that al-Jadani would be reluctant" to identify these detainees to U.S. authorities. Moreover, the panel majority found it significant that al-Jadani knew specific details regarding the capture of a "Hussain al-Aden" by Iranian authorities and his subsequent transfer first to Afghan and then to U.S. custody. The panel majority characterized the circumstances as matching "Almerfedi's unique experiences and therefore mak[ing] clear that Hussain Almerfedi and Hussain al-Adeni are the same man," buttressing the credibility of al-Jadani and that of the unnamed detainees who purportedly identified Almerfedi as an Al Qaeda facilitator.

Writing separately, D.C. Circuit Judge Judith W. Rogers concurred with the panel majority in its ruling that the government had satisfied the evidentiary burden needed to support Almerfedi's detention. However, Judge

Rogers disagreed with the majority's analysis of the recorded statements of al-Jadani. The district court's determination that al-Jadani's statements were unreliable was a factual one that could only be reversed for clear error, and an examination of the record evidenced did "not lead to a 'firm conviction' that the district court's analysis of alJadani's statements was mistaken, much less implausible."

The Supreme Court declined to review the circuit court's decision.

Al Alwi v. Obama, 653 F.3d 11 (D.C. Cir. 2011), Cert. Denied, 132 S. Ct. 2739 (2012)

In this case, a circuit panel found that although the corroboration of hearsay statements has proved useful to establish their reliability, corroboration of statements made by the petitioner himself during interrogations is not necessary to find that he is lawfully detained. The district court had sustained Al Alwi's detention based on admissions he made during interrogation that established he had traveled to Afghanistan to join the fight against the Northern Alliance, had stayed in at least three guesthouses associated with enemy forces, received military training and participated in hostilities against the Northern Alliance, and was part of a unit that was bombed by U.S. forces in late 2001.[40] Al Alwi sought to have the denial of his habeas petition reversed on the basis that his statements were insufficiently corroborated by other evidence, which he argued was required under the "corroboration rule" applicable in criminal trials. The appellate court expressed skepticism that such a rule still exists in the criminal context, but regarded it as irrelevant to habeas proceedings,[41] where other indicia of reliability could satisfy the requirement to assess the probative value of such statements. In this case, the interrogation reports were found to be sufficiently reliable because Al Alwi's statements were consistent and he did not contend that he gave false answers during any specific session due to the coercive interrogation methods he alleged were used. Moreover, the government did submit evidence other than the petitioner's statements to demonstrate the connection between the admissions and inferences that could be drawn from them (i.e., such conduct was typical of Taliban and Al Qaeda recruits).[42]

The appellate court declined to review the petitioner's argument that his detention was no longer lawful because the "associated force" of which he was allegedly a member is no longer engaged in hostilities, stating that he had failed to raise the argument before the lower court and that there was sufficient evidence to establish he was a part of the Taliban or Al Qaeda.[43] The court also rejected Al Alwi's argument that the government must prove not only that he was "part of" Al Qaeda or the Taliban, but also that he "substantially supported" one of those entities. Although the district court had not squarely addressed whether Al Alwi was a part of any group of combatants, the appellate court found that enough facts had been established for it to make that determination on review, without remanding the case for further finding of fact. Finally, the circuit panel rejected the petitioner's contention that the district court's denial of his unopposed request for a 30-day continuance amounted to an abuse of discretion. He had asked for extra time because he had been unable to meet with his attorneys due to his having begun a hunger strike, but the court denied the request because Al Alwi was himself responsible for the delay. While the appellate court agreed that the denial of Al Alwi's request was difficult to understand in light of the fact that the district court had granted the government a similar continuance without objection, it stated that the petitioner must be able to demonstrate actual prejudice from the denial, which he had failed to do. The district judge had permitted his attorneys to submit an amended response, and at any rate, according to the panel, it could not be demonstrated that 30 days would have made an appreciable difference given the amount of time his counsel had been working with him through the CSRT and habeas proceedings.

The Supreme Court declined to accept an appeal of the case.

Latif v. Obama, 666 F.3d 746 (D.C. Cir. 2011), 677 F.3d 1175 (Reissued), Cert. Denied, 132 S. Ct. 2741 (2012)

In this case a three-judge circuit panel reviewed a district court ruling granting the habeas petition of a Guantanamo detainee whom the government claimed was subject to detention under the AUMF. The district court had found that the government failed to satisfy its evidentiary burden to demonstrate its allegation that Latif, a Yemeni national who had travelled to Afghanistan and was subsequently captured in Pakistan, had fought with the Taliban and was subject to detention. In a 2-1 decision, the panel vacated the district court's ruling and remanded the case for further proceedings.[44] The panel's published decision was initially heavily redacted, but much of the discussion centered on classified government intelligence documents that served as the primary evidentiary basis supporting the government's allegations. The opinion was later reissued with fewer redactions.[45]

The panel majority found that the district court erred by not affording a "presumption of regularity" to the intelligence documents proffered by the government, and that Latif had not presented evidence to satisfactorily rebut the presumption that the intelligence documents accurately recorded the statements made therein.

The controlling opinion in *Latif*, written by Judge Brown, described the presumption of regularity as applicable to "the official acts of public officers and, in the absence of clear evidence to the contrary, courts presume that they have properly discharged their official duties." Judge Brown distinguished a presumption of regularity from a presumption of truthfulness, and suggested that confusion over the distinction might explain the prior reluctance of lower courts to accord a presumption of regularity to government intelligence documents:

> The confusion stems from the fact that intelligence reports involve two distinct actors—the non-government source and the government official who summarizes (or transcribes) the source's statement. The presumption of regularity pertains only to the second: it presumes the government official accurately identified the source and accurately summarized his statement, but it implies nothing about the truth of the underlying non-government source's statement. There are many conceivable reasons why a government document might accurately record a statement that is itself incredible. A source may be shown to have lied, for example, or he may prove his statement was coerced. The presumption of regularity—to the extent it is not rebutted—requires a court to treat the Government's record as accurate; it does not compel a determination that the record establishes what it is offered to prove.[46]

The majority characterized the application of a presumption of regularity to intelligence documents as being supported by separation of powers principles; because "courts have no special expertise in evaluating the nature and reliability of the Executive branch's wartime record...it is appropriate to defer to Executive branch expertise."[47] The majority also noted that this presumption regularly given to government documents in other contexts, including in ordinary criminal cases. It also discussed prior D.C. Circuit rulings which it characterized as being consistent with or lending support to the panel's holding.

Reviewing the evidence before the district court, the panel majority found that the intelligence report proffered by the government, if reliable, provided sufficient evidence to demonstrate the lawfulness of Latif's detention. Because the majority held that this report was entitled to a presumption of regularity, and because Latif "challenge[d] only the reliability of the Report," the majority found that it could only uphold the district court's grant of habeas if

Latif was able to rebut the government's evidence "with more convincing evidence of his own."[48] The majority found that he had not done so, and in addition, it found that the district court had failed to consider properly relevant evidence in assessing Latif's credibility, including the similarity between Latif's travel route and that commonly used by Al Qaeda and Taliban fights, as well as potentially incriminating statements that he made. The panel remanded the case back to the district court for further consideration of the evidence.

Judge Henderson wrote a separate concurrence to the panel decision, agreeing with the controlling opinion's analysis but arguing that remand was unnecessary and that the panel should have simply reversed the lower court's grant of habeas.

Writing in dissent, Judge Tatel argued that the district court's factual findings were subject to a deferential clear error standard of review, and that employing this standard would have resulted in affirming the lower court's grant of habeas. He also disputed the majority's holding that a presumption of regularity should apply to government intelligence documents in habeas cases. He characterized the presumption as typically being applied to those government documents which are "familiar, transparent, generally understood as reliable, or accessible." Judge Tatel argued that presumption should not apply to intelligence documents of the kind at issue here, which "was produced in the fog of war by a clandestine method that we know almost nothing about." He further expressed fear that application of this presumption would in practice come "perilously close to suggesting that whatever the government says must be treated as true.... "[49]

The Supreme Court denied certiorari to review the *Latif* decision.[50]

Transfer and Release of Detainees

The D.C. Circuit has also considered a number of cases involving issues related to the transfer or release of Guantanamo detainees. Some of these cases concern the remedy available to persons whom a reviewing court has determined to be unlawfully held, but who cannot be resettled or repatriated to a foreign country in the near future due to legal or practical obstacles.[51] Other cases involve challenges by detainees to their impending transfer to a specific foreign country, where detainees claim that they would be tortured or unlawfully detained by the government of the receiving country. The D.C. Circuit has also indicated that it is highly unlikely that a detainee may challenge his designation as an enemy combatant after being released from U.S. custody and transferred to a foreign country.

Kiyemba v. Obama, 555 F.3d 1022 (D.C. Cir. 2009) ("Kiyemba I"), Vacated, 130 S. Ct. 1235 (2010), Reinstated as Amended, 605 F.3d 1046 (D.C. Cir. 2010) ("Kiyemba III"), Cert. Denied, 131 S. Ct. 1631 (2011)

In October 2008, a federal district court ordered the release into the United States of several Guantanamo detainees who were no longer considered enemy combatants but who could not be returned to their home country (China) because of the likelihood they would be subjected to torture there, finding that the political branches' plenary authority in the immigration context did not contravene the petitioners' entitlement to an effective remedy to their unauthorized detention.[52] However, the D.C. Circuit panel stayed the district court's order pending appellate review,[53] and subsequently reversed the district court's decision in the case of *Kiyemba v. Obama* ("*Kiyemba I*"), decided in February 2009. The majority held that although the constitutional writ of habeas enables Guantanamo detainees to challenge the legality of their detention, habeas courts lack authority (absent the enactment of an authorizing statute) to compel the transfer of a non-citizen detainee into the United States, even if that detainee is found to be unlawfully held and the government has been unable to effectuate his release to a foreign county. The *Kiyemba I* panel's decision was primarily based on long-standing jurisprudence in the immigration context which recognizes that the political branches have plenary authority over whether arriving aliens may enter the United States. The majority of the panel also found that Guantanamo detainees were not protected by the Due Process Clause of the Constitution, as they are non-citizens held outside the U.S. and lack significant ties to the country.

As discussed *supra*, the Supreme Court granted certiorari to review the *Kiyemba* ruling, and subsequently vacated the appellate court's opinion and remanded the case in light of the fact that several countries had thereafter agreed to resettle the petitioners. In May 2010, the D.C. Circuit panel reinstated its earlier opinion, as modified to take into account subsequent congressional enactments limiting the use of funds to release any Guantanamo detainee into the United States (the panel's reinstatement is commonly referred to as "*Kiyemba III*," to distinguish it from the Circuit panel's initial ruling and an intervening case also entitled *Kiyemba v. Obama*). The detainees at issue in *Kiyemba III* have filed a petition for writ of certiorari with the Supreme Court, seeking review of the circuit court's ruling.

Kiyemba v. Obama, 561 F.3d 509 (D.C. Cir. 2009) ("Kiyemba II"), Cert. Denied, 130 S.Ct. 1880 (2010)

In another case entitled *Kiyemba v. Obama* (commonly referred to as "*Kiyemba II*"), a D.C. Circuit panel considered habeas petitions by detainees who were no longer considered enemy combatants, and who sought to prevent their transfer to any country where they would likely face further detention or torture. The *Kiyemba II* panel rejected the government's argument that the MCA stripped the court of jurisdiction to hear claims related to the petitioners' proposed transfer. The panel interpreted *Boumediene* as invalidating the MCA's court-stripping provisions with respect "to all *habeas* claims brought by Guantanamo detainees, not simply with respect to so-called 'core' *habeas* claims" relating to the legality of the petitioners' detention. However, the panel held that an executive branch determination that a detainee will not be tortured if transferred to a particular country is binding on the court, and a habeas court may not second-guess this assessment. The circuit panel also reversed a district court ruling that required the government to provide 30 days' notice to detainees' counsel before any proposed transfer. As a result of this ruling, the detainees' ability to challenge their proposed transfer from Guantanamo may be quite limited. On March 22, 2010, the Supreme Court denied a petition for writ of certiorari to review the appellate court's ruling.

The *Kiyemba II* decision has been relied upon by the D.C. Circuit in subsequent rulings concerning detainees' right to challenge the executive's determination that they would not face torture if transferred to a particular country and receive advance notice of their proposed transfer. Some of these cases are the subject of ongoing litigation.

Gul v. Obama, 652 F.3d 12 (D.C. Circ. 2011), Cert. Denied, 132 S. Ct. 1906 (2012)

This case involved two former Guantanamo detainees who sought to challenge their designation as "enemy combatants" by the U.S. government, despite the fact that they were no longer in U.S. custody. Following the detainees' transfer to foreign government custody, the lower court dismissed their habeas petitions as moot. The detainees appealed to the D.C. Circuit, arguing that dismissal was improper and that they had suffered collateral consequences even after leaving U.S. custody because of their enemy combatant designation.

The three-judge panel upheld the lower court's dismissal. The court held that even assuming that courts may retain habeas jurisdiction over former detainees who suffer collateral consequences as a result of their detention, the consequences identified by the petitioners did not constitute the kind of injuries sufficient to give the court jurisdiction. Although petitioners claimed that their designation as enemy combatants caused the countries to which they were transferred to restrict their travel, the *Gul* panel did not find this to be an injury redressible by the court, because the restrictions were imposed by the foreign governments rather than the United States. The panel also was not persuaded by petitioners' claim that they suffered a cognizable injury because their "enemy combatants" designation barred their travel to the United States. As an initial matter, the panel noted that there was no evidence that petitioners actually wanted to enter the United States. Moreover, the court ruled that even the plaintiffs' designation as enemy combatants was rescinded, this would not remove the barriers to U.S. travel; by statute, all Guantanamo detainees were placed on the government's "no fly" list, regardless of enemy combatant status, and U.S. immigration law's restrictions on the admission of aliens posing security risks was not dependent upon an enemy combatant designation. The panel also deemed petitioners' claim that their designation meant that they remained subject to possible targeting by the United States as "the most speculative [claim] of all," as the petitioners had "no basis whatsoever for believing" the government might still pursue them after releasing them from custody. Finally, the court found that binding precedent foreclosed consideration of petitioners' argument that they suffered a cognizable injury on the basis of the stigma caused by their designation.

The Supreme Court declined to review the case.

Other Notable Rulings

Besides the rulings discussed above, the appellate court for the D.C. Circuit has also issued opinions on several other distinct issues related to U.S. detention policy. These rulings have involved issues including, *inter alia*, the continuing application of the judicial review procedures established under DTA following the Supreme Court's ruling in *Boumediene v. Bush*; the ability of former Guantanamo detainees to bring civil suit against U.S. officials based on the detainees' allegedly wrongful treatment while in U.S. custody; and the application of the constitutional writ of habeas to persons held by the United States in foreign locations other than Guantanamo.

Parhat v. Gates, 532 F.3d 834 (D.C. Cir. 2008)

In June 2008, a three-judge panel of the D.C. Circuit ruled in the case of *Parhat v. Gates* that the petitioner had been improperly deemed an "enemy combatant" by a Combatant Status Review Tribunal (CSRT), the first ruling of its kind by a federal court. The ruling, which occurred prior to the Supreme Court's decision in *Boumediene*, was made under the judicial review process that had been established by the DTA. Although the D.C. Circuit has since held that the DTA review process is no longer in effect, the *Parhat* decision continues to be cited within the D.C. Circuit for its holding that evidence presented by the government must be in a form that permits a reviewing court to assess its reliability.[54]

The petitioner in *Parhat*, an ethnic Chinese Uighur captured in Pakistan in December 2001, was found by a CSRT to be subject to detention on account of his affiliation with a Uighur independence group known as the East Turkistan Islamic Movement (ETIM), which was purportedly "associated" with Al Qaeda and the Taliban and engaged in hostilities against the United States and its coalition partners (the petitioner denied membership in the ETIM). The *Parhat* panel found that the evidence presented by the government to support its claims regarding the ETIM was insufficient to support the CSRT's determination that Parhat was an enemy combatant. Most significantly, the court found that the principal evidence presented by the government regarding the ETIM being associated with Al Qaeda and the Taliban and engaged in hostilities against the United States and its coalition allies—four government intelligence documents describing ETIM activities and the group's relationship with Al Qaeda and the Taliban—did not "provide any of the underlying reporting upon which the documents' bottom-line assertions are founded, nor any assessment of the reliability of that reporting."[55] As a result, the Circuit Court found that neither the CSRT nor the reviewing court itself were capable of assessing the reliability of the assertions made by the documents. Accordingly "those bare assertions cannot sustain the determination that Parhat is an enemy combatant,"[56] and the CSRT's designation was therefore improper. The circuit court stressed that it was not suggesting that hearsay evidence could never reliably be used to determine whether a person was an enemy combatant, or that the government must always submit the basis for its factual assertions to enable an assessment of its claims. However, evidence "must be presented in a form, or with sufficient additional information, that permits the [CSRT] and court to assess its reliability."[57]

The *Parhat* panel also denied without prejudice a government motion to protect from public disclosure any nonclassified information raised in the litigation that the executive branch had labeled "law enforcement sensitive," along with names and identifying information of U.S. personnel mentioned in the record. While the panel acknowledged that information falling under both of these categories warranted protection from public disclosure, it characterized the government's argument for nondisclosure as being supported only upon "a generic explanation of the need for protection, providing no rationale specific to the information actually at issue in this case." In particular, the panel faulted the government motion for failing either to "give the court a basis for withholding" a specific category of information, or a basis upon which the court could "determine whether the information it has designated properly falls within the categories it has described."

Bismullah v. Gates, 551 F.3d 1068 (D.C. Cir. 2009)[58]

This case concerned the continuing availability of DTA review procedures in light of the Supreme Court's ruling in *Boumediene v. Bush* that the constitutional privilege of habeas corpus extends to non-citizen detainees held at Guantanamo. As discussed *supra*, following the Supreme Court's ruling in *Gates v. Bismullah*, the D.C. Circuit reinstated two earlier rulings concerning the scope of judicial review of CSRT determinations available under the DTA. The government subsequently petitioned for a rehearing of the case, arguing that the Supreme Court's ruling in *Boumediene* effectively nullified the review system established by the DTA, as Congress had not intended for detainees to have two judicial forums in which to challenge their detention. The D.C. Circuit granted the government's motion for rehearing, and in *Bismullah v. Gates*, a three-judge panel held that, in light of the Supreme Court's ruling in *Boumediene* restoring detainees' ability to seek habeas review of the legality of their detention, the appellate court no longer had jurisdiction over petitions for review filed pursuant to the DTA.

Rasul v. Myers, 563 F.3d 527 (D.C. Cir. 2009) (per Curiam), Cert. Denied, 130 S.Ct. 1013 (2009)

Four British nationals formerly detained at Guantanamo sued the Secretary of Defense and various military officers for damages, alleging that their treatment while in U.S. military custody violated their rights under the Fifth and Eighth Amendments to the Constitution, the Geneva Conventions, and other provisions of law. The district court dismissed the *Bivens*[59] claims on the basis of qualified immunity, holding that the officers could not reasonably be expected to have anticipated that the plaintiffs, as aliens held overseas, would be entitled to rights under the U.S. Constitution.[60] The D.C. Circuit twice affirmed,[61] interpreting *Boumediene* (on remand) as "disclaim[ing] any intention to disturb existing law governing the extraterritorial reach of any constitutional provisions, other than the Suspension Clause,"[62] which, in the circuit court's view, appears to mean that those detained at Guantanamo have no rights under the Constitution (other than the right to petition for habeas corpus). It rested its holding, however, on its analysis of qualified immunity under *Bivens*, agreeing with the lower court that even if the Constitution does provide some protections to the plaintiffs, the defendants were protected by qualified immunity. Even were this not so clear, the D.C. Circuit noted a "special factor" precludes extending a *Bivens* remedy to plaintiffs; namely, the "[t]he danger of obstructing U.S. national security policy."[63]

Having found that the claims for damages were barred by the Federal Tort Claims Act, the circuit court did not address whether *Boumediene*'s holding invalidating Section 7 of the MCA encompassed only the portion of the provision that stripped courts of jurisdiction over habeas claims, or whether the language eliminating other causes of action against the government had also been invalidated.[64] Subsequently in *Al-Zahrani v. Rodriguez*, discussed *infra*, the D.C. Circuit held that the language in the MCA eliminating causes of action other than habeas corpus survived *Boumediene*. [65]

Maqaleh v. Gates, 605 F.3d 84 (D.C. Cir. 2010)

This case concerned the application of the constitutional writ of habeas corpus to non-citizens detained by the United States in Afghanistan. In 2009, a federal district court ruled that constitutional writ of habeas may extend to non-Afghan detainees held in a U.S.-operated facility in Bagram, Afghanistan, when those detainees had been captured outside of Afghanistan but were transferred to Bagram for long-term detention as enemy combatants. The district court held that the circumstances surrounding the detention of the petitioners in *Maqaleh* were "virtually identical to the detainees in *Boumediene*—they are [non-U.S.] citizens who were ... apprehended in foreign lands far from the United States and brought to yet another country for detention."[66]

A three-judge panel of the D.C. Circuit Court of Appeals reversed, and held that the constitutional writ of habeas did not extend to non-citizens detained in the Afghan theater of war. In making this determination, the circuit court applied factors listed by the Supreme Court in *Boumediene* as being relevant to analysis of the writ's extraterritorial application, namely, (1) the citizenship and status of the detainee and the adequacy of the status determination process; (2) the nature of the site where the person is seized and detained; and (3) practical obstacles inherent in resolving the prisoner's entitlement to the writ. According to the circuit panel, consideration of the first factor weighed in favor of extending the writ of habeas to the petitioners, because the status determination process employed in Afghanistan to determine whether persons were subject to detention afforded fewer procedural protections than the process used at Guantanamo.[67] However, the circuit panel found that the application of the other two enumerated factors conclusively weighed against extending the constitutional writ of habeas to non-citizens held at Bagram. In particular, the circuit panel found that the degree and likely duration of U.S. control over Bagram were more limited than U.S. control over Guantanamo. The panel also found that significant practical obstacles would be inherent in attempting to resolve the habeas claims of Bagram detainees, including the petitioners' location in an active theater of war. The court considered it pertinent that the Unites States held persons at Bagram pursuant to a cooperative agreement with the Afghan government, and suggested that extending constitutional protections to Bagram detainees could be disruptive to the U.S.-Afghan relationship.

Although the *Maqaleh* panel held that the constitutional writ of habeas did not extend to persons in petitioners' situation, it suggested that its analysis might be different if evidence were presented that the executive branch opted to transfer detainees into a theater of war to evade judicial review. Relying on this statement, the *Maqaleh* petitioners sought a rehearing of their habeas claims. In February 2011, a lower district court permitted the petitioners to amend their habeas complaint to take into account new evidence that purportedly undercut the reasoning of the *Maqaleh* panel. The petitioners argued before the district court that the U.S. plan to turn the Bagram prison facility to Afghan control while retaining non-Afghan detainees in U.S. custody undermines the rationale for the appellate decision and warranted a conclusion that habeas review should be available. The district court was not persuaded, however, and granted the government's motion to dismiss.[68]

Al-Zahrani v. Rodriguez, 669 F.3d 315 (D.C. Cir. 2012)

In *Al-Zahrani*, a three-judge panel of the D.C. Circuit upheld the dismissal of a civil suit brought against federal officials by the fathers of two foreign nationals who had been detained as "enemy combatants" at Guantanamo and died in U.S. custody. The circuit panel held that dismissal was warranted under Section 7(a)(2) of the MCA, which stripped federal courts of jurisdiction over non-habeas claims brought against the government concerning the detention of aliens designated as "enemy combatants." While the Supreme Court in *Boumediene* had struck down the MCA's bar on federal court jurisdiction over habeas claims, the *Al-Zahrani* panel recognized that the MCA's separate jurisdictional bar over non-habeas claims remained in effect. Although plaintiffs' contended that Section 7(a)(2) was unconstitutional because it denied plaintiffs "a proper remedy for violations of their constitutional rights." The panel rejected this claim because the only remedy that plaintiffs sought was money damages, and "such remedies are not constitutionally required" and may be barred by statutory or common law immunities.

In re Guantanamo Bay Detainee Continued Access to Counsel, Misc. No. 12–398 (RCL) (D.D.C. September 6, 2012)

Habeas counsel for Guantanamo detainees who had lost—or were not actively pursuing—their habeas cases contesting detention brought this action to challenge the government's plan to condition the detainees' right of access to counsel on counsel's agreement to abide by a Memorandum of Understanding (MOU). The court agreed with the petitioners that detainees' access to counsel should continue to be governed by the Protective Order the court issued in 2008 to cover all Guantanamo detainee habeas cases. The Justice Department took the view that the Protective Order expired with respect to a detainee once his case was terminated; that is, finally adjudicated, withdrawn or dismissed. The judge, however, agreed with attorneys for the detainees, who argued that continued privileged access to their clients was necessary to pursue further petitions or otherwise vindicate their clients' rights.

The government had represented to the court that the procedures in the MOU were, for all practical purposes, the same as those in the Protective Order. The court, however, discerned a few critical differences, chief among them that the MOU gave military authorities sole discretion to permit counsel to visit their clients, leaving no role for the courts. While the terms of the Protective Order were enforceable through the court, disputes regarding the MOU were to be settled under the "final and unreviewable discretion" of the Commander of Joint Task Force-Guantanamo Bay, with no written obligation to render a timely decision, and it expressly avoided creating "any right or benefit enforceable at law or in equity" for detainees or their lawyers.

The court also noted that the Protective Order assumed that counsel for detainees have a "need to know" classified information relevant to their cases, and permits the discussion of such information with clients "to the extent necessary for [their] effective representation." In contrast, the MOU made no such presumption ("need to know" would be determined by the Department of Defense Office of General Counsel) and required the attorneys to justify the need to view their own work product created during the pendency of the habeas case in order to gain access to it. The judge predicted such a requirement would cause lengthy delays and force attorneys to divulge strategy to opposing counsel merely to review their own work. Moreover, the MOU required counsel to seek permission from appropriate government personnel in order to share information with one another.

The court explained its view that permitting the Executive to create its own counsel-access provisions would "allow the Government to transgress on the Court's duty to safeguard individual liberty by 'calling the jailer to account.'"[69] The court also expressed puzzlement that the government saw a need to replace the Protective Order, which had functioned smoothly for more than four years without drawing complaints from either side. For its part, the government argued that the vacuum left by the expiration of the Protective Order in inactive cases called for the new rules, which led the court to observe that "when it comes to power, the Government, as much as nature, abhors a vacuum."[70] The court, however, felt its own power was more than sufficient to fill any perceived void, and reinstated the judicially created Protective Order.

RULINGS BY THE FOURTH CIRCUIT COURT OF APPEALS

Although most judicial activity concerning U.S. detention policy has occurred in the D.C. Circuit, a few notable cases have been decided in the Fourth Circuit Court of Appeals. Each case concerned the military detention of a U.S. person within the United States—one a U.S. citizen and the other an alien lawfully admitted into the country on a student visa—following the Executive's determination that the person was an unlawful enemy combatant. In each case, the individual was ultimately transferred to civilian custody, and thereafter tried and convicted for terrorism-related activity. Nonetheless, it is possible that the circuit court's analysis of the scope of executive detention authority may inform subsequent judicial rulings on the matter.

Padilla v. Hanft, 423 F.3d 386 (4th Cir. 2005)

After the Supreme Court vacated an earlier ruling in his favor by the Second Circuit (see above), Jose Padilla filed a new petition in the District Court for the District of South Carolina. The district court granted Padilla's motion for summary judgment and ordered the government to release him from military detention, while suggesting Padilla could be kept in civilian custody if charged with a crime or determined to be a material witness.[71] Padilla's attorneys had based their argument on the dissenting opinion of four Supreme Court Justices, who would have found Padilla's detention barred by the Non-Detention Act, 18 U.S.C. §4001(a), and the language in *Hamdi* seemingly limiting the scope of detention authority under the AUMF to combatants captured in Afghanistan. The government argued that Padilla's detention was covered under the *Hamdi* decision's interpretation of the AUMF as an act of Congress authorizing his detention because he is alleged to have attended an Al Qaeda training camp in Afghanistan before traveling to Pakistan and then to the United States.[72] The judge disagreed with the government, finding that more express authority from Congress would be necessary and that the AUMF contains no such authority. Accordingly, the court found Padilla's detention barred by 18 U.S.C. §4001(a). The court also disagreed that the President has inherent authority as Commander-in-Chief of the Armed Forces to determine wartime measures.[73]

The Fourth Circuit Court of Appeals reversed, finding that Padilla, although captured in the United States, could be detained pursuant to the AUMF because he had been, prior to returning to the United States, "'armed and present in a combat zone' in Afghanistan as part of Taliban forces during the conflict there with the United States."[74] As the Supreme Court again considered whether to grant review, the government charged Padilla with conspiracy based on evidence unrelated to the original "dirty bomb" plot allegations and petitioned for leave to transfer him from military custody to a federal prison for civilian trial.[75] The Court granted the government permission to transfer Padilla[76] and later denied certiorari.[77] Padilla was found guilty and sentenced to 17 years and three months' imprisonment, the trial court having rejected his motion to dismiss charges against him due to his alleged mistreatment at the hands of the military.[78]

al-Marri v. Pucciarelli, 534 F.3d 213 (4th Cir. 2008) (*per Curiam*)[79]

In *al-Marri*, the Fourth Circuit sitting *en banc* considered whether the AUMF and the law of war permit the detention of a resident alien alleged to have engaged in activities within the United States in support of Al Qaeda, but who had not been part of the conflict in Afghanistan. Four of the nine judges would have held that even if the allegations were true, al-Marri did not fit within the legal category of "enemy combatant" within the meaning of *Hamdi*, and that the government could continue to hold him only if it charged him with a crime, commenced deportation proceedings, or obtained a material witness warrant in connection with grand jury proceedings (as a majority of the original three-judge panel had found). A plurality of the fractured *en banc* court, however, found that the AUMF and the law of war give the President the power to detain persons who enter the United States as "sleeper agents" on behalf of Al Qaeda for the purpose of committing hostile and war-like acts such as those carried out on 9/11 (although the judges did not arrive at a common definition of "enemy combatant"). The case was remanded to the district court for further consideration of the evidence to determine whether the government had established that al-Marri was a sleeper agent.

The *en banc* panel also considered the evidentiary burden that the government would be required to fulfill to detain al-Marri as an enemy combatant. In his controlling opinion, Judge Traxler wrote that the lower court had erred in applying the relaxed evidentiary standards of *Hamdi* to persons captured in the United States. While the *Hamdi* plurality suggested that hearsay evidence might be sufficient to support detention of a person apprehended in combat zone, Judge Traxler wrote that *Hamdi* does not establish a "cookie-cutter procedure appropriate for every alleged enemy-combatant, regardless of the circumstances of the alleged combatant's seizure or the actual burdens the government might face in defending the *habeas* petition in the normal way."[80] However, he recognized that some relaxation of normal procedural safeguards may be warranted if the government demonstrates the need for this relaxation on account of national security interests and an undue burden that would result if it was compelled to produce more reliable evidence.

After the Supreme Court granted review, the government brought charges against al-Marri in federal court and asked the Court to dismiss the case as moot and to vacate the decision below, which the Court agreed to do, leaving the applicability of the AUMF to persons captured in the United States uncertain. Al-Marri pled guilty to conspiring to provide material support to terrorists and was sentenced to eight and a half years in prison.

Lebron v. Rumsfeld, 670 F.3d 540 (4th Cir. 2012), *Cert. Denied*, 132 S. Ct. 2751 (2012)

This 2012 decision concerned a civil suit brought by Jose Padilla and his mother against current and former government officials based on Padilla's prior military detention as an enemy combatant (Padilla's habeas challenge to military detention is discussed *supra*). The petitioners sought a declaration that Padilla's detention was unconstitutional, an order enjoining any future designation as an enemy combatant, and nominal damages. The district court dismissed the suit, and a three-judge circuit panel affirmed.

The panel construed all but one of petitioners' claims to ask the judiciary to imply a cause of action for constitutional violations by federal officials (i.e., a *Bivens* claim). The panel stated that special factors "counsel judicial hesitation in implying causes of action for enemy combatants held in military detention."[81] The Constitution designates the political branches with authority over military affairs, with no comparable role accorded to the judiciary. According to the panel, judicial involvement in such matters would "stray from the traditional subjects of judicial competence,"[82] and risk impingement upon the explicit constitutional responsibilities of the political branches. The panel also characterized the judiciary as ill-equipped to administer a *Bivens* remedy the case before it, as litigation would risk interrupting the military chain of command by requiring members of the Armed Forces and their civilian superiors to testify about each other's decisions and actions, and could also interfere with military and intelligence operations on a wide scale. Finally, the panel found that Padilla had "extensive opportunities to challenge the legal basis for his detention"[83] in prior habeas litigation, and the existence of alternative avenues for protecting his interests counseled against recognition of a *Bivens* action.

In addition to his *Bivens* claims, Padilla also brought action under the Religious Freedom Restoration Act (RFRA) for alleged burdens to his free exercise of religion that were caused by his military detention. While not going so far as to absolutely rule that RFRA did not apply to persons held in military detention, the panel found that there were "strong reasons for defendants to believe that RFRA did not apply to enemy combatants," and it was appropriate to recognize an immunity defense in the present situation because "it would run counter to basic notions of notice and fair warning to hold that personal liability in such an unsettled area of law might attach."[84]

The panel also upheld the lower court's ruling that Padilla lacked standing to seek an order enjoining the government from designating him as an enemy combatant in the future. The panel held that the lower court had properly found that Padilla suffered no real and immediate risk of harm from this designation, as he was in the process of serving a long-term prison sentence due to his criminal conviction for terrorist activities. Any additional reputational harm that Padilla suffered on account of his designation as an enemy combatant was also deemed to be inadequate to provide Padilla with standing.

The Supreme Court declined to review the case.

OTHER CITIZEN DETENTION CASES

Hedges v. Obama, No. 12-CV-331 (S.D.N.Y. 2012)

Although there are currently no persons detained in the United States under AUMF authority, plaintiffs in *Hedges v. Obama*[85] were able to persuade a federal judge to issue a preliminary injunction enjoining enforcement of Section 1021(b)(2) of the 2012 NDAA, which includes among "covered persons" subject to detention under the authority of the AUMF:

> A person who was a part of or substantially supported al-Qaeda, the Taliban, or associated forces that are engaged in hostilities against the United States or its coalition partners, including any person who has committed a belligerent act or has directly supported such hostilities in aid of such enemy forces.[86]

The *Hedges* plaintiffs are a group of activists and journalists who sued the government arguing that the provision caused them to alter their lawful conduct in order to avoid being subject to military detention without trial under the provision. Reporter Christopher Hedges stated that his work in the past involved coverage of Al Qaeda and the Taliban and other groups that might be considered to be engaged in hostilities against the United States or its coalition partners. Another journalist, Alexa O'Brien, testified that she feared that her work reporting in particular on Guantanamo detainees and WikiLeaks disclosures of U.S. government documents could lead to her detention under

Section 1021. Two foreign plaintiffs also provided testimony, both basing their concerns in part on their past activities in support of WikiLeaks. One of them, Icelandic parliament member Birgitta Jonsdottir, noted her participation in the release by WikiLeaks of a leaked video depicting a U.S. Apache helicopter attack on a group of men who turned out to be civilians, pointing out that the accused leaker, Bradley Manning, is being tried by court-martial for having aided terrorists.

The Obama Administration sought to deflect the lawsuit on the basis that Section 1021 of the NDAA does "nothing new," but merely reaffirms detention authority conferred by the AUMF as it has been practiced by the executive branch and affirmed by the U.S. Court of Appeals for the D.C. Circuit. Read in this light, the government argued in essence, Section 1021 cannot give rise to reasonable fears of imminent detention for the conduct the plaintiffs cited because these activities did not result in detention during the time that passed between enactment of the AUMF and the 2012 NDAA, and the plaintiffs did not report similar fears under the AUMF standing alone. Accordingly, the government urged the court to declare the plaintiffs to be without standing and to dismiss the action.

The court rejected the argument that Section 1021 is merely an affirmation of the AUMF that does not change the law regarding detention, noting that to hold otherwise "would be contrary to basic principles of legislative interpretation that require Congressional enactments to be given independent meaning."[87] The court also noted differences in language describing the scope of application in the two statutes that make the NDAA language seem broader, including the addition of "substantial support" of Al Qaeda and the Taliban and the inclusion of "associated forces" (who might not have had direct involvement in the 2001 terrorist attacks), as well as mention of "direct support of hostilities" engaged in by any such groups against the United States or its coalition partners. While the court noted that the NDAA language was consistent with a government filing in the D.C. Circuit describing detention authority under the AUMF,[88] it also agreed that the government filing did not itself have the force of law, and that cases from the D.C. Circuit upholding the standard have not yet construed the meaning of substantial support. The court also took note of the fact that the Obama Administration has stated that it will not indefinitely detain U.S. citizens under the authority conferred by either the AUMF or the NDAA, but found the promise insufficient to cure the vagueness of the statutory language.

Each of the plaintiffs gave testimony demonstrating how Section 1021 had produced a chilling effect over their professional activities. The government, however, told the court in each case that it was unprepared to state whether the activities in question constitute "substantial support" to Al Qaeda or associated forces of the type that could subject the plaintiffs to military detention. Largely in light of the government's responses, the court credited the plaintiffs' fears as reasonable and concluded that the statute must also be too vague to satisfy the Fifth Amendment's requirement that a statute provide adequate notice regarding the nature of conduct to be avoided. Given the government's representations that Section 1021 does not add anything to previous law, the court presumed that a preliminary injunction would not cause the government undue burdens.

The government moved for reconsideration of the court's opinion with respect to the plaintiffs' standing, stating that "law of war detention" does not apply to persons solely on the basis of independent journalistic activities or independent public advocacy as described by the plaintiffs. The court issued an order clarifying that the injunction is not limited to the detention of the plaintiffs named in the case, but rather, because the judge treated the lawsuit as a facial challenge and found the provision constitutionally infirm on the basis of the First Amendment and the Due Process Clause of the Fifth Amendment, the injunction applies nationwide.[89] It does not, however, apply to persons whose detention is based on Section 1021(b)(1), which essentially restates the scope of the AUMF. The court granted the plaintiffs' motion to make the injunction,[90] and the government immediately appealed. The Court of Appeals for the Second Circuit granted the government's motion for a stay of the injunction pending appeal.

Some observers predict a reversal on appeal. Issues to be raised include whether overbreadth and vagueness considerations under the First and Fifth Amendments can be applied by analogy to noncriminal provisions such as Section 1021; whether these constitutional requirements necessarily apply to the foreign plaintiffs; whether the court should have supplied a limiting construction to avoid invalidating the provision (the court gave several reasons for not doing so); and perhaps, assuming that no further amendments to the provision are forthcoming, what effect invalidating Section 1021(b)(2) permanently would have with respect to detention operations connected with hostilities against Al Qaeda and its associates.

Vance v. Rumsfeld, Nos. 10–1687, 10–2442 (7th Cir. November 7, 2012) (*En Banc*)

This case was a suit for damages involving two U.S. citizens who were detained by U.S. forces in Iraq as "security internees" after they were accused of conducting illicit arms sales. They asserted they were whistle-blowers and that the accusations were retaliation against them for reporting suspicious activity to the FBI. According to their complaint, they were held in solitary confinement and denied access to counsel, interrogated under severely abusive conditions, and denied due process before a Detainee Status Board. Neither was charged with a crime, and both were eventually released. They brought suit against the Secretary of Defense at the time, Donald Rumsfeld, and other officials they felt bore responsibility for their mistreatment.

The district court denied Secretary Rumsfeld's motion to dismiss the complaint,[91] and he appealed. The United States also appealed the district court's rejection of its motion to dismiss on the basis that the Administrative Procedure Act prohibits judicial review of "military authority exercised in the field in time of war or in occupied territory."[92] An appellate panel reversed the decision with respect to the U.S. claim and affirmed the decision with respect to Secretary Rumsfeld.[93] Rehearing en banc was granted and both decisions set aside.

On rehearing, the full circuit court agreed with the merits panel that there was no right of action against the United States for activities in Iraq. With respect to the claim against Secretary Rumsfeld and others in the chain of command, the majority framed the question as "whether the federal judiciary should create a right of action for damages against soldiers (and others in the chain of command) who abusively interrogate or mistreat military prisoners, or fail to prevent improper detention and interrogation."

Noting that the other appellate courts who have addressed the question answered it in the negative[94] and that the Supreme Court has only rarely allowed new *Bivens* action, the majority declined to permit the suit to go forward. The majority interpreted Supreme Court precedent to establish a principle that civilian courts should not interfere with the military chain of command without statutory authority.[95] Even assuming that the plaintiffs' constitutional rights were violated and that law prohibiting mistreatment of prisoners—the Detainee Treatment Act and possibly some treaties[96]—were violated, the majority assessed that permitting the lawsuit would "come at an uncertain cost in national security," and declined to find a right of action where relevant statutes failed to provide one.[97] Moreover, even if a right of action were to be created under the circumstances present, liability would not extend to the Secretary of Defense and others far removed from the actual conduct at the heart of the complaint.

Three judges dissented from the opinion, arguing that the majority essentially created absolute immunity for members of the military from *Bivens* civil liability even in cases involving the torture of civilians.[98]

Criminal Cases

Although numerous cases have been brought in federal civilian court involving persons who allegedly engaged in terrorist activity, relatively few involve persons who were captured abroad by U.S. forces during operations against either Al Qaeda or the Taliban, and only one case has been tried in civilian court involving a person involved in the September 11, 2001, terrorist attacks. This section discusses notable rulings made in criminal cases involving Zacharias Moussaoui, who was tried and convicted for his role in the September 11, 2001, terrorist attacks, but was never officially designated as an "enemy combatant"; John Walker Lindh, thus far the only person captured abroad and tried and convicted in federal civilian court for belligerent activities occurring on the Afghan battlefield; and Ahmed Khalfan Ghailani, a suspect in the 1998 African Embassy bombings who was incarcerated at Guantanamo and charged at a military commission, but was later transferred to the Southern District of New York for trial on terrorism charges. Ghailani is the only Guantanamo prisoner to have been transferred for civilian trial in the United States.

Moussaoui Litigation

Zacharias Moussaoui, a French citizen, was arrested by immigration authorities for overstaying his visa after he raised suspicions at a Minnesota flight school where he was enrolled. Less than a month after he was taken into custody, a group of Al Qaeda terrorists carried out the September 11, 2001, attacks, and Moussaoui was charged in connection with the conspiracy to commit those attacks. On January 7, 2002, after Moussaoui's arraignment, the Department of Justice (DOJ) imposed Special Administrative Measures (SAMs) to prevent his communication with other terrorists. Moussaoui was permitted unmonitored attorney/client and consular communications and mail, and monitored communications with others. The court also issued a protective order under the Classified Information Procedures Act (CIPA; 18 U.S.C. app. 3, §3), which permitted defense counsel to access classified information, but did not permit Moussaoui to receive such information unless the government consented or the judge determined that it was necessary to protect his right to prepare a defense.

After a competency hearing in which the judge explained that the lack of personal access to classified information could impede Moussaoui's ability to defend himself without counsel appropriately cleared for access to such information, the judge permitted the defendant to proceed *pro se*, and appointed the public defenders who had been assigned to the case to act as standby counsel. After Moussaoui refused to cooperate with his appointed lawyers, the judge replaced some of them, but ultimately concluded that Moussaoui was unlikely to approve any court-appointed attorneys, and also held that he was not entitled to unmonitored access to "advisory counsel" of his choice. Despite Moussaoui's rejection of virtually all efforts by standby counsel to assist him, the lawyers continued to file motions on his behalf, including motions seeking relief from the SAMs or to revoke his *pro se* status on the grounds that he was not in a position to take advantage of exculpatory information in the government's possession. Moussaoui attempted to plead guilty in July 2002, but was unwilling to admit to the facts necessary to support the plea and withdrew it.

Moussaoui then sought access to several persons held overseas by the government as enemy combatants who might provide information that would be useful to his defense by testifying that Moussaoui was not involved in the September 11 attacks. (The government had advanced theories that Moussaoui was the intended "20th hijacker" or pilot of a fifth plane intended to target the White House, whose participation in the actual attack was thwarted due to his incarceration, and that Moussaoui's refusal to provide agents information about the plot that might have prevented the attacks from taking place contributed to the deaths of the several thousand victims, a factor relevant to death penalty eligibility. Moussaoui claimed to be part of a plan for subsequent terrorist operations and to have had no knowledge regarding the September 11 plot.) The government offered to provide redacted summaries of reports presumably based on intelligence interrogations of the enemy combatant witnesses,[99] but the judge rejected the proffered substitutions as possibly unreliable and inadequate to protect Moussaoui's Sixth Amendment right to compulsory process.

The government appealed the district court's order requiring the government to make three of the requested enemy combatant witnesses available for deposition to be conducted by remote video. The United States Court of Appeals for the Fourth Circuit affirmed the district court's holding that that the enemy combatants in question could be reached through judicial process (directed at their custodians) for the purpose of providing testimony and that their testimony would be relevant to the case, but reversed the order for depositions and the sanctions the court had imposed for the government's refusal to comply.[100] The appellate court held that substitutions for depositions could be prepared that would provide substantially the same ability to prepare a defense, although it agreed with some of the objections the district court had articulated regarding the government's proposed substitutions. The majority viewed the intelligence reports as possessing adequate indicia of reliability because they were produced through methods designed to produce accurate analyses of foreign intelligence.[101] Consequently, the court remanded the case to the district court with instructions to prepare substitutions for the deposition testimony by a process involving collaboration with the parties,[102] noting that adequate jury instructions would be necessary in some cases to permit the jury to assess the reliability of the evidence.

In the meantime, the district court revoked Moussaoui's *pro se* privilege for his continued submission of improper filings, some of which contained veiled or overt threats, political statements with no relevance to the case, attempts at communicating to persons overseas, and insulting language, despite repeated warnings that such conduct would result in sanctions. After the Supreme Court denied certiorari with respect to the appellate court's ruling on his right to depose enemy combatant witnesses in the custody of the United States, Moussaoui again decided, over his counsel's objections, to plead guilty as an apparent tactic to avoid the death penalty. After a hearing in which Moussaoui demonstrated to the court's satisfaction that he understood a guilty plea would result in forfeiting his right to appeal based on any violation of his constitutional rights that might have occurred prior to the plea, the court accepted his plea. Moussaoui admitted to the government's allegations, including some he had previously denied, and signed the statement of facts supporting the guilty plea, adding the designation of "20th Hijacker" below his signature. During the sentencing phase, Moussaoui claimed that his mission on September 11 was to have been piloting a commercial airliner into the White House, although statements by enemy combatant witnesses introduced by the government contradicted that claim, along with some other allegations Moussaoui had admitted as true. In the bifurcated sentencing proceeding, the jury found Moussaoui to be eligible to receive the death penalty but declined to impose it, sentencing him instead to life in prison.

Just days after receiving his sentence, Moussaoui filed a motion to withdraw his guilty plea, claiming that his understanding of the American legal system had been "completely flawed" and asking for a new trial "[b]ecause I now see that it is possible that I can receive a fair trial ... even with Americans as jurors and that I can have the opportunity to prove that I did not have any knowledge of and was not a member of the plot to hijack planes and crash them into buildings on September 11, 2001."[103] He then appealed the court's denial of his motion for a new trial, arguing among other things that his plea was not voluntary as a matter of law because of district court rulings that violated his constitutional rights, and that it was not knowing because he did not have access to classified information in the government's possession that contradicted the government's theory of the case. Finding that his guilty plea was entered with full knowledge and understanding of its ramifications and that his objections to constitutional claims were waived, the circuit court affirmed. The circuit court reviewed the procedural history regarding Moussaoui's access to classified information because these claims were relevant to the adequacy of the plea and were therefore not waived for purposes of appeal, but reiterated its earlier view that adequate substitutions under CIPA would have protected Moussaoui's rights had the CIPA process not been cut short by the guilty plea. Moreover, it noted that CIPA information had been made available during the sentencing phase for establishing death-eligibility factors, and that not only did Moussaoui make no effort to withdraw his plea upon receiving the information, but he contradicted the supposedly exculpatory statements at trial. Finally, the circuit court rejected Moussaoui's contention that plain error had resulted in the jury's false belief that the only sentencing options available to them were the death penalty or life imprisonment without possibility of parole, in violation of his right to have his sentence decided by the jury, on the basis that Moussaoui had requested the jury be instructed that the sentencing options were limited as part of an apparently successful strategy to avoid the death penalty.

United States v. Lindh, 227 F. Supp. 2d 565 (E.D. Va. 2004)

John Walker Lindh, a U.S. citizen, was captured in Afghanistan and charged with 10 counts of supplying services to the Taliban under various statutes. He moved to have the charges dismissed, arguing, *inter alia* that he was entitled to combatant immunity as part of the Taliban. While the judge refused to accept the government's argument that the President's designation of Lindh as an "unlawful combatant" was not subject to second-guessing by the court, he nevertheless concluded that the Taliban is not entitled to combatant immunity under international law and rejected the defense.[104]

Lindh was also unsuccessful in his bid to avoid the government's request for a protective order covering unclassified but sensitive information as well as classified information that the government had concluded was subject to discovery by the defendant.[105] At issue was whether the defendant could adequately prepare a defense given the government's proposal to restrict certain information from the government's redacted reports of relevant interviews with detainees held at Guantanamo. Rule 16(d) of the Federal Rules for Criminal Procedure permits the court to restrict discovery with respect to any information for good cause, including cases where the government claims the protection of such information is vital to the national security. The court found good cause to issue a protective order to prohibit the public dissemination of the detainee interview reports, which would serve to prevent Al Qaeda members from learning "the status of, the methods used in, and the information obtained from the ongoing investigation of the detainees."[106] Lindh objected to the order on the basis that it would burden his ability to prepare for trial by requiring the pre-screening of investigators and expert witnesses before he would be permitted to disclose unclassified information to them, which he argued could reveal his defense strategy to the prosecution. The judge found the needs of both parties could be accommodated by amending the proposed order to require investigators or expert witnesses for the defense to sign a memorandum of understanding, under oath, promising not to disclose information provided under the order, rather than requiring pre-screening. Lindh also objected to the proposed protective order because he believed it would impair his ability to use the media to influence public opinion, as he contended the government had done. Noting that the "[d]efendant has no constitutional right to use the media to influence public opinion concerning his case so as to gain an advantage at trial" under either the Sixth Amendment right to a public trial or the public's First Amendment right to a free press,[107] the judge rejected the argument, but cautioned that information that turned out to be relevant and material to the trial as the case progressed might eventually require unsealing to further those rights.[108]

Prior to the beginning of the merits phase of the trial, Lindh struck a plea deal with prosecutors, admitting to one count of carrying an explosive during the commission of a felony, and was sentenced to 20 years' imprisonment.

United States v. Ghailani, No. S10 98 Crim. 1023 (S.D.N.Y.)

Alleged Al Qaeda member Ahmed Khalfan Ghailani was indicted in 1998 and charged with conspiracy to kill Americans abroad in connection with the bombing the United States Embassies in Nairobi, Kenya, and Dar es Salaam, Tanzania. He was arrested in Pakistan in 2004 and turned over to U.S. custody to be held and interrogated at an undisclosed site abroad by Central Intelligence Agency (CIA) officials. In 2006, he was transferred to DOD custody and held as an enemy combatant at Guantanamo. He was charged before a military commission for his role in one of the embassy bombings, but the charges were later withdrawn so that he could be transferred to the Southern District of New York to be tried on the earlier indictment. The transfer occurred in May 2009. Ghailani has since been convicted and sentenced to life imprisonment for his part in the conspiracy.

The case has resulted in a number of rulings on constitutional issues that are likely to be pertinent to the debate as to whether to try similar crimes in federal court or before military commissions, including such issues as the right to effective assistance of counsel, the right to a speedy trial, the privilege against self-incrimination and the right to counsel in custodial interrogation, and the consequences of a jury trial. How these issues might be resolved in a military commission or by reviewing courts remains to be seen. A military commission would also have had to resolve the issue of whether crimes committed prior to the 9/11 attacks can properly be charged as war crimes, a highly charged question for which arguments can be made either way, but which appears to be lacking in precedent.

After his transfer to New York, Ghailani moved for an injunction or other relief against the Secretary of Defense to prevent the reassignment of the military defense attorneys who had been detailed to serve as his defense counsel before the military commission. Ghailani urged the court to order the government to permit the two officers to act as his appointed counsel in federal court, arguing that depriving him of the assistance of the counsel he had grown to trust amounted to a violation of his Sixth Amendment right to the effective assistance of counsel. The government urged the court to decline to adjudicate the motion or grant relief based on the political question doctrine, arguing that the assignment of military officers to particular duties is the prerogative of the executive branch alone. The judge did not think the political question doctrine prevented his consideration of the matter, since he was not considering the propriety of the reassignment as much as he was assessing the impact of the decision on the defendant's rights, but ultimately denied the motion, holding that an indigent defendant's right to appointed representation does not mean the right to continuous representation by counsel of his choice.[109]

Ghailani also filed a motion for dismissal of his indictment based on his claim that the government violated his Sixth Amendment right to a speedy trial. In connection with this motion, Ghailani sought discovery of documents in the government's possession that demonstrate the government delayed his prosecution from 2004 until his transfer to New York for reasons other than national security. Rule 16 of the Federal Rules for Criminal Procedure permits discovery of items "within the government's custody, possession, or control" that are material to the case, excluding documents that were prepared by government attorneys or agents that constitute work product connected to the prosecution. The judge excluded one document specifically requested by the defendant as attorney work product, but approved a more general request for information relating to the reasons behind the timing of Ghailani's transfer for trial based on a Supreme Court ruling that makes the "reason for delay" one part of the test for determining whether charges must be dismissed for failure to provide a speedy trial.[110] The judge defined the scope of "in the government's possession, custody, or control" as reaching beyond the officials of the U.S. Attorney's Office who had worked on the case to include higher-level DOJ officials who were not intimately involved in the case but were involved in the decision about where to prosecute Ghailani. This requirement will not unduly burden the prosecution with unreasonable discovery requirements, according to the court, because the embassy bombing crime had "commanded the attention of the highest levels" of the government long before Ghailani was in American custody. Under these circumstances, high-level officials involved in the important decisions involving Ghailani's treatment can be included within the meaning of "government" in Rule 16.[111] Accordingly, the judge issued an order requiring production of documents held by the DOJ that are material to the case and not otherwise privileged under the rule.

The court ultimately denied the speedy trial motion after applying the multi-factor balancing test established by the Supreme Court in *Barker v. Wingo*,[112] which takes into account the length of the delay, the reason for the delay, the defendant's assertion of the right, and the prejudice to the defendant.[113] The court held that the time Ghailani spent in CIA detention was justified by the need to interrogate him for intelligence purposes, a process that was incompatible with prosecution in federal court.[114] The time between Ghailani's transfer to Guantanamo in 2006 and his transfer to New York in

2009, however, was held insufficient to justify postponement of trial, because the need to prevent the defendant from returning to hostilities was not incompatible with federal prosecution.[115] The aborted military commission prosecution did not justify delay because the government had complete discretion as to where to prosecute the defendant.[116] However, although the Guantanamo portion of the delay was attributable to the government, it was assessed as a "neutral factor" because there was no evidence that its purpose had to do with a "quest for tactical advantage."[117] Because Ghailani was detainable as an "enemy combatant" with or without prosecution, the need to avoid excessive incarceration was not a relevant factor under *Barker* analysis, either. The court was not persuaded that Ghailani was prejudiced by the delay, and it held there was no violation of his Sixth Amendment rights.

Although Ghailani's overseas detention by the CIA did not preclude his prosecution, it did result in the exclusion of a government witness whose identity was uncovered during Ghailani's interrogation and whose cooperation with prosecutors was less than willing.[118] The government having stipulated that any statements Ghailani made to CIA interrogators were coerced, the judge held that the Fifth Amendment's privilege against self-incrimination would permit the government to introduce such witness testimony only if it had proven that the connection between Ghailani's coerced statements and the witness's testimony was sufficiently remote or attenuated to purge the taint of illegality, or if it could establish another basis upon which the testimony could be admitted. The government failed to establish the inevitability of its identification of the witness independent of the defendant's coerced statement, and it did not persuade the judge that the "core application" doctrine applicable to the exclusionary rule in the Fourth Amendment search and seizure context should hold sway in the Fifth Amendment context.[119] Consequently, the court held hearings to examine whether the witness's testimony was truly voluntary; the extent to which the coerced statements played a role in securing the witness's cooperation; and whether the lapse of time between the illegal government action and contact with the witness established a sufficient attenuation to avoid the exclusion of his testimony. The judge ultimately found each of these criteria weighed in favor of the defendant, but the facts leading to this determination remain largely classified.[120]

After a jury trial, Ghailani was found guilty of conspiracy to destroy buildings and property of the United States, but not guilty of 284 other counts—one count of murder or attempted murder for each of the Americans killed or injured in the attacks, one count each for the bombing the U.S.

embassies in Dar es Salaam, Tanzania, and Nairobi, Kenya, and various other charges related to the bombings.[121] The jury concluded that Ghailani's participation in the property destruction conspiracy was a direct or proximate cause of the death of a person other than a conspirator. After rejecting the defendant's motion for acquittal or a new trial on the property conspiracy charge,[122] which the defense argued was necessary in light of the seemingly inconsistent verdict,[123] the judge sentenced Ghailani to life imprisonment based on the aggravating factor the jury found.

The results of Ghailani's trial have fueled the debate over whether military commissions or federal court trials are appropriate in terrorism cases. Some observers view the trial as a demonstration that federal trial courts using the ordinary tools of criminal justice are up to the task of meting out justice to terrorists, while others characterize the outcome as a "near acquittal" that demonstrates the superiority of military commissions. The judge's post-trial opinion denying the defendant's motion for acquittal sheds some light on what may seem to be a curious verdict. Ghailani's defense throughout the trial was that he had been unknowingly duped into carrying out what he thought were innocent acts, but which in hindsight turned out to be acts in furtherance of the bombing conspiracy. The charge of conspiracy to destroy property, however, did not require that the government prove beyond a reasonable doubt that Ghailani was aware of the exact objective and targets of the plot; it merely required proof that Ghailani understood that his activities would very likely result in the bombing of American facilities somewhere, for which the judge agreed there was abundant evidence. The jury was instructed that willful blindness on the part of the accused to the precise objective of the conspiracy would invalidate a defense based on the lack of requisite knowledge, and that conviction was therefore proper if the facts demonstrated that the defendant "was aware of a high probability of the fact in dispute and consciously avoided confirming that fact"[124] In contrast, the charge for participating in the Dar es Salaam embassy bombing required proof that "Ghailani knew that the embassy was a target and that he acted to further that goal."[125] Apparently the jury did not agree that the government's evidence adequately established these elements.

Hamdan v. United States, 696 F.3d 1238 (D.C. Cir. 2012)

After Salim Hamdan won his earlier habeas case at the Supreme Court,[126] which led the Supreme Court to invalidate the military commission system set up by President Bush, Congress enacted the Military Commission Act of 2006.[127] Hamdan was then charged under the new system with conspiracy and material support of terrorism. In 2008, Salim Hamdan was found guilty of one count of providing material support for terrorism and sentenced to 66 months' imprisonment, but was credited with five years' time served and subsequently returned to Yemen.[128] Despite his release, Hamdan continued his appeal through the system established by the MCA, arguing that his conviction on the material support charge was invalid because the charge was not recognized as a violation of the international law of war at the time he committed it.

After determining the appeal was not moot by reason of Hamdan's release, the U.S. Court of Appeals for the D.C. Circuit overturned Hamdan's conviction as contrary to the MCA. In its unanimous opinion, the three-judge panel found that Congress did not intend for the offenses it defined in the MCA to apply retroactively. Because the court agreed that the crime of material support of terrorism did not exist as a war crime under the international law of war at the time the relevant conduct occurred (a requirement under the previously existing military commissions statute[129]), it vacated the decision below of the Court of Military Commissions Review (CMCR), which had unanimously affirmed Hamdan's conviction.[130]

The MCA declares that it "codif[ies] offenses that have traditionally been triable by military commissions," and that "because the provisions ... codify offenses that have traditionally been triable under the law of war or otherwise triable by military commission, this subchapter does not preclude trial for offenses that occurred before the date of the enactment.... "[131] Where the CMCR had deferred to Congress in its determination that material support for terrorism, as defined, is a pre-existing violation of the law of war, the D.C. Circuit interpreted the language quoted above as evincing an intent to preclude retroactive enforcement of any offenses in the event Congress was mistaken about their pre-existence, as the court determined was the case with respect to the material support offense. This interpretation was based not only on the plain language of the statute (an interpretation the government brief shared), but also on the canon of constitutional avoidance, which in this case called for a reading that would not require the court to decide whether the offense was retroactive in violation of the Ex Post Facto clause of the Constitution.

The government had asserted that ample precedent for the charge of material support for terrorism could be found in analogous charges under the "U.S. common law of war" as practiced in Civil War military commissions and during other conflicts. The court rejected that theory, instead regarding the "U.S. common law of war" as distinct from the international law of war which

Congress intended for military commissions to apply. Because the charge of material support has been the most frequently charged of the offenses before military commissions, and because all charges to date have involved conduct that occurred prior to the enactment of the MCA, the effect of the opinion is bound to have an effect on upcoming cases, charging decisions, and possibly opportunities for plea agreements. The court also hinted that other offenses proscribed by the MCA might fall into the retroactive category. To avoid that fate, the court suggested, an offense must be shown to be "based on norms firmly grounded in international law."[132]

The government may opt to appeal the decision to the full court or to the Supreme Court, but has as of yet not commented on its plans.

CONCLUSION

Although the political branches of government have been primarily responsible for shaping U.S. wartime detention policy in the conflict with Al Qaeda and the Taliban, the judiciary has also played a significant role in clarifying elements of the rights and privileges owed to detainees under the Constitution and existing federal statutes and treaties. These rulings may have longterm consequences for U.S. detention policy, both in the conflict with Al Qaeda and the Taliban and in future armed conflicts. Judicial decisions concerning the meaning and effect of existing statutes and treaties may compel the executive branch to modify its current practices to conform with judicial opinion. For example, judicial opinions concerning the scope of detention authority conferred by the AUMF may inform executive decisions as to whether grounds exist to detain an individual suspected of involvement with Al Qaeda or the Taliban. Judicial decisions concerning statutes applicable to criminal prosecutions in Article III courts or military tribunals may influence executive determinations as to the appropriate forum in which to try detainees for criminal offenses.

Judicial rulings may also invite response from the legislative branch, including consideration of legislative proposals to modify existing authorities governing U.S. detention policy. The 2012 NDAA, for example, contains provisions which arguably codify aspects of existing jurisprudence regarding U.S. authority to detain persons in the conflict with Al Qaeda. Judicial activity with respect to the present armed conflict may also influence legislative activity in future hostilities. For example, Congress may look to judicial rulings interpreting the meaning and scope of the 2001 AUMF for guidance when drafting legislation authorizing the executive to use military force in some future conflict.

While the Supreme Court has issued definitive rulings concerning certain issues related to wartime detainees, many other issues related to the capture, treatment, and trial of suspected enemy belligerents are either the subject of ongoing litigation or are likely to be addressed by the judiciary. Accordingly, the courts appear likely to play a significant role in shaping U.S. policies relating to enemy belligerents in the foreseeable future.

End Notes

[1] For further discussion of the detention provisions in the 2012 NDAA, see CRS Report R42143, The National Defense Authorization Act for FY2012: Detainee Matters, by Jennifer K. Elsea and Michael John Garcia. For an analysis of their application to U.S. persons, see CRS Report R42337, Detention of U.S. Persons as Enemy Belligerents, by Jennifer K. Elsea.

[2] The Obama Administration has discontinued the use of the term "enemy combatant" to describe persons detained pursuant to the law of war or the Authorization for Use of Military Force ("AUMF"). See Department of Justice (DOJ), "Department of Justice Withdraws 'Enemy Combatant' Definition for Guantanamo Detainees," press release, March 13, 2009, http://www.usdoj.gov/opa/pr/2009/March/09-ag-232.html (hereinafter "DOJ Press Release"); In re Guantanamo Bay Detainee Litigation, Respondents' Memorandum Regarding the Government's Detention Authority Relative to Detainees Held At Guantanamo Bay, No. 08-0442, filed March 13, 2009 (D.D.C.) (hereinafter "Detention Authority Memorandum"). We use the terms "enemy combatant" or "enemy belligerent" broadly to describe persons who might be subject to detention or prosecution in connection with the conflict authorized by the AUMF as interpreted by the executive branch.

[3] For further discussion of Hamdi, see CRS Report RS21884, The Supreme Court 2003 Term: Summary and Analysis of Opinions Related to Detainees in the War on Terrorism, by Jennifer K. Elsea; CRS Report R42337, Detention of U.S. Persons as Enemy Belligerents, by Jennifer K. Elsea.

[4] Hamdi v. Rumsfeld, 542 U.S. 507, 518 (2004) (O'Connor, J., plurality opinion); id. at 588-589 (Thomas, J., dissenting).

[5] Id. at 518, 533 (O'Connor, J., plurality opinion, joined by Breyer, J., Kennedy, J., and Rehnquist, C.J.); 553 (Souter, J., concurring in part and dissenting in part, joined by Ginsburg, J.). Justices Scalia and Stevens supported a more limited view concerning the Executive's authority to detain U.S. citizens, believing that detention without criminal charge was only permissible if Congress suspended the writ of habeas corpus. Id. at 554 (Scalia, J., dissenting, joined by Stevens, J.).

[6] Id. at 533-534 (O'Connor, J., plurality opinion).

[7] For further discussion of the Padilla decision, see CRS Report RS21884, supra footnote 3; CRS Report R42337, supra footnote 1.

[8] For a more detailed summary of the Rasul opinion, see CRS Report RS21884, supra footnote 3.

[9] P.L. 109-148, Title X; P.L. 109-163, Title XIV.

[10] P.L. 109-366.

[11] For further discussion of the Hamdan opinion, see CRS Report RS22466, Hamdan v. Rumsfeld: Military Commissions in the "Global War on Terrorism," by Jennifer K. Elsea.

[12] Hamdan v. Rumsfeld, 548 U.S. 557, 602 (2006) (Stevens, J., plurality opinion, joined by Souter, J., Ginsburg, J., and Breyer, J.).

[13] A more extensive discussion of Boumediene is found in CRS Report RL34536, Boumediene v. Bush: Guantanamo Detainees' Right to Habeas Corpus, by Michael John Garcia.

[14] Boumediene v. Bush, 553 U.S. 723, 764 (2008).

[15] The D.C. Circuit in July 2007 issued an order rejecting the government's motion to limit the scope of the court's review to the official record of the CSRT hearings. Bismullah v. Gates, 501 F.3d 178 (Bismullah I). The circuit court decided that in order to determine whether a preponderance of evidence supported the CSRT determinations, it must have access to all the information a CSRT is "authorized to obtain and consider, pursuant to the procedures specified by the Secretary of Defense." The court thereafter denied the government's request for rehearing, explaining its view that its previous order would not require a search for information that was not "reasonably available." Bismullah v. Gates, 503 F.3d 137(D.C. Cir. 2007) (Bismullah II).

[16] See generally Benjamin Wittes, Robert Chesney & Rabea Benhalim, The Emerging Law of Detention: The Guantánamo Habeas Cases as Lawmaking, Brookings Institute, January 22, 2010, available at http://www.brookings.edu/papers/2010/0122_guantanamo_wittes_chesney.aspx (discussing different approaches taken by district courts in the handling of habeas petitions brought by Guantanamo detainees); Wittes, Chesney, & Larkin Reynolds, The Emerging Law of Detention 2.0: The Guantánamo Habeas Cases as Lawmaking, Brookings Institute, May 2011, available at http://www.brookings.edu/papers/2011/05_guantanamo_wittes.aspx (discussing more recent trends in Guantanamo habeas cases, including the effects that appellate rulings have had upon habeas litigation).

[17] A third member of the panel issued a separate opinion concurring with the majority's judgment. However, the opinion did not clearly endorse the majority's view as to the scope of the executive's detention authority. See Al-Bihani v. Obama, 590 F.3d 866, 883-885 (D.C. Cir. 2010) (Williams, J., concurring) (arguing that petitioner was detainable on account of being "part of" an AUMF-targeted organization, but not deciding whether a person could be detained on account of "support" for a targeted organization that he was not also a "part of").

[18] Id. at 872 (quoting 2006 MCA, P.L. 109-366, §3, and 2009 MCA, P.L. 111-84, Div A, §1802).

[19] Id. at 872-873. The panel found that even if petitioner was not a member of an AUMF-targeted organization, his service as a cook for a military brigade affiliated with Taliban and Al Qaeda forces, in addition to his accompaniment of the brigade during military operations, constituted sufficient grounds for his detention. Id.

[20] Al-Bihani v. Obama, 590 F.3d 866, 877 (D.C. Cir. 2010).

[21] The preponderance standard is generally interpreted to require that the evidence presented by both sides taken together makes the facts in question more likely true than not. See 29 AM. JUR. 2d Evid. §173.

[22] See Hamdi v. Rumsfeld, 542 U.S. 507, 533-34 (2004) (O'Connell, J., plurality opinion) ("exigencies of the circumstances may demand" that procedural rules be tailored to avoid undue burden on the government, and that hearsay "may need to be accepted as the most reliable available evidence from the Government").

[23] The court distinguished the petitioner's case from any case involving a U.S. citizen or one in which an alien is detained within the United States, suggesting it might reach a different conclusion in such a case. Al-Bihani, 590 F.3d at 877.

[24] Id. at 879.

[25] Al-Bihani v. Obama, 619 F.3d 1 (D.C. Cir. 2010) (Sentelle, C.J., concurring).

[26] See, e.g., Almerfedi v. Obama, 654 F.3d 1, 4 n.2 (D.C. Cir. 2011) ("As we have explained [in Al-Bihani], the government may detain any individual 'engaged in hostilities ... against the United States,' who 'purposefully and materially supported hostilities against the United States or its coalition partners,' or who 'is part of the Taliban, al Qaeda, or associated forces.'"); Hatim v. Gates, 632 F.3d 720 (D.C. Cir. 2011) (per curiam panel decision) (finding that district court ruling that military could only detain person who was "part of" Al Qaeda or the Taliban was "directly contrary to Al-Bihani v. Obama, which held that 'those who purposefully and materially support' al-Qaida or the Taliban could also be detained").

[27] 2012 NDAA, P.L. 112-81, §1021(b).

[28] Al Bihani v. Obama, No. 10-5352, 2011 U.S. App. LEXIS 2600 (D.C. Cir., February 11, 2011) (summarily affirming lower court's denial of habeas petition), cert. denied, 132 S. Ct. 2739 (2012).

[29] Al-Adahi v. Obama, 613 F.3d 1102, 1105-1106 (D.C. Cir. 2010) (omitting some citations contained in original).

[30] In support of its finding that the government had demonstrated by a preponderance of evidence that the petitioner was a member of Al Qaeda, the circuit panel cited, inter alia, evidence relating to the petitioner's travel to Afghanistan in 2001, his subsequent meetings with Osama Bin Laden, his stay at an Al Qaeda guesthouse, his presence at an Al Qaeda-affiliated training camp, and his wearing of a watch at the time of capture that was of the same model as that used by Al Qaeda operatives.

[31] See also Khan 655 F.3d 20, 26 (D.C. Cir. 2011) (preponderance of the evidence standard is constitutional in cases involving detention under the AUMF); Alsabri v. Obama, 684 F.3d 1298, 1309 (D.C. Cir. 2012) (same).

[32] Al Odah v. United States, 611 F.3d 8, 14 (D.C. Cir. 2010) (citing 648 F. Supp. 2d 1, 10 (D.D.C. 2009)).

[33] Al Kandari v. United States, 462 Fed. Appx. 1 (2011) (in an unpublished opinion, ruling that petitioner's argument that the Federal Rules of Evidence applied to Guantanamo habeas litigation was foreclosed by Al-Odah), cert. denied, 132 S. Ct. 2741 (2012).

[34] Boumediene v. Bush, 579 F. Supp. 2d 191 (D.D.C. 2008).

[35] Salahi v. Obama, 625 F.3d 745, 752 (D.C. Cir. 2010) (italics in original).

[36] Almerfedi v. Obama, 654 F.3d 1, 5 n.4 (D.C. Cir. 2011).

[37] Id. at 4 (claiming that [T] the government's evidence may well have been stronger in previous cases than in this case. But that is irrelevant; all of those cases were not close.").

[38] Id. at 3. 39 Id. at 6.

[40] Al Alwi v. Obama, 653 F.3d 11, 16-17 (D.C. Cir. 2011).

[41] Id. at 18-19.

[42] Id. at 20.

[43] Id. at 18 n.7.

[44] Latif v. Obama, 666 F.3d 746, 750-751 (D.C. 2011).

[45] 677 F.3d 1175 (D.C. Cir. 2012).

[46] Id. at 1180.

[47] Id. at 1182.

[48] Id. at 1185. The panel majority expressly declined to "decide precisely how much more the detainee must show to overcome the presumption of regularity." Id. at 1186 n5.

[49] Id. at 1215 (Tatel, J., dissenting) (quoting Parhat v. Gates, 532 F.3d 834, 849 (D.C. Cir. 2008)).

[50] 132 S. Ct. 2741 (2012).

[51] For discussion of U.S. policy relating to the transfer or release of Guantanamo detainees to foreign countries, see CRS Report R40139, Closing the Guantanamo Detention Center: Legal Issues, by Michael John Garcia et al.

[52] In re Guantanamo Bay Detainee Litigation, 581 F. Supp. 2d 33 (D.D.C. 2008).

[53] Kiyemba v. Bush, No. 08-5424, 2008 WL 4898963, Order (D.C. Cir., October 20, 2008) (per curiam).

[54] Indeed, the D.C. Circuit in Bismullah implied that, despite its determination that the DTA review process was no longer available to detainees, the circuit court's ruling in Parhat remained in force. Bismullah, 551 F.3d 1068, 1075, n. 2 (D.C. Cir. 2009). See also Bensayah v. Obama, 610 F.3d 718, 725-726 (D.C. Cir. 2010) ("In Parhat we made clear that the reliability of evidence can be determined not only by looking at the evidence alone but, alternatively, by considering 'sufficient additional information ... permit[ting the fact finder] to assess its reliability.'"); Ameziane v. Obama, 620 F.3d 1 (D.C. Cir. 2010) (holding that district court had failed to properly apply Parhat in its consideration of government motion to designate certain information as "protected" under the governing protective order).

[55] Parhat v. Gates, 532 F.3d 834, 846-47 (D.C. Cir. 2008).

[56] Id. at 847.

[57] Id. at 849.

[58] A more detailed discussion of the Bismullah case is found in CRS Report RL33180, Enemy Combatant Detainees: Habeas Corpus Challenges in Federal Court, by Jennifer K. Elsea and Michael John Garcia.

[59] Bivens v. Six Unknown Agents of Fed. Bureau of Narcotics, 403 U.S. 388 (1971) (providing for cause of action in tort for violation of certain constitutional rights).

[60] Rasul v. Rumsfeld, 414 F. Supp. 2d 26 (D.D.C. 2006).

[61] Rasul v. Myers, 512 F.3d 644 (D.C. Cir. 2008) ("Rasul I") was vacated by the Supreme court and remanded for reconsideration in light of Boumediene. 129 S.Ct. 763 (2008) Rasul v. Myers, 563 F.3d 527 (D.C. Cir. 2009) ("Rasul II") reinstated the earlier opinion but limited its scope to rest the holding on qualified immunity without adjudicating the constitutional questions. The appellate court reversed a holding by the district court that would have enabled plaintiffs to pursue claims based on the Religious Freedom Restoration Act (RFRA), 42 U.S.C. §§2000bb et seq.

[62] Rasul II, 563 F.3d at 529.

[63] Id. at 532 & n.5.

[64] 28 U.S.C. §2241(e)(2), provides that "[n]o court ... shall have jurisdiction to hear or consider any other action against the United States or its agents relating to any aspect of the detention, transfer, treatment, trial, or conditions of confinement of an alien who is or was detained by the United States and has been determined by the United States to have been properly detained as an enemy combatant or is awaiting such determination."

[65] Prior to this decision, district court judges appeared to have uniformly agreed that Boumediene only invalidated the provision of the MCA stripping federal courts of habeas jurisdiction over Guantanamo detainees. See, e.g., Khadr v. Bush, 587 F. Supp. 2d 225, 235-36 (D.D.C. 2009); In re Guantanamo Bay Detainee Litig., 577 F. Supp. 2d 312, 314 (D.D.C. 2008); In re Guantanamo Bay Detainee Litig., 570 F. Supp. 2d 13, 18 (D.D.C. 2008)). See also Kiyemba v. Obama, 561 F.3d 509, 512 n.1 (D.C. Cir. 2009) (in habeas case, noting that

Boumediene "referred to §7 without specifying a particular subsection of §2241(e) but its discussion of the Suspension Clause clearly indicates it was referring only to that part of §7 codified at §2241(e)(1)")).

[66] Maqaleh v. Gates, 604 F. Supp. 2d 205 (D.D.C. 2009).

[67] After the district court's initial ruling in Maqaleh, the DOD announced modifications to the administrative process used to review the status of aliens held at Bagram, which would afford detainees greater procedural rights. The modified process does not contemplate judicial review of administrative determinations regarding the detention of persons at Bagram. See Letter from Phillip Carter, Dep. Asst. Sec. Defense for Detainee Policy, to Sen. Carl Levin, Chairman of Sen. Armed Serv. Comm., July 14, 2009, available at http://www.scotusblog.com/wp/wp-content/uploads/ 2009/09/US-Bagram-brief-9-14-09.pdf. The circuit panel stated that its analysis was not informed by these new procedures, as those procedures were not in place when the case was appealed to the circuit court.

[68] Maqaleh v. Gates, 2012 WL 5077483 (D.D.C., Oct., 9, 2012).

[69] In re Guantanamo Bay Detainee Continued Access to Counsel, 2012 WL 4039707 at *5 (D.D.C. Sept. 6, 2012).

[70] Id. at *6.

[71] Padilla v. Hanft, 389 F. Supp. 2d 678 (D.S.C. 2005).

[72] See Respondents' Answer to the Petition for a Writ of Habeas Corpus at 2, Padilla v. Hanft, C/A No. 02:04 2221- 26AJ (D.S.C. filed 2004).

[73] 389 F. Supp. 2d at 690.

[74] 423 F.3d 386, 390-91 (4th Cir. 2005).

[75] The government initially asked the Fourth Circuit to approve Padilla's transfer and suggested it should vacate its opinion, but the judges preferred to defer to the Supreme Court to make that determination. In rejecting the government's application, Circuit Judge Luttig (who has since stepped down from the bench) issued a harsh opinion expressing disappointment at the government's decision abruptly to abandon its position that national security imperatives demanded Padilla's continued military detention:

[A]s the government surely must understand, although the various facts it has asserted are not necessarily inconsistent or without basis, its actions have left not only the impression that Padilla may have been held for these years, even if justifiably, by mistake—an impression we would have thought the government could ill afford to leave extant. They have left the impression that the government may even have come to the belief that the principle in reliance upon which it has detained Padilla for this time, that the President possesses the authority to detain enemy combatants who enter into this country for the purpose of attacking America and its citizens from within, can, in the end, yield to expediency with little or no cost to its conduct of the war against terror—an impression we would have thought the government likewise could ill afford to leave extant.

Padilla v. Hanft, 432 F.3d 582, 587 (4th Cir. 2005)(order).

[76] Padilla v. Hanft, 546 U.S. 1084 (2006).

[77] 547 U.S. 1062 (2006).

[78] United States v. Padilla, 2007 WL 1079090 (S.D.Fla. 2007) (unreported opinion). While one district court held Padilla can pursue civil damages against a former government official for his treatment in military detention, Padilla v. Yoo, 633 F. Supp. 2d 1005 (N.D.Cal. 2009), the Fourth Circuit has rejected a civil suit on the basis of qualified immunity for the government officials involved, Lebron v. Rumsfeld, 670 F.3d 540 (4th Cir. 2012)

[79] For further discussion of al-Marri, see CRS Report RL33180, Enemy Combatant Detainees: Habeas Corpus Challenges in Federal Court, by Jennifer K. Elsea and Michael John Garcia;

CRS Report R42337, Detention of U.S. Persons as Enemy Belligerents, by Jennifer K. Elsea.

[80] al-Marri v. Pucciarelli, 534 F.3d 213, 221 (2008) (Traxler, J., concurring).

[81] Lebron v. Rumsfeld, 670 F.3d 540, 548 (4th Cir. 2012).

[82] Id.

[83] Id. at 556.

[84] Id. at 557.

[85] Hedges v. Obama, No. 12-CV-331, 2012 WL 1721124 (S.D.N.Y. May 16, 2012).

[86] For further discussion of Section 1021 of the 2012 NDAA, see CRS Report R42143, The National Defense Authorization Act for FY2012: Detainee Matters, by Jennifer K. Elsea and Michael John Garcia.

[87] Hedges at *2.

[88] In re Guantanamo Bay Detainee Litigation, Respondents' Memorandum Regarding the Government's Detention Authority Relative to Detainees Held at Guantanamo Bay, No. 08-0442, filed March 13, 2009 (D.D.C), available at http://www.justice.gov/opa/documents/memo-re-det-auth.pdf.

[89] Hedges v. Obama, No. 12-CV-331 (S.D.N.Y. June 6, 2012).

[90] Hedges v. Obama, No. 12-CV-331 (S.D.N.Y September 12, 2012).

[91] Vance v. Rumsfeld, . 694 F. Supp. 2d 957 (N.D.Ill.2010).

[92] 5 U.S.C. §701(b)(1)(G).

[93] Vance v. Rumsfeld, 653 F.3d 591 (7th Cir.2011).

[94] Vance v. Rumsfeld, 2012 WL 5416500 at *1 (7th Cir. Nov. 7, 2012) (en banc) (citing Lebron v. Rumsfeld, 670 F.3d 540 (4th Cir.2012); Doe v. Rumsfeld, 683 F.3d 390 (D.C.Cir.2012); Ali v. Rumsfeld, 649 F.3d 762 (D.C.Cir.2011).

[95] Id. at *5.

[96] Id. at *3.

[97] The majority noted that a portion of the Detainee Treatment Act codified at 42 U.S.C. §2000dd–1(a), which provides a defense for federal officials against damages liability for violation, only applies to suits by non-U.S. nationals. Id. at *7. But the court did not find that citizenship was dispositive for the viability of a Bivens suit. Id. at *8. Judge Wood, concurring because the Secretary of Defense was too far removed from the conduct to be personally liable, pointed out that a Bivens action is the only possible action for citizens harmed on foreign land under control of the United States, while non-citizens and U.S. citizens harmed by foreign officials can sue under the Torture Victim Protection Act. Id. at *14 (Woods, C.J., concurring). The dissenting judges made a similar point by arguing that the court should not attribute to Congress the "improbable" intent to "deny U.S. civilians a right that Congress has expressly extended to the rest of the world." Id. at *23 (Hamilton, C.J., dissenting).)

[98] Id. at *16 (Hamilton, C.J., dissenting).

[99] The exact nature of the information and its acquisition by the government is obscured by the many redactions in the reported opinions.

[100] United States v. Moussaoui, 382 F.3d 453, 456-57 (4th Cir. 2004) ("Moussaoui II"). In "Moussaoui I," 333 F.3d 509, 517 (4th Cir. 2003), the circuit court dismissed the appeal of the discovery order as unripe and remanded for the government to propose substitutions for the witness testimony similar to those available under CIPA. (CIPA applies to the production of documents during discovery but does not address witnesses). The district court imposed sanctions on remand after the government refused to make the enemy combatant witnesses available for deposition. The judge rejected the parties' proposal for an

order of dismissal, the ordinary sanction under CIPA in cases in which the government declines to provide classified information the court has determined is necessary for the defense. Instead, she dismissed the death notice on the grounds that the witnesses could provide testimony that might preclude a jury from finding Moussaoui eligible for the death penalty. Because the testimony could exonerate Moussaoui of involvement in the September 11 attacks, the district court prohibited the government "from making any argument, or offering any evidence, suggesting that the defendant had any involvement in, or knowledge of, the September 11 attacks." United States v. Moussaoui, 282 F. Supp. 2d 480, 327 (E.D. Va. 2003). Evidence that would have been excluded under the order included cockpit voice recordings, video footage showing the collapse of the World Trade Center Towers, and photographs of victims.

[101] 382 F.3d at 487 n. 31. Judge Gregory noted in dissent that such information may be reliable for intelligence purposes and yet omit relevant information that might be helpful to the defense because such information was not deemed to have any actionable foreign intelligence value. Id. at 488, n. 6.

[102] As noted by a dissenting judge of the appellate panel, the procedures crafted by the majority deviate from CIPA procedures by having the district judge, rather than the government, prepare the substitutions for the potential testimony, arguably making the district court judge an advocate in the proceedings. 382 F.3d. at 484-85 (Gregory, J., concurring in part and dissenting in part).

[103] Moussaoui v. Obama, 591 F.3d 263, 278 (4th Cir. 2010).

[104] United States v. Lindh, 212 F. Supp. 2d 541, 557-58 (E.D. Va. 2002). The judge also rejected Lindh's contention that media publicity had rendered a fair trial for him impossible, at least in that particular court, and that the International Economic Emergency Powers Act ("IEEPA") (50 U.S.C. §1701 et seq.) regulations he was charged with violating were not valid.

[105] United States v. Lindh, 198 F. Supp. 2d 739 (E.D. Va. 2002).

[106] Id. at 742.

[107] Id. at 743.

[108] Id. at 744.

[109] United States v. Ghailani, 686 F. Supp. 2d 279, 298-99 (S.D.N.Y 2009) (citing Morris v. Slappy, 461 U.S. 1, 14 (1983); Wheat v. United States, 486 U.S. 153, 159 (1988)).

[110] United States v. Ghailani, 687 F. Supp. 2d 365, 369 (S.D.N.Y. 2010) (citing Barker v. Wingo, 407 U.S. 514 (1972)).

[111] Id. at 372.

[112] Barker v. Wingo, Warden 407 U.S. 514, 519 (1972).

[113] See id. at 530. Courts have recognized at least three types of prejudice, including "'oppressive pretrial incarceration,' 'anxiety and concern of the accused,' and 'the possibility that the [accused's] defense will be impaired' by dimming memories and loss of exculpatory evidence." See Doggett v. United States, 505 U.S. 647, 654 (1992) (citing Barker, 407 U.S. at 532; Smith v. Hooey, 393 U.S. 374, 377-379 (1969); United States v. Ewell, 383 U.S. 116, 120 (1966).

[114] United States v. Ghailani, 751 F. Supp. 2d 515, 534 (S.D.N.Y. 2010).

[115] Id. at 535. The court pointed out that the defendant had been "no more able to engage in hostilities against the United States while in the custody of the Bureau of Prisons pending trial on this indictment than he was at Guantanamo in the custody of the DoD. He could have been brought to this Court in 2006 or any subsequent date to face this 1998 indictment

and, at the same time, prevented from engaging in hostilities against this country." Id. at 536.

[116] Id. at 538. The judge contrasted this factor against situations where delay is justified by ongoing state investigations and prosecutions.

[117] Id. at 540.

[118] United States v. Ghailani, 743 F. Supp. 2d 261 (S.D.N.Y. 2010).

[119] United States v. Ghailani, 743 F. Supp. 2d 242 (S.D.N.Y. 2010) (order). Under the "core application" doctrine, the exclusionary rule should be limited to cases where it serves as a deterrent to unlawful police actions, which typically means barring the use of unlawfully seized evidence in the government's case in chief for the offense that precipitated the search, and that extension of the rule to cases where the remedial purpose is not served (such as cases in which a search is defective due to clerical error) must be justified by weighing the additional marginal deterrence against the cost to the public interest in pursuing the truth. See Arizona v. Evans, 514 U.S. 1 (1995). The government argued that the exclusion of any evidence obtained as a result of Ghailani's coerced statements would not serve any deterrent purpose because the interrogation was conducted as part of a CIA effort to gather intelligence necessary for national security purposes rather than part of a law enforcement operation., and that CIA interrogators did not contemplate nor were motivated by the prospect of a criminal investigation. Judge Kaplan rejected the government's rationale, noting that a Fourth Amendment violation occurs at the time of an unlawful search or seizure, while the Fifth Amendment's Self-Incrimination Clause is violated whenever a coerced statement or its fruit is introduced at trial. Accordingly, he reasoned that the direct protection of a constitutional right rather than the deterrence of future violations was at stake in the case before him, and that the rationale of the core application doctrine did not apply.

[120] United States v. Ghailani, 743 F. Supp. 2d 261 (S.D.N.Y. 2010).

[121] For a complete list of charges, see Press Release, U.S. Justice Department, "Ahmed Ghailani Transferred from Guantanamo Bay to New York for Prosecution on Terror Charges," June 9, 2009, available at http://www.justice.gov/ opa/pr/2009/June/09-ag-563.html.

[122] United States v. Ghailani, 761 F. Supp. 2d 167 (S.D.N.Y. 2011).

[123] The defense argued in essence that a conviction for conspiracy to commit a substantive offense is improper where a defendant is acquitted of committing the substantive offense itself and the proof necessary to support the substantive charge is identical to that required for a conspiracy conviction. The judge rejected that theory as a valid statement of the law. See id. at 190-191.

[124] Id. at 194.

[125] Id.

[126] See supra "Hamdan v. Rumsfeld, 548 U.S. 557 (2006)."

[127] P.L. 109-366, 120 Stat. 2600, codified as amended at Chapter 47a of Title 10, U.S. Code. For an overview, see CRS Report R41163, The Military Commissions Act of 2009: Overview and Legal Issues, by Jennifer K. Elsea.

[128] Press release, Department of Defense, Detainee Transfer Announced (Nov. 28, 2008), available at http://www.defenselink.mil/releases/release.aspx?releaseid=12372.

[129] 10 U.S.C. §821.

[130] Hamdan v. United States, 09-002 (CMCR 2011), available at http://www.lawfareblog.com/wp-content/uploads/ 2011/06/hamdan.pdf.

[131] 10 U.S.C. §950p(d).

[132] Hamdan v. United States, 696 F.3d 1238, 1250 n. 10 (D.C. Cir. 2012).

In: Law and Legal Issues in the United States ISBN: 978-1-63117-827-6
Editor: Laurent B. Landers

Chapter 6

THE IRAN HOSTAGES: EFFORTS TO OBTAIN COMPENSATION*

Jennifer K. Elsea

SUMMARY

Even today, after the passage of some three decades, the 1979-1981 Iran Hostage Crisis remains an event familiar to most Americans. Many might be unaware that the 52 American mostly military and diplomatic personnel held hostage in Tehran for 444 days continue to strive for significant compensation for their ordeal. The former hostages and their families did receive a number of benefits under various civil service laws, and each hostage received from the U.S. government a cash payment of $50 for each day held hostage. The hostages have never received any compensation from Iran through court actions, all efforts having failed due to foreign sovereign immunity and an executive agreement known as the Algiers Accords, which bars such lawsuits. Congress took action to abrogate Iran's sovereign immunity in the case *Roeder v. Islamic Republic of Iran*, but never successfully abrogated the executive agreement, leaving the plaintiffs with jurisdiction to pursue their case but without a judicial cause of action.

Having lost their bids in the courts to obtain recompense, the former hostages have turned to Congress for relief. This report outlines the history of various efforts, including legislative efforts and court cases,

* This is an edited, reformatted and augmented version of Congressional Research Service Publication, No. R43210, dated November 1, 2013.

and describes three bills currently before Congress (H.R. 904, S. 559, H.R. 3200).

INTRODUCTION

Even today, after the passage of some three decades, the 1979-1981 Iran Hostage Crisis remains an event familiar to most Americans. Many might be unaware that the 52 American mostly military and diplomatic personnel held hostage in Tehran for 444 days or their survivors continue to strive for significant compensation for their ordeal. The former hostages and their families did receive a number of benefits under various civil service laws, and each hostage received from the U.S. government a cash payment of $50 for each day held hostage. The hostages have never received any compensation from Iran through court actions, all efforts having failed due to foreign sovereign immunity and an executive agreement known as the Algiers Accords, which bars such lawsuits. Congress took action to abrogate Iran's sovereign immunity in the case, but never successfully abrogated the executive agreement, leaving the plaintiffs with jurisdiction to pursue their case but without a judicial cause of action.

Having lost their bids in the courts to obtain recompense, the former hostages have turned to Congress for relief.[1] This report outlines the history of various efforts, including legislative efforts and court cases, and describes three bills currently before Congress (H.R. 904, S. 559, H.R. 3200).

THE HOSTAGE RELIEF ACT

The 52 Americans taken hostage in Tehran in November 1979 and held until January 1981[2] included civilian foreign service diplomats and other government employees, as well as military service members and one private citizen. Concern about the effects of the ordeal on the hostages and their families led Congress to enact legislation in 1980 designed to make the hostages and their families eligible for the same benefits that were available to prisoners of war and soldiers missing in action during the Vietnam conflict, including their dependents. The Hostage Relief Act of 1980[3] did not provide for a cash payment to hostages or their families; however, benefits under the act included

- creation of an interest-bearing salary savings fund including retroactive interest;
- reimbursement of medical expenses of the hostages and their family members;
- extension of relief under the Soldiers and Sailors Act to hostages;
- tax relief, including deferred assessment of taxes and penalties, tax forgiveness during the period of captivity, and refunding of tax collected prior to enactment;
- educational expenses for family members of hostages and retraining of hostages.[4]

These benefits were supplemental to benefits to which government employees and service members and their families were already entitled.[5] The Congressional Budget Office estimated that the cost of additional medical benefits for the 1981 fiscal year would amount to $390,000; educational benefits would cost from $80,000 to $307,000 depending on the version of the bill enacted; and internal revenue would decrease by less than $1 million due to the tax benefits.[6] A proposal to provide the hostages each with $1,000 per day to be paid from frozen Iranian assets in the United States met with the objection of the State Department on the grounds that it could complicate negotiations to secure the hostages' release, and it was not adopted.[7]

Algiers Accords

In order to secure the release of the hostages and bring the crisis to an end, the U.S. government sought the good offices of Algeria to broker a deal with the new Iranian government. The result was a set of executive agreements known collectively as the Algiers Accords.[8] The agreements provided not only for the release of the hostages, but also the unfreezing of Iranian assets in the United States and the creation of an international tribunal to settle claims between the two governments, as well as certain private claims against either government by a national of the other, mostly arising as a result of contracts disrupted by the revolution in Iran.

The Algiers Accords contain the following provisions respecting claims arising out of the hostage taking:

> [T]he United States ... will thereafter bar and preclude the prosecution against Iran of any pending or future claim of the United

> States or a United States national arising out of events occurring before the date of this declaration related to (A) the seizure of the 52 United States nationals on Nov. 4, 1979, (B) their subsequent detention, (C) injury to United States property or property of the United States nationals within the United States embassy compound in Tehran after Nov. 3, 1979, and (D) injury to the United States nationals or their property as a result of popular movements in the course of the Islamic Revolution in Iran which were not an act of the Government of Iran. The United States will also bar and preclude the prosecution against Iran in the courts of the United States of any pending or future claims asserted by persons other than the United States nationals arising out of the events specified in the preceding sentence.[9]

To fulfill this commitment, President Carter issued Executive Order 12283,[10] citing the International Emergency Economic Powers Acts (IEEPA),[11] among other authorities, to order the Secretary of the Treasury to promulgate regulations prohibiting any person subject to U.S. jurisdiction from bringing any court claim against Iran arising out of the hostage seizure or subsequent detention.[12] The Office of Foreign Assets Control (OFAC) at the Treasury Department amended the Iranian Assets Control Regulations (31 C.F.R. Part 535) accordingly.[13]

PRESIDENT'S COMMISSION ON HOSTAGE COMPENSATION

On the same day the Algiers Accords were signed to secure the release of the hostages, President Carter created the President's Commission on Hostage Compensation[14] and tasked it to provide recommendations as to whether the United States should provide financial compensation to the former hostages.[15] The Commission reviewed prior practice regarding governmental compensation for prisoners of war and the value of benefits already received by the former hostages under other laws in making its recommendation.[16] The Commission focused on the obligations it found the U.S. government owes as an employer, and concluded that "compensation in the tort sense" was not appropriate.[17] It did, however, recommend a "token" payment of tax-exempt detention benefits in the amount of $12.50 per day of captivity, similar to benefits paid to Vietnam prisoners of war and interned civilians as well as to the crew of the USS *Pueblo* who were detained by the government of North Korea for 11 months in 1968.[18]

In making this recommendation, the Commission was mindful of the fact that the Algiers Accords precluded the former hostages from suing Iran for damages,[19] but agreed with the government's position that this did not constitute a "taking" within the meaning of the Fifth Amendment because

> (1) the President had statutory and constitutional authority to settle the potential hostage claims;
>
> (2) the hostages could not establish for purposes of a taking claim that they suffered an actual uncompensated loss since (a) their claims were settled for considerable value, i.e., their release and (b) their right of action against Iran was of dubious value because of the unlikelihood that the U.S. courts would have been available as a forum in which to sue Iran in light of certain provisions of the Foreign Sovereign Immunities Act.[20]

The Commission recommended that the government "assume the costs of restoring the hostages to health, provide disability compensation if their health cannot be restored, provide compensation for material losses and safeguard their employment rights and career prospects."[21]

COURT ACTIONS

Notwithstanding the Algiers Accords' provision barring lawsuits, many of the former hostages brought suit against Iran for damages.[22] These lawsuits failed for lack of jurisdiction under the Foreign Sovereign Immunities Act (FSIA)[23] or because of the Algiers Accords, or both.

In *Persinger v. Islamic Republic of Iran*,[24] the U.S. Court of Appeals for the D.C. Circuit initially found jurisdiction based on the non-commercial tort exception to the FSIA,[25] on the notion that U.S. embassy grounds are within the jurisdiction of the United States. On the merits, however, the court found that the President's order implementing the Algiers Accords extinguished any claim the plaintiff may have had. Despite having won the case, the U.S. government petitioned for rehearing on the foreign sovereign immunity question. The court granted the motion and vacated its earlier opinion, agreeing with the government that the tort exception to sovereign immunity applies only to injuries occurring within the territorial jurisdiction of the United States, which did not include U.S. embassies abroad. The court held it could not, without jurisdiction over the case, reach the question regarding the legitimacy of the President's action.[26]

Some of the former hostages brought suit against the United States seeking compensation for what they viewed as an unconstitutional taking of their claim against Iran, but were ultimately unsuccessful.[27] In *Belk v. United States*,[28] the United States Claims Court entered summary judgment in favor of the government, holding that the signing of the Algiers Accords did not effect a "taking" of private property because it primarily benefited the plaintiffs, the barring of claims was not novel or unexpected or outside the recognized authority of the President, and alternatively, that the presidential decision to bar claims amounted to a political question. The Court of Appeals for the Federal Circuit affirmed, agreeing that the extinguishment of the plaintiffs' claims was not novel or unexpected,[29] and "cannot be said to have 'interfered with distinct investment-backed expectations.'"[30] The appellate court also agreed that the matter was non-justiciable as a political question:

> It involves a policy decision made by the President during a time of crisis. The appellants apparently contend that the President should not have entered into the Algiers Accords because he could have obtained better terms, and that the Accords themselves were illegal because the President was coerced into agreeing to them. The determination whether and upon what terms to settle the dispute with Iran over its holding of the hostages and obtain their release, necessarily was for the President to make in his foreign relations role. That determination was "of a kind clearly for nonjudicial discretion," and there are no "judicially discoverable and manageable standards" for reviewing such a Presidential decision. A judicial inquiry into whether the President could have extracted a more favorable settlement would seriously interfere with the President's ability to conduct foreign relations.[31]

The court concluded that if any compensation of the plaintiffs for their mistreatment and suffering were to be forthcoming, it would have to be provided by "one of the other 'coordinate branches of government.'"[32]

THE OMNIBUS DIPLOMATIC SECURITY AND ANTI-TERRORISM ACT OF 1986

When Congress returned to the issue of compensation for former hostages in 1985, the House Foreign Affairs Committee rejected the amount recommended by the Commission in favor of a per diem payment based on the average government allowance for travel.[33] As referred to the House floor, Section 802 of the Omnibus Diplomatic Security and Anti-Terrorism Act of 1986 provided for compensation in an amount deemed appropriate by the President taking into account the treatment the hostages received during captivity or other factors, but not less than the worldwide per diem rate under 5 U.S.C. Section 5702.[34] The committee explained that

> In determining a level of cash compensation for civilian captives, the committee attempted to weigh the issues presented in the debate over the rate of compensation for the Iran hostages. At the time that the President's Commission on Hostage Compensation presented its findings, many felt that the Commission's recommendation that the hostages receive $12.50 per day for every day in captivity vastly underestimated both the captivity itself and the sympathy of the American people for the captives' plight. Others suggested that any cash award should be upward of $100 per day or more. The per diem rate chosen by the committee is a uniform rate which is a reliable gauge of the Government's obligation to its employees when they are engaged in official business away from the normal duty station.[35]

This formula would have provided compensation in the amount of $66 per day for each former hostage. A floor amendment to reduce the amount to $20 failed,[36] but the provision was amended in conference to provide $50 per day to the Iran hostages and to reduce the minimum per-diem based rate for future victims by half.[37] The conference report provides no explanation for the substitution.[38]

Foreign Sovereign Immunities Act Amendment

After Congress amended the FSIA in 1996[39] to include a new exception to immunity for acts of terrorism conducted or sponsored by designated terrorist states, the former hostages again brought suit against Iran.

Roeder v. Islamic Republic of Iran

In late 2000 a suit was filed in federal district court on behalf of the 52 embassy staffers and on behalf of their families. *Roeder v. Islamic Republic of*

Iran[40] sought both compensatory and punitive damages from Iran. In August of 2001, the trial court granted a default judgment to the plaintiffs and scheduled a hearing on the damages to be awarded. In October 2001, however, the U.S. government intervened in the proceeding and moved that the judgment be vacated and the case dismissed. The government contended that the suit did not meet all of the requirements of the terrorist State exception to the FSIA (notably, that Iran had not been designated as a state sponsor of terrorism at the time the U.S. personnel were held hostage) and that the suit was barred by the explicit provisions of the 1981 Algiers Accords that led to the release of the hostages.

While that motion was pending before the court, Congress passed as part of the Hollings amendment to the FY2002 Appropriations Act for the Departments of Commerce, Justice, and State a provision specifying that *Roeder* should be deemed to be included within the terrorist State exception to the FSIA. As amended, the pertinent section of the FSIA excluded suits against terrorist states from the immunity generally accorded foreign states but directed the courts to decline to hear such a case (with the amendment in italics): "if the foreign state was not designated as a state sponsor of terrorism ... at the time the act occurred, unless later so designated as a result of such act *or the act is related to Case Number 1:00CV03110 (ESG) in the United States District Court for the District of Columbia.*"[41]

The conference report on the bill explained the provision as follows: "Subsection (c) quashes the State Department's motion to vacate the judgment obtained by plaintiffs in Case Number 1:00CV03110 (ESG) in the United States District Court for the District of Columbia. Consistent with current law, subsection (c) does not require the United States government to make any payments to satisfy the judgment."[42]

In signing the appropriations act into law on November 28, 2001, however, President George W. Bush took note of this provision and commented as follows:

> [S]ubsection (c) ... purports to remove Iran's immunity from suit in a case brought by the 1979 Tehran hostages in the District Court for the District of Columbia. To the maximum extent permitted by applicable law, the executive branch will act, and will encourage the courts to act, with regard to subsection 626(c) of the Act in a manner consistent with the obligations of the United States under the Algiers Accords that achieved the release of U.S. hostages in 1981.[43]

The government continued to pursue its motion to dismiss the case, arguing, *inter alia*, that the suit was barred by the Algiers Accords. During the course of the proceeding the judge expressed concern regarding the lack of clarity of the recent congressional enactment with respect to whether Congress had intended to abrogate the Algiers Accords. A week later, in the fiscal 2002 appropriations act for the Department of Defense, the 107th Congress included a provision making a minor technical correction in the reference to the *Roeder* case.[44] The accompanying conference report elaborated on what it said was the effect and intent of the earlier amendment of the FSIA with respect to *Roeder*, seemingly in response to the judge's expression of concern. The conference report explained that

> The language included in Section 626(c) of P.L. 107-77 quashed the Department of State's motion to vacate the judgment obtained by plaintiffs in Case Number 1:00CV03110(EGS) and reaffirmed the validity of this claim and its retroactive application.... The provision included in Section 626(c) of P.L. 107-77 acknowledges that, notwithstanding any other authority, the American citizens who were taken hostage by the Islamic Republic of Iran in 1979 have a claim against Iran under the Antiterrorism Act of 1996 and the provision specifically allows the judgment to stand for purposes of award damages consistent with Section 2002 of the Victims of Terrorism Act of 2000 (P.L. 106-386, 114 Stat. 1541).[45]

Nonetheless, in signing the Department of Defense appropriations measure into law on January 10, 2002, President Bush asserted that

> Section 208 of Division B makes a technical correction to subsection 626(c) of P.L. 107-77 (the FY2002 Commerce, Justice, State, the Judiciary and Related Agencies Appropriations Act), but does nothing to alter the effect of that provision or any other provision of law. Since the enactment of sub-section 626(c) and consistent with it, the executive branch has encouraged the courts to act, and will continue to encourage the courts to act, in a manner consistent with the obligations of the United States under the Algiers Accords that achieved the release of U.S. hostages in 1981.[46]

The judge granted the government's motion to vacate the default judgment against Iran and to dismiss the suit.[47] In a lengthy opinion the court concluded that

- at the time it entered a default judgment for plaintiffs on August 17, 2001, it did not have jurisdiction over the case and should not have entered a judgment;[48]
- the cause of action which Congress had adopted in late 1996 did not apply to suits against terrorist states but only against the officials, employees, and agents of those states who perpetrate terrorist acts;[49]
- the provision of the Algiers Accords committing the United States to bar suits against Iran for the incident constitutes the substantive law of the case, and Congress's two enactments specifically concerning the case were too ambiguous to conclude that Congress specifically intended to override this international commitment.[50]

In addition, the court in *dicta* suggested that Congress's enactments on the *Roeder* case might have interfered with its adjudication of the case in a manner that raised constitutional separation of powers concerns.[51] It also chastised the plaintiffs' attorneys for what it said were serious breaches of their professional and ethical responsibilities.[52]

The U.S. Court of Appeals for the District of Columbia affirmed the decision of the lower court, placing emphasis on the fact that the legislative history plaintiffs sought to use—the joint explanatory statement prepared by House and Senate conferees—is not part of the conference report voted on by both houses of Congress and thus does not carry the force of law.[53]

> Executive agreements are essentially contracts between nations, and like contracts between individuals, executive agreements are expected to be honored by the parties. Congress (or the President acting alone) may abrogate an executive agreement, but legislation must be clear to ensure that Congress—and the President—have considered the consequences. The "requirement of clear statement assures that the legislature has in fact faced, and intended to bring into issue, the critical matters involved in the judicial decision." The kind of legislative history offered here cannot repeal an executive agreement when the legislation itself is silent. [Citations omitted].

The appellate court denied that its interpretation rendered any act of Congress futile. On the contrary, it stated that, "[i]f constitutional ... the amendments had the effect of removing Iran's sovereign immunity, which the United States had raised in its motion to vacate."[54]

Efforts to Abrogate the Algiers Accords

Subsequent to the trial court's original decision in *Roeder*, efforts were made in the 107th through the 111th Congresses to enact legislation that would explicitly abrogate the provision of the Algiers Accords barring the hostages' suit. On July 24, 2002, the Senate Appropriations Committee reported the Fiscal 2003 Appropriations Act for the Departments of Commerce, Justice, and State (S. 2778). Section 616 of that bill proposed to amend the FSIA as follows:

> SEC. 616. Section 1605 of title 28, United States Code is amended by adding a new subsection (h) as follows:
>
> (h) CAUSE OF ACTION FOR IRANIAN HOSTAGES- Notwithstanding any provision of the Algiers Accords, or any other international agreement, any United States citizen held hostage in Iran after November 1, 1979, and their spouses and children at the time, shall have a claim for money damages against the government of Iran. Any provision in an international agreement, including the Algiers Accords that purports to bar such suit is abrogated. This subsection shall apply retroactively to any cause of action cited in 28 U.S.C. 1605(a)(7)(A).

In explaining the provision, the report of the committee stated that "Section 616 clarifies section 626 of P.L. 107-77 that the Algiers Accord is abrogated for the purposes of providing a cause of action for the Iranian hostages."[55] The measure received no further action prior to the adjournment of the 107th Congress.

In the 108th Congress the Senate added amendments to three appropriations bills that expressly would have abrogated the Algiers Accords, but in each case the amendment was deleted in conference.[56] The 109th Congress did not take up any legislation to abrogate the Algiers Accords. One bill, H.R. 3358, would have declared the Algiers Accords abrogated and inapplicable, and would have directed the Secretary of the Treasury to pay the *Roeder* plaintiffs $1,000 per day of captivity (family members were to be awarded $500 per day of captivity of the hostages), to be paid out of Iran's Foreign Military Sales (FMS) Fund[57] and frozen assets belonging to Iran. No action was taken on the bill, but new versions were introduced in the 110th Congress as H.R. 394 and in the 111th Congress as H.R. 4025.

There were also some efforts to provide compensation for the former hostages without abrogating the Algiers Accords. H.R. 6305/S. 3878, 109th

Congress, would have provided up to $500,000 for victims of hostage-taking, including specifically the Iran hostages and family members named in the *Roeder* case, who would have been eligible for additional compensation from the FMS account. The bill did not mention the Algiers Accords, and it would have prohibited recipients from commencing or maintaining a civil action in U.S. court against a foreign state. Similar legislation was introduced in the 110th Congress as H.R. 3369 and H.R. 3346. The Justice for the American Diplomats Held Hostage in Tehran Act, H.R. 5796 (112th Congress), would not have directly abrogated the Algiers Accords, but would have found that liquidating any property in which Iran or its surrogates has an interest in order to pay compensation to former hostages is consistent with the Algiers Accords. It would have barred prosecution of hostage claims against Iran only after such payments were made. None of these bills received committee action. H.R. 5796 has been introduced in the 113th Congress as H.R. 904 (see below).

Roeder II

When Congress again amended the FSIA in 2008[58] to overhaul the terrorist state exception to immunity, it retained the language granting jurisdiction to the *Roeder* plaintiffs but did not mention the Algiers Accords or clearly indicate whether the refiling of a suit no longer pending in any court would be permitted.[59] Nothing in the statute expressly abrogated the Algiers Accords, and the conference report explained only that "The provision would also provide for courts to hear a claim under this section if the terrorist act is related to Case Number 1:00CV03110 (EGS) in the United States District Court for the District of Columbia. The conferees intend that nothing in this section would prejudice the claimants or their representatives in that case."[60]

The former hostages and their families attempted to revive their suit[61] on the basis that the new exception permitted pending suits against state sponsors of terrorism to be refiled under certain conditions.[62] Plaintiffs sought to persuade the district court that the 2008 amendment, by providing a cause of action and permitting revival of the lawsuit, unambiguously conflicted with the terms of the agreement and should therefore be read to abrogate them, but the district court disagreed, declaring "with an equal measure of frustration, regret, and compassion," that "Congress has failed to provide plaintiffs with a cause of action against Iran."[63] The standard for clarity necessary for abrogation of the Algiers Accords was not met.

The appellate court affirmed the decision on the basis that language describing how "pending cases" and "related actions" are to be treated does not clearly permit the plaintiffs to revive their lawsuit,[64] and that language in the new exception covering jurisdiction over the hostages' claim does not differ meaningfully from the version in effect when that court dismissed the suit in 2003. While the 2008 amendment to the FSIA preserved jurisdiction for the case, it did not include the case in the language providing for a cause of action. Thus, the statute was found too ambiguous to overcome the bar presented by the Algiers Accords. The Supreme Court denied certiorari in May 2012.

CURRENT LEGISLATIVE PROPOSALS

S. 559

The Senate Committee on Foreign Relations reported favorably on S. 559, the Justice for Former American Hostages in Iran Act of 2013, which would establish a fund to compensate the former hostages (S.Rept. 113-104). The American Hostages in Iran Compensation Fund would pay to each former hostage[65] or estate of a former hostage $150,000 plus $5,000 per each day of captivity ($2.37 million total per former hostage). The Secretary of State would administer claims, and each recipient would be required to "waive and forever release all existing claims against Iran and the United States" arising out of the hostage crisis. It appears that the Secretary of State would have some discretion to deny claims or reduce the amount of the award, although the bill does not clarify the basis for such an action. An individual whose claim is denied or who receives a reduced award would be entitled to submit further information, but would not be permitted to challenge the decision in court. The Secretary of State would be required to submit to Congress an annual report describing the status of the fund, including deposits, payments, and the rules and processes established to administer the fund.

The bill would finance the fund through a 30% surcharge on "any fine or monetary penalty assessed, in whole or in part, on a person for a violation of a law or regulation" or "the monetary amount of a settlement entered into by a person with respect to a suspected violation of a law or regulation" that "provides for a civil or criminal fine or other monetary penalty for any economic activity relating to Iran that is administered by the Department of the Treasury, the Department of Justice, or the Department of Commerce." It is unclear which entity would be responsible for regulating the payment of surcharges into the fund. Surcharges would cease five years after enactment or, if later, once all payments to recipients are completed, with any surplus to be deposited into the general fund of the Treasury.

Table 1. Proceeds from Iran Sanctions Violations 2005-2012

Year	Total Penalties and Settlements, and Forfeitures in USD	30% surcharge
2005	$7,360,417.25	$2,208,125.18
2006	$41,862,309.32	$12,558,692.80
2007	$4,202,142.19	$1,260,642.66
2008	$3,951,951.80	$1,185,585.54
2009	$766,444,618.50	$229,933,385.55
2010	$195,207,477.00	$58,562,243.10
2011	$95,626,867.72	$28,688,060.32
2012	$1,162,033,172.00	$348,609,951.60
Total	$2,279,049,115.65	$683,006,686.73

Source: CRS.

Notes: Information was obtained from the website of the Treasury Department, Office of Foreign Assets Control (OFAC), Civil Penalties and Enforcement Information, http://www.treasury.gov/resource-center/sanctions/CivPen/Pages/civpen-index 2.aspx; the annual reports of the Department of Commerce, Bureau of Industry and Security (BIS) to Congress for the years 2005-2011, available at http://www.bis.doc.gov/news/ indexnewsarchives.html; and a report from the Department of Justice entitled *Summary of Major U.S. Export Enforcement, Economic Espionage, Trade Secret and Embargo-Related Criminal Cases* (January 2007 to the present: updated February 14, 2013), available at http://www.pmddtc.stateOngoingExportCase FactSheet022013.pdf.

In order to assess how much revenue the fund could likely be expected to accrue, CRS has compiled data available from several sources in order to estimate the total revenue from penalties and settlement agreements connected with violations of regulations proscribing economic activity with Iran for the calendar years 2005-2012.

Information was obtained from the Department of the Treasury, Office of Foreign Assets Control (OFAC) website; the Department of Commerce, Bureau of Industry and Security (BIS) Annual Reports to Congress for the years 2005-2012; and a report of major violations from the Department of Justice. CRS identified 321 penalties stemming at least in part from violations of sanctions against Iran (there may be more than one penalty per violation).

Table 2. Major Penalties for Iran Sanctions Violations

Name	Violation	Penalty	Date
HSBC Holdings, PLC	violation of Cuban, Burmese, Sudanese, Libyan, and Iranian sanctions programs by processing wire transfers	$375,000,000.00	12/11/2012
Standard Chartered Bank	violation of Iranian, Burmese, Sudanese, Libyan, and Foreign Narcotics Kingpin sanctions regulations by processing wire transfers	$132,000,000.00	12/10/2012
ING Bank, NV (Amsterdam)	conspiring to violate Iranian, Burmese, Sudanese, Libyan, and Cuban sanctions programs as well as New York State laws by moving funds through U.S. financial system	$619,000,000.00	6/12/2012
Barclays Bank PLC of United Kingdom	"a systemic pattern of conduct giving rise to apparent violations of OFAC sanctions involving Burma, Cuba, Iran, and Sudan."	$176,000,000.00	8/10/2010
Lloyds TSB Bank PLC of London, United Kingdom	violation of Iran, Sudan, and Libya sanctions	$217,000,000.00	12/22/2009
Credit Suisse of Zurich, Switzerland	payments involving Iran, Sudan, Burma, Cuba, North Korea, and persons whose property is blocked pursuant to OFAC regulations	$536,000,000.00	12/16/2009
Total		$2,055,000,000.00	

Source: CRS.

Notes: See note to Table 1 for source materials.

The data include criminal fines, forfeitures, special assessments, and civil penalties that were reported to have some connection with Iran. Because the data sets are not complete through the time covered, and because it is not always easily ascertained whether the enforcement action summarized pertained to Iran, the following should be considered an estimate only.

It should be noted that a few large penalties against banks account for the bulk of the total, as shown in **Table 2**. These large penalties involved violations of other sanctions programs in addition to the Iran sanctions. All of them resulted from settlement agreements. The imposition of a 30% surcharge could result in a restructuring of future similar settlement agreements in order to isolate the violations related to Iran.

For 2013, OFAC reports a total of $7,569,303.00 in penalties for Iran sanctions through the end of October. (The offenses themselves occurred in prior years.)

H.R. 3200

The Justice for Former American Hostages in Iran Act of 2013, a companion bill to S. 559, was introduced on September 27, 2013, and referred to the Subcommittee on the Constitution and Civil Justice. The bill would establish a fund based on the same 30% surcharge proposed by S. 559, but it would cover penalties for activities that began prior to enactment of the bill so long as the activities continue past that date, and would cover settlement agreements entered into after the date of enactment regardless of when the illegal activity took place. The bill specifies that terrorism judgments against Iran would not be subject to the surcharge. The House bill would award each former hostage or estate of a former hostage (including those held at locations other than the U.S. Embassy in Tehran) the amount of $4.59 million, and to each qualifying spouse or child of a former hostage the amount of $2.22 million. The bill would require the President to propose an alternative program for financing the fund if the surcharges are insufficient to satisfy the awards within two years or if the President were to determine that the relevant laws and regulations are reduced in scope or effect.

H.R. 904

The Justice for the American Diplomats Held Hostage in Tehran Act, H.R. 904, was introduced in the House of Representatives and referred to the Subcommittee on the Constitution and Civil Justice. It would require the Secretary of the Treasury, in consultation with the Secretary of State, to establish a common fund to be administered by the class representatives and agents for the former hostages, their survivors, and their family members—all of whom were identified as plaintiffs in *Roeder I*. Each former hostage or estate of a former hostage would receive $10,000 for each day of captivity

($4.44 million each); each spouse or child of a former hostage would receive half that amount.

The fund would have two possible sources for financing: half of all amounts collected from certain fines and penalties imposed for violations related to Iran; or, at the President's discretion, the vesting and liquidation of property with certain connections to Iran. After the amounts described above have been collected and disbursed to claimants, the President could use any excess in the fund to reimburse those whose assets were seized; otherwise, such excess remaining two years after enactment or the date on which payments to claimants is complete would be paid to the Treasury. Claimants would thereafter be barred from prosecuting any claims against Iran related to the hostage crisis. The President would be required to pursue the subrogated rights of claimants against the government of Iran, the Iranian Revolutionary Guard Corps, or its affiliates or agents, apparently even to the extent that Iran's assets are used to augment the common fund.

In order to provide a source for the common fund, H.R. 904 would double the maximum fines and penalties authorized "in whole or in part, for violations of any conduct or activities with respect to any government or person by reason of their connection with or sponsorship by Iran." Half of the amounts collected on or after the date of enactment, apparently irrespective of when the conduct occurred, would be paid to the fund administrator until the total of all claims are paid. It is not clear which fines or penalties are meant to be covered. It appears to cover sanctions violations with respect to persons and governments subject to sanctions by reason of their connection with Iran, but not violations with respect to sanctions against Iran itself. It does not appear to cover settlements between the government and violators, and may not cover forfeitures. (The bulk of amounts listed in **Table 1** are the result of settlement agreements.)

The President would be authorized—but not required—to pay into the common fund any funds or property in which Iran has an interest or in which any person or entity subject to any Iran-related sanctions law has an interest that is held by the United States or that is subject to any prohibition or regulation with respect to transactions. The President would be authorized to vest and liquidate such property not later than 60 days after enactment or after the property becomes subject to such treatment. However, if the President determines that the claims can be satisfied through fines and penalties within one year of enactment, he would be able to defer payments of any property that is held by the United States in the form of a trust until one year after enactment, but must ensure that any such funds are not transferred, disbursed, or otherwise constrained for payment in the meantime.

End Notes

[1] See Matthew L. Wald, Iran Hostages See Renewed Focus on Their 17-Year Bid for Compensation, NY TIMES, May 9, 2013, at A18.

[2] All but three of these individuals were confined at the U.S. Embassy for the duration of their captivity. The three exceptions were those detained at the Iranian Foreign Ministry until 17 days before the hostages' repatriation. Thirteen other hostages were released during the first several weeks of the hostage crisis, and one was released after 86 days. See THE FINAL REPORT AND RECOMMENDATIONS OF THE PRESIDENT'S COMMISSION ON HOSTAGE COMPENSATION 3 (1981) [hereinafter FINAL REPORT].

[3] P.L. 96-449, 94 Stat. 1967 (1980).

[4] The benefits for family members were cut off after the semester during which the captivity ended, while benefits for the hostages themselves continued for 10 years, similar to educational benefits for veterans. Id. §104.

[5] Under the Missing Persons Act, 5 U.S.C. §§5661 et seq., the hostages were entitled to receive continued pay and benefits, including special pay and incentive pay as well as basic allowances for quarters and subsistence, and a per diem allowance for up to 90 days. They were also permitted to accrue leave without limit and have forfeited leave restored.

[6] H.Rept. 96-1349, pt. 1 at 13-14 (estimate of H.R. 7085, 96th Cong., for the Committee on Post Office and Civil Service); pt. 2 at 13-15 (estimate for the Committee on Foreign Affairs) (1980). The version of the bill that was eventually enacted contained the educational benefits provision pointing toward the lower end of the estimate.

[7] The Hostage Relief Act of 1980, Hearings and Markup of H.R. 7085 before the Subcomm. on International Operations of the H. Comm. on Foreign Affairs, 96th Cong. 28-29 (1980) (statement of Rep. Mica). The Carter Administration noted that it was preparing claims resolution legislation that would "establish a mechanism to ensure that the hostages and their families are fully compensated for the grievous wrongs they have endured." Id. at 29 (memorandum from the Department of State).

[8] The Algiers Accords consists of five documents: The Declaration of the Government of the Democratic and Popular Republic of Algeria ("General Declaration"); Declaration of the Democratic and Popular Republic of Algeria Concerning the Settlement of Claims by the Government of the United States of America and the Government of the Islamic Republic of Iran ("Claims Settlement Declaration"); The Undertakings of the Government of the United States of America and the Government of the Islamic Republic of Iran with Respect to the Declaration of the Government of the Democratic and Popular Republic of Algeria; The Escrow Agreement; and The Technical Arrangement Between Banque Centrale D'algerie as Escrow Agent and the governor and Company of the Bank of England and the Federal Reserve Bank of New York as Fiscal Agent of the United States, United States-Iran, January 19, 1981, reprinted at 20 I.L.M. 223 (1981).

[9] See General Declaration, supra footnote 8, at 11, 20 I.L.M. at 224.

[10] Exec. Order No. 12,283, 46 Fed. Reg. 7927 (January 19, 1981).

[11] P.L. 95-223, codified at 50 U.S.C. 1701 et seq.

[12] Exec. Order No. 12,283 at 1-101.

[13] See 31 C.F.R. 535.216 (1981).

[14] Exec. Order No. 12,285, 46 Fed. Reg. 7931 (January 19, 1981).

[15] See FINAL REPORT, supra footnote 2, App. A (Charter), September 21, 1981.

[16] The value of benefits received is set forth in an appendix to the report. The Commission estimated the total aggregate benefits, including compensation for property losses and benefits mentioned above that amounted to extra benefits (that is, excluding pay or medical benefits to which they were already entitled), to amount to $2,243,792 as of August 15, 1981. Id. appendix H.

[17] Id. preface (Commission letter to President); see also id. at 35-36 ("The Commission recommends that the United States Government make no payment to the Iranian hostages or their family members of any compensation intended to be the equivalent to compensatory damages for injuries incurred as the result of the unlawful detention of the hostages by the Iranian Government.").

[18] Id. preface; id. at 33. The U.S. Navy vessel Pueblo and 82 members of its crew (one was killed during the capture) were captured and detained by North Korea on the basis of an alleged incursion into that state's territorial waters for purposes of espionage. The crew was released after the United States negotiated an apology. Several members of the crew sued North Korea in 2006 for torture and hostage-taking and were awarded a $65 million judgment. See Massie v. Government of Democratic People's Republic of Korea, 592 F. Supp. 2d 57 (D.D.C. 2008); see also Del Quentin Wilber, USS Pueblo's William Massie Seeks Retribution From N. Korea, WASH. POST, October 8, 2009, available at http://www.washingtonpost.com/wp-dyn/content/article/2009/10/07/AR2009100703890. html?sid=ST2009100703955. It does not appear that the plaintiffs have succeeded in enforcing their judgment.

[19] FINAL REPORT, supra footnote 2, at 29-31; see also Id. app. F, 110-11 (explaining that the primary purpose of previous legislation for the benefit of prisoners of war and civilian internees since World War II had been to provide token payments as "a symbolic gesture ... expressing recognition of the hardship suffered by the beneficiaries" that was "not to be commensurate with the actual injury").

[20] Id. at 31.

[21] Id.

[22] See, e.g., Persinger v. Islamic Republic of Iran, 729 F.2d 835 (D.C. Cir.), cert. denied, 469 U.S. 881 (1984); McKeel v. Islamic Republic of Iran, 722 F.2d 582 (9th Cir. 1983), cert. denied, 469 U.S. 880 (1984); Williams v. Iran, 692 F.2d 151 (D.C. Cir. 1982); Lauterbach v. Iran, 692 F.2d 150 (D.C. Cir. 1982); Ledgerwood v. State of Iran, 617 F. Supp. 311 (D.D.C. 1985).

[23] 28 U.S.C. §§1602 et seq.

[24] 729 F.2d 835.

[25] 28 U.S.C. 1605(a)(5) provides that a foreign state shall not be immune in cases in which "money damages are sought against a foreign state for personal injury or death, or damage to or loss of property, occurring in the United States and caused by the tortious act or omission of that foreign state or of any official or employee of that foreign state while acting within the scope of his office or employment.... "

[26] 729 F.2d at 838.

[27] McKeel, 722 F.2d at 590 (finding lack of jurisdiction over taking action); Cooke v. United States, 1 Cl. Ct. 695 (1983).

[28] Belk v. United States, 12 Cl. Ct. 732 (1987), aff'd, 858 F.2d 706 (Fed. Cir. 1988).

[29] 858 F.2d at 709.

[30] Id. at 710 (citing Penn Central Transp. Co. v. New York City, 438 U.S. 104, 124 (1978)).

[31] Id. (citation omitted).

[32] Id.

[33] H.R. 4151 (99th Cong.).

[34] See 132 CONG. REC. 5248 (March 18, 1986).

[35] H.Rept. 99-494, at 31 (1986). During hearings on a similar measure, the Family Liaison Action Group (FLAG—an advocacy group formed by the hostages' families) suggested that an amount equal to or greater than $192.50 per day would be adequate, a sum that corresponded to the amount the members of the President's Commission were paid per day at the going consultancy rate. H.R. 1956 and H.R. 2019, Benefits to Federal Employees who are Victims of Terrorism, Joint Hearings before the subcommittee on Civil Service and the Subcomm. on Compensation and employee Benefits of the Comm. on Post Office and Civil Service and the Subcomm. on International Operations of the Comm. on Foreign Affairs, 99th Cong. at 31 (1985) (statement of Katherine Keough).

[36] 132 CONG. REC. 5257 (March 18, 1968). Rep. McCain introduced the amendment, arguing that the bill under consideration strayed from precedent and the Commission's recommendation to such an extent that it would be perceived as unfair among those held prisoner during the Vietnam conflict, and that government employees and service members do not expect such compensation. Id. at 5253.

[37] Victims of Terrorism Compensation Act §802, P.L. 99-399, Title VIII. The act extended benefits similar to those enacted in the Hostage Relief Act of 1981 to cover future terrorist acts, and provided for cash compensation for future hostages in the amount of "not less than half of the amount of the world-wide average per diem rate.... " 5 U.S.C. §5569(d)(1).

[38] Conference report to accompany H.R. 4151, H.Rept. 99-738, at 82. There was no similar provision in the Senate version of the bill.

[39] P.L. 104-132, Title II, §221 (April 24, 1996); 110 Stat. 1241; previously codified at 28 U.S.C. §1605(a)(7).

[40] Case Number 1:00CV03110 (ESG) (D.D.C., filed December 29, 2000).

[41] P.L. 107-77, Title VI, §626(c) (November 28, 2001), amending 28 U.S.C. §1605(a)(7)(A).

[42] H.Rept. 107-278 (2001).

[43] Statement on Signing the Departments of Commerce, Justice, and State, the Judiciary, and Related Agencies Appropriations Act, 2002, 37 WEEKLY COMP. PRES. DOC. 1723, 1724 (November 28, 2001).

[44] The amendment inverted two letters in the case reference to Roeder that had been contained in P.L. 107-17, changing "1:00CV03110 (ESG)" to "1:00CV03110 (EGS)." See P.L. 107-117, Title II, §208 (January 10, 2002). This technical correction had originally been included in the Department of Defense appropriations bill as reported and adopted by the Senate but without explanation. See H.R. 3338 as reported by the Senate Appropriations Committee (S.Rept. 107-109 (2001)) and Senate floor debate at 147 CONG. REC. S12476-S12529 (daily ed. December 6, 2001), S12586-S12676 and S12779-S12812 (daily ed. December 7, 2001).

[45] H.Rept. 107-350 (2001).

[46] Remarks on Signing the Department of Defense and Emergency Supplemental Appropriations for Recovery from and Response to Terrorist Attacks on the United States Act, 2002, in Arlington, Virginia, 38 WEEKLY COMP. PRES. DOC. 44 (January 10, 2002).

[47] Roeder v. Islamic Republic of Iran, 195 F. Supp. 2d 140 (D.D.C. 2002).

[48] The court said that it did not have jurisdiction over the suit until Congress amended the FSIA by means of Section 626(c) of the FY2002 appropriations act for the Departments of

Justice, Commerce, and State, which was signed into law on November 28, 2001. Prior to that amendment, it said, the suit did not fall within the terrorist state exception to the FSIA because Iran had not been declared to be a terrorist state at the time it seized and held the American personnel hostage. The court said also that, absent an "express statement of intent by Congress," it could not apply §626(c) retroactively.

[49] The court stressed that the terrorist state exception which Congress had added to the FSIA in 1996 meant only that U.S. courts could exercise jurisdiction over such cases. Traditional foreign state immunity, in other words, was eliminated as a jurisdictional barrier. But that amendment to the FSIA did not in itself, the court said, provide a cause of action for such suits. The specific statute providing for such a cause of action which Congress enacted later in 1996, it said, provided only for a cause of action against an official, employee, or agent of a terrorist state, not against the terrorist State itself. (See P.L. 104-208, Div. A, Title I, §101(c) (September 30, 1996) ("Flatow Amendment"); 110 Stat. 3009-172; 28 U.S.C. §1605 note).

[50] The court stressed that an act of Congress "ought never to be considered to violate the law of nations, if any other possible construction remains." None of the statutes Congress had adopted relating to a cause of action generally or to Roeder itself, the court said, unambiguously declared an intent either to override the Algiers Accords or to preserve it. They, and their "scant" legislative history, were ambiguous on the question, it held, and, consequently, must be construed not to conflict with the Accords. Roeder, 195 F. Supp. 2d at 177. The court also rejected the argument that the United States had entered into the Algiers Accords under duress, making the Accords "an unenforceable illegal contract." "Whatever emotional appeal and rhetorical flourish this argument contains," the court said, "it is absolutely without basis in law." Id. at 168.

[51] The court did not base its decision on any separation of powers considerations. It said, however, that if it had construed Section 626(c) to apply retroactively, Congress's "post-judgment retroactive imposition of jurisdiction [would raise] serious separation of powers concerns" and might be "an impermissible encroachment by Congress into the sphere of the federal courts.... " Id. at 161. "By expressly directing legislation at pending litigation, Congress has arguably attempted to determine the outcome of this litigation," it said. Id. at 163.

[52] In commenting on what it called the "repeated ethical failures by class counsel," the court stated that "[p]laintiffs' counsel in this case repeatedly presented meritless arguments to this Court, repeatedly failed to substantiate their arguments by reference to any supporting authority, and repeatedly failed to bring to the Court's attention the existence of controlling authority that conflicted with those arguments." Id. at 185.

[53] Roeder v. The Islamic Republic of Iran, 333 F.3d 228, 238 (D.C. Cir. 2003) ("While legislative history may be useful in determining intent, the joint explanatory statements here go well beyond the legislative text of §208, which did nothing more than correct a typographical error.").

[54] The court noted, but did not decide, whether the amendments were an impermissible intrusion by Congress into the role of the courts. Id. at 237 & n.5.

[55] S.Rept. 107-218 at 167 (2002).

[56] H.J.Res. 2149 (108th Cong.); S. 762 (108th Cong.); S. 1689 (108th Cong.).

[57] A Foreign Military Sales Fund is a Treasury holding account established to facilitate the sale of military items to foreign countries or international organizations, pursuant to the Arms Control Export Act, 22 U.S.C. §§2751 et seq. Foreign purchasers place monies in the fund under individual sub-accounts from which the Department of Defense pays for military

equipment and services provided to the purchaser by the Department of Defense or private suppliers. Iran's FMS account held about $377 million as of 2000. The account originally contained funds deposited by Iran to pay for military equipment and services during the reign of the Shah. However, Congress also provided funds for the account in order to continue to pay contractors for goods and services after Iran terminated contracts under the FMS program. Disposition of military equipment procured for Iran through the FMS fund and the money remaining in the FMS account is an unresolved issue between the United States and Iran before the U.S.-Iran Claims Tribunal.

[58] P.L. 110-181, §1083. The act created 28 U.S.C. Section 1605A, which provides in pertinent part:

(a) In General.—(1) No immunity.—A foreign state shall not be immune from the jurisdiction of courts of the United States or of the States in any case not otherwise covered by this chapter in which money damages are sought against a foreign state for personal injury or death that was caused by an act of torture, extrajudicial killing, aircraft sabotage, hostage taking, or the provision of material support or resources for such an act if such act or provision of material support or resources is engaged in by an official, employee, or agent of such foreign state while acting within the scope of his or her office, employment, or agency.

(2) Claim heard.—The court shall hear a claim under this section if—

(A)(i) (I) the foreign state was designated as a state sponsor of terrorism at the time the act described in paragraph (1) occurred, or was so designated as a result of such act, and, subject to subclause (II), either remains so designated when the claim is filed under this section or was so designated within the 6-month period before the claim is filed under this section; or

(II) in the case of an action that is refiled under this section by reason of section 1083(c)(2)(A) of the National Defense Authorization Act for Fiscal Year 2008 or is filed under this section by reason of section 1083(c)(3) of that Act, the foreign state was designated as a state sponsor of terrorism when the original action or the related action under section 1605 (a)(7) (as in effect before the enactment of this section) or section 589 of the Foreign Operations, Export Financing, and Related Programs Appropriations Act, 1997 (as contained in section 101(c) of division A of Public Law 104–208) was filed;

...

(B) the act described in paragraph (1) is related to Case Number 1:00CV03110 (EGS) in the United States District Court for the District of Columbia.

(b) Limitations.—An action may be brought or maintained under this section if the action is commenced, or a related action was commenced under section 1605 (a)(7) (before the date of the enactment of this section) or section 589 of the Foreign Operations, Export Financing, and Related Programs Appropriations Act, 1997 (as contained in section 101(c) of division A of Public Law 104–208) not later than the latter of—

(1) 10 years after April 24, 1996; or

(2) 10 years after the date on which the cause of action arose.

(c) Private Right of Action.—A foreign state that is or was a state sponsor of terrorism as described in subsection (a)(2)(A)(i), and any official, employee, or agent of that foreign state while acting within the scope of his or her office, employment, or agency, shall be liable to—

(1) a national of the United States,

(2) a member of the armed forces,

(3) an employee of the Government of the United States, or of an individual performing a contract awarded by the United States Government, acting within the scope of the employee's employment, or

(4) the legal representative of a person described in paragraph (1), (2), or (3), for personal injury or death caused by acts described in subsection (a)(1) of that foreign state, or of an official, employee, or agent of that foreign state, for which the courts of the United States may maintain jurisdiction under this section for money damages. In any such action, damages may include economic damages, solatium, pain and suffering, and punitive damages. In any such action, a foreign state shall be vicariously liable for the acts of its officials, employees, or agents.

...

[59] Section 1083(c) permitted the refiling of prior actions or the filing of new suits related to pending actions, under certain circumstances. 28 U.S.C. §1605A note.

[60] H.Rept. 110-477, at 1001 (2007).

[61] Roeder v. Islamic Republic of Iran, 742 F. Supp. 2d 1 (D.D.C. 2010), aff'd, 646 F.3d 56 (D.C. Cir. 2011), cert. denied, 132 S. Ct. 2680 (2012) ("Roeder II").

[62] For an explanation of the law, see CRS Report RS22094, Lawsuits Against State Supporters of Terrorism: An Overview, by Jennifer K. Elsea.

[63] Roeder II, 742 F. Supp. 2d at 3.

[64] Roeder II, 646 F.3d at 62.

[65] "Former hostage" refers to those held at the U.S. Embassy in Tehran for the duration of the hostage crisis (444 days), but apparently excludes those three hostages held at locations other than the embassy, as well as the 14 hostages who were released prior to January 20, 1981. See supra footnote 2. Former hostages must also have been listed as plaintiffs in the Roeder case.

In: Law and Legal Issues in the United States
Editor: Laurent B. Landers
ISBN: 978-1-63117-827-6

Chapter 7

SEXUAL ABUSE OF CHILDREN: FEDERAL CRIMINAL OFFENSES*

Richard M. Thompson II

SUMMARY

Over the past 100 years, Congress has sought to prohibit acts of sexual abuse of minors and punish those who harm the nation's children. These efforts began in the early 20th century when Congress prohibited the transportation of a minor in interstate commerce for the purpose of sexual exploitation, and continue to more modern measures such as outlawing the use of the Internet to lure children for sexual purposes. Nevertheless, Congress's power in this area does have constitutional limits.

The power to create criminal laws in the United States resides most broadly with the states. The states retain a general police power to regulate for the health, safety, and welfare of their citizens. By contrast, Congress may only act within its express and implied powers, including the power to legislate for federal enclaves and in areas within its enumerated powers (e.g., commerce, spending, taxing). Congress has exercised both strands of authority to criminalize sexual abuse of children.

Congress began outlawing sexual abuse of minors in 1910 with the Mann Act, which outlawed the use of a common carrier to transport a

---

* This is an edited, reformatted and augmented version of Congressional Research Service Publication, No. R42132, dated July 13, 2012.

minor in interstate commerce for an illegal sexual purpose. In subsequent enactments, including the Sexual Exploitation of Children Act of 1977, the Sexual Abuse Act of 1986, and the Protection of Children from Sexual Predators Act of 1998, Congress increased penalty provisions (including repeat offender provisions), expanded jurisdictional clauses, and broadened the list of prohibited acts, including aggravating factors warranting an increased penalty.

Presently, federal sexual abuse law is a hierarchy based on the age of the victim and whether the act involved aggravating circumstances. The most serious offense is when a child is murdered during the commission of a sexual offense. The penalty is death or up to life imprisonment. The least serious is sexual *contact* (as opposed to a sexual *act*) with a minor at least 12 years of age but younger than 16. This crime requires no aggravating circumstances and carries a possible four-year maximum prison sentence. Between these two crimes falls a host of other offenses prohibiting sexual abuse or contact. These include sexual abuse of a child at least 12 years of age but younger than 16, sexual contact with a child under the age of 12 years, and use of the mail or other facility of interstate commerce to persuade a minor under the age of 18 to engage in an illegal sexual act.

Because much of the prohibited conduct in these statutes overlaps, courts must consider the lesser-included offense doctrine when handling sexual abuse cases. This doctrine permits a court to instruct the jury on not only the offense charged by the government, but also a lesser offense that is "necessarily included" in the charged offense. This doctrine has been used to aid the prosecution in obtaining a conviction when proof of the charged offense is insufficient, but also assists defendants by allowing the jury to convict on the lesser included offense.

INTRODUCTION

Prompted by reported cases of child sexual abuse, Congress periodically evaluates whether federal law adequately protects the nation's children from sexual abuse and properly punishes those who seek to harm them. Congress has passed many criminal laws that prohibit acts such as aggravated sexual abuse of a minor, sexual contact with a minor, and transporting minors across state lines with the intent to commit sexual acts. Congress's power to outlaw sexual abuse, however, is not limitless. The federal government may only proscribe abuse when it occurs in a federal enclave (a statutorily and constitutionally defined federal territorial jurisdiction) or is within Congress's enumerated powers, such as commerce, taxing, or spending, or its implied powers (those arising from the necessary and proper clause).

To clarify at the outset, this report does not cover issues such as sex offender registration and grant programs covered under the Adam Walsh Child Protection and Safety Act of 2006,[1] and only generally discusses programs for reporting child abuse under the Child Abuse Prevention and Treatment Act.[2] Those issues are covered comprehensively in other CRS reports.[3]

Instead, this report focuses on a narrow subset of substantive criminal offenses that outlaw and punish sexual abuse of children, and certain procedural aspects under these laws. First, the report will briefly discuss the federal government's authority (as opposed to state authority) to enact criminal laws. Next, it will briefly discuss child abuse reporting requirements under the Child Abuse Prevention Treatment Act. Third, it will provide a general overview of the various laws Congress has passed to address sexual abuse of children, including the Sexual Abuse Act of 1986,[4] the Amber Hagerman Child Protection Act of 1996,[5] and the Protection of Children from Sexual Predators Act of 1998.[6] Fourth, it will take an in-depth look at each sexual abuse offense, including its substantive elements, potential punishments, and procedural aspects. Finally, this report includes an **Appendix** that lists federal child sexual abuse crimes, including each prohibited act, its jurisdictional clause, its punishment, and its statute of limitations.

LIMITS OF FEDERAL AUTHORITY TO PUNISH LOCAL CRIMINAL ACTS

The power to create criminal laws in the United States rests with both the federal and state governments. Under this system of dual sovereigns, the "States possess primary authority for defining and enforcing the criminal law."[7] They have retained "inherent police power,"[8] meaning the power to legislate for the "health, safety, and morals" of the citizenry.[9] The federal government, on the other hand, is allocated a more limited role. The Constitution does not grant it a broad police power to outlaw local acts generally, but instead confines its authority to a limited bundle of powers, both express and implied.[10] Nonetheless, the federal government does have power to create and enforce criminal laws under both its territorial and enumerated powers.

Respecting its territorial power, Congress can criminalize acts that occur within certain federal enclaves—those areas carved out by the Constitution for congressional administration. These include the District of Columbia,[11] territories of the United States,[12] and land purchased by the federal government from the states.[13] Also, with this power, Congress has created a host of offenses applicable to the "special maritime and territorial jurisdiction of the United States."[14] This area includes the high seas, any land acquired by the United States from one of the several states or land generally reserved or acquired by the United States, military posts, and crimes occurring on an aircraft while in-flight over the high seas and out of the jurisdiction of the several states.[15]

Congress can also criminalize acts that occur within the states if the desired prohibition is within its enumerated powers. These powers include the commerce clause, the spending power, and the taxing power.[16] Under its power "[t]o regulate Commerce ... among the several States,"[17] Congress can regulate three broad categories: (1) the use of the channels of interstate commerce, (2) instrumentalities, or persons or things in interstate commerce, and (3) activities that have a substantial effect on interstate commerce.[18] Congress has employed the first and second categories to outlaw crimes occurring in interstate commerce including domestic violence,[19] stalking,[20] and child sexual abuse.[21]

While Congress's power under the Commerce Clause is broad, it is not without limits. In *United States v. Lopez*, the Court held that a provision of the Gun-Free School Zones Act of 1990 that prohibited possession of a firearm in a school zone, was beyond Congress's commerce power because the "Act neither regulate[d] a commercial activity nor containe[d] a requirement that the possession be connected in any way to interstate commerce" (sometimes referred to as a "jurisdictional hook").[22] But 10 years later in *Gonzales v. Raich*, the Court upheld a provision of the Controlled Substances Act (CSA) that prohibited a person from possessing, obtaining, or manufacturing marijuana for medical use.[23] The Court sustained this use of Congress's power to regulate a wholly intrastate activity because the CSA was part of a "larger scheme" designed to regulate an act that "in the aggregate, substantially affect[ed] interstate commerce."[24]

Under its spending power, Congress has conditioned receipt of federal money by states upon their passage of criminal statutes.[25] Describing this process, the Court stated that "legislation enacted pursuant to the spending power is much in the nature of a contract: in return for federal funds, the States agree to comply with federally imposed conditions."[26] The Court upheld in

South Dakota v. Dole Congress's condition of state receipt of highway funds upon the states passage of a 21-year old minimum drinking age.[27] In the child sexual abuse context, Congress conditioned law enforcement funds to the states upon the state's passage of Megan's Law,[28] which required states to release information to the public about convicted sex offenders.[29]

Exercising both its territorial power in the federal enclaves, and its express and implied powers under its Article I commerce and spending powers, Congress has criminalized certain acts of sexual abuse towards children.

CHILD ABUSE REPORTING LAWS

Though not a focal point of this report, it is necessary to briefly discuss child abuse reporting laws. In 1974, Congress enacted the Child Abuse Prevention and Treatment Act (CAPTA)[30] to establish procedures for the "prevention, identification, and treatment of child abuse and neglect."[31] Among other provisions, CAPTA created a uniform definition for child abuse and established minimum child abuse reporting standards the states were required to institute as a condition of receiving grant funds.[32] All fifty states have enacted definitions that meet CAPTA's minimum definition of "child abuse," while some states have exercised their discretion to expand on CAPTA's definition.[33]

In addition to CAPTA, Congress enacted as Title II of the Crime Control Act of 1990, the Victims of Child Abuse Act,[34] which extended mandatory reporting requirements to "covered professionals" while engaged in their work on "[f]ederal land or in a federally operated (or contracted) facility."[35] A person who fails to report an act of child abuse under this act is subject to fines and imprisonment of not more than one year.[36]

OVERVIEW OF FEDERAL CHILD SEXUAL ABUSE LAWS

Although Congress's role in the field of criminal law is limited, it has made an effort to target sexual abuse, with an emphasis on sexual abuse of children, a "particularly vulnerable section of our society."[37] Congress's movement to prohibit the sexual exploitation of minors began in 1910 with the White Slave Traffic Act or "Mann Act."[38] This act outlawed a person from inducing or enticing a female under the age of 18 to engage in "prostitution, debauchery, or any other immoral practice" while knowingly causing her to be transported in interstate commerce upon a common carrier.[39] This law was later expanded by the Sexual Exploitation of Children Act of 1977, which prohibited the transportation of any minor (making the offense gender neutral) in interstate commerce or within the District of Columbia or a territory of the United States, with the intent that the minor engage in prostitution or in prohibited sexual conduct if that person knew or had reason to know that such conduct would be commercially exploited.[40]

Then in 1986, in an effort to "modernize and reform Federal rape statutes" and "protect[] children of very tender years," Congress enacted the Sexual Abuse Act of 1986.[41] This act added a new chapter to Title 18 entitled "Sexual Abuse" and contained five new sections creating sexual abuse offenses within the special maritime and territorial jurisdiction of the United States or a federal prison. Of these five, several targeted sexual abuse of children, including aggravated sexual abuse of a child under the age of 12 years and sexual abuse of a minor at least 12 years of age but younger than 16.[42] This act is tiered, in that the seriousness of the offenses escalates depending on whether the defendant engaged in a "sexual act" or "sexual contact" and whether there are aggravating factors present.[43] The greatest offense is contained in Section 2241 (aggravated sexual abuse), which requires a sexual act coupled with serious aggravating circumstances.[44] Also requiring a sexual act but with less serious aggravating factors are Sections 2242 (sexual abuse) and 2243 (sexual abuse of a minor or ward).[45] Finally, the least serious is Section 2244 (abusive sexual contact), which requires sexual *contact*, and not a sexual *act*.[46]

The offenses created under the Sexual Abuse Act, however, were limited to crimes occurring in the special maritime or territorial jurisdiction of the United States or in a federal prison.[47] Seeking to expand the reach of these statutes, Congress passed the Amber Hagerman Child Protection Act of 1996, which, among other provisions, broadened existing statutes to cover crimes that occurred not only in the federal enclaves, but also when the defendant crossed state lines.[48] Also enacted that year as part of the Communications Decency Act of 1996, Congress made it unlawful to use the mail or other facility of interstate commerce or within the defined federal jurisdiction to persuade a minor under 18 years of age to engage in sexual activity if that act constituted a criminal offense.[49]

Two years later Congress passed the Protection of Children from Sexual Predators Act of 1998, which increased the penalties for several sexual abuse offenses including sexual abuse of a child under the age of 12 years and also added a repeat offender penalty.[50] Previously, 18 U.S.C. Section 2244 (abusive sexual contact) did not expressly distinguish between adult and child victims in setting maximum penalties for violations of it.[51] This act amended Section 2244 to add a separate penalty provision, doubling the sentence if the victim of the abusive sexual contact is under the age of 12.[52] For example, under Section 2244(a)(1) a person can receive up to 10 years imprisonment for abusive sexual contact regardless of the victim's age.[53] Under the amended version, the same abusive sexual contact of a child under the age of 12 may receive 20 years.[54]

This act increased the penalty from a maximum of 10 years to a maximum of 15 years under both Section 2422(b) (using the mail or other facilities of interstate commerce or within a federal enclave to coerce or entice a minor under the age of 18 to engage in illegal sexual activity) and Section 2423(a) (transporting a minor in interstate commerce with the intent to engage in illegal sexual activity).[55] This law also doubled the prison sentence for repeat offenders who committed a sexual abuse offense found in Chapter 109A of Title 18.[56] Finally, this law made it a crime to use the mail or other facility of interstate commerce to transmit personal information about a minor under the age of 16 with the intent to entice or encourage any person to engage in any sexual activity for which any person can be charged with a crime.[57]

In 2003, Congress enacted the PROTECT Act, increasing the minimum and maximum penalty for several sexual abuse offenses.[58] The minimum penalties under Section 2422(b) (coercing or enticing a minor under the age of 18 to engage in an illegal sexual act) and Section 2423(a) (transporting a minor in interstate commerce with intent to engage in illegal sexual activity) were set at five years and the maximum penalties were increased from 15 to 30 years.[59] The PROTECT Act also created the "Two Strikes You're Out" section,[60] which requires a sentence of life imprisonment if a person is convicted of a "federal sex offense"[61] and had a "prior sex conviction."[62]

Finally, Congress enacted the Adam Walsh Protection and Safety Act in 2006, which, in addition to establishing a system of sex offender registration, increased the terms of imprisonment of existing offenses.[63] As an example of the increased sentences for sexual abuse of a child, Section 204 of the act increased the sentence for transporting a minor in interstate commerce for sexual activity from five to 30 years to 10 years to life.[64] Likewise, the offense of aggravated sexual abuse was increased from any term of years to a minimum of 30 years to life.[65]

Specific Federal Offenses

As shown above, Congress's efforts to combat the sexual exploitation and abuse of minors spans from 1910 with the Mann Act, which prohibited enticing minors to travel on a common carrier in interstate commerce for illegal sexual purposes, to more modern laws that prohibit the use of the Internet to entice minors to engage in sexual acts. At each point, Congress has sought to modernize and expand the laws to better effectuate its goals of preventing child abuse and punishing those who engage in it. Such changes include stronger penalty provisions (including repeat offender provisions), extension of jurisdictional clauses, and expansion of the acts prohibited under the laws. This section explores current federal offenses (as opposed to a historical review) pertaining to child sexual abuse.

Aggravated Sexual Abuse of Children

Enacted as part of the Sexual Abuse Act of 1986,[66] and amended multiple times since, 18 U.S.C. Section 2241(c) outlaws two categories of aggravated sexual abuse of children. The first category prohibits a person from committing aggravated sexual abuse of a child under the age of 12. This section has two alternative jurisdictional elements: the first requires interstate travel and the second requires the act be committed in a federal jurisdiction. Specifically, the first offense makes it unlawful to cross a state line with the intent to engage in a sexual act with a child under the age of 12 and either commit or attempt to commit the sexual act.[67] Similarly, the second offense prohibits a person from committing or attempting to commit a sexual act on a child under the age of 12 while in the territorial or special maritime jurisdiction of the United States or in a federally run or contracted prison.[68]

The second category under Section 2241(c) prohibits aggravated sexual abuse of a minor at least 12 years of age but younger than 16 while in the special maritime or territorial jurisdiction of the United States, or in a federally run or contracted prison. This category can be further divided into three subcategories. First, it is unlawful to knowingly cause a minor to engage in a sexual act by the use of force or "threatening or placing that other person in fear that any person will be subjected to death, serious bodily injury, or kidnapping," if the child is at least four years younger than the offender.[69] Second, it is unlawful to render a minor unconscious and engage in a sexual act with that minor.[70] Third, Section 2241(c) prohibits a person from administering a drug to a minor through the use of force, threat of force, or without the minor's knowledge, which substantially impairs that minor's ability to apprise or control her conduct, and then engaging in a sexual act with that minor.[71] An attempt to commit any of these three crimes is sufficient for a conviction under Section 2241(c).

In addition to the substantive elements, there are attendant procedural aspects to these two categories. As to first category, Congress intended the offenses require no force or threats on the part of offender.[72] Likewise, the age of the offender is of no consequence.[73]

There are similar procedural rules that apply to both categories. For example, each distinct sexual act under Section 2241(c) can be charged as a separate offense.[74] If a perpetrator performs one sexual act as defined in Section 2246(2) (e.g., contact between the penis and the vulva) and then performs another distinct act (e.g., intentional touching of the genitalia), he can be prosecuted for each separate count. Also, mistake of age is not a defense under Section 2241(c).[75] Nor is there a statute of limitations under Section 2241(c), meaning there is no time limit to when cases may be brought against an offender.[76] A person who violates any of the offenses in Section 2241(c) may be fined and imprisoned for a minimum of 30 years up to life.[77] Furthermore, if the offender has committed a previous aggravated sexual abuse of a child under Section 2241(c), or a state offense that would have been an offense under this subsection had it occurred in a federal jurisdiction, the punishment for the second offense will be life imprisonment (unless the death penalty is imposed).[78]

Abusive Sexual Contact with Minor or Ward

In 1998, Congress enacted the Protection of Children from Sexual Predators Act "to respond to the horrifying menace of sex crimes against children" and to provide "law enforcement with the tools it needs to investigate and bring to justice those individuals who prey on our nation's children."[79] This act doubled the punishment for crimes committed under 18 U.S.C. Section 2244 if the victim was under the age of 12.[80] To determine the elements of each offense under Section 2244, one must refer back to Sections 2241(a)-(b), 2242, and 2243(a)-(b). For each of these offenses, Section 2244 requires that the prohibited conduct currently in the text—"sexual *act*"— be replaced with a different prohibited conduct—"sexual *contact*."[81] As one moves up or down the levels of offenses, Congress has increased or decreased the penalty depending on the level of force and violence involved.

Applying this process to Section 2244(c) produces the following offenses. It is unlawful for any person while in the special maritime and territorial jurisdiction of the United States, or in a federally run or federally contracted prison facility, to knowingly engage in sexual contact with a child under the age of 12 years by use of force against that child or by threatening or placing the child in fear that "any person will be subject to death, serious bodily injury, or kidnapping."[82] Likewise, it is unlawful for any person while in this defined federal jurisdiction to render a child unconscious, or administer a drug or intoxicant to this child, substantially impairing her, and then initiating sexual contact with her.[83] A sexual offender who violates either of these offenses is subject to not more than 20 years imprisonment.[84]

Similarly, it is a federal offense for a person, while in the special maritime and territorial jurisdiction of the United States, to knowingly cause a child under the age of 12 years to engage in sexual *contact* by threatening or placing that child in fear (other than by threatening another person who is not the child).[85] Also, it is unlawful while in this same defined federal jurisdiction to knowingly[86] cause a child under the age of 12 to engage in sexual contact if the child is "incapable of appraising the nature of the conduct" or is "physically incapable of declining participation in, or communicating unwillingness to engage in, that sexual contact."[87] Violators of either of these offenses are subject to fines and not more than six years of imprisonment.[88]

As a lesser tiered offense, it is unlawful while in the special maritime and territorial jurisdiction of the United States or in a federally run or contracted prison to engage or attempt to engage in sexual contact with a child under 12 years of age.[89] Violators of this section are subject to fines and not more than four years imprisonment.[90] Further, it is also unlawful to commit such an act on a child when the child is in official detention and under the custody of the offender.[91] There is no time limit for when a prosecution may be brought for any of the offenses under Section 2244.[92]

Sexual Abuse of Child at Least 12 Years of Age but Younger Than 16

Congress has also enacted several crimes for sexual acts and sexual contact committed on children at least 12 years of age but younger than 16, what has traditionally been called statutory rape. Congress wanted these laws to reach "older, mature persons who take advantage of younger, immature persons, but not to reach sexual activity between persons of comparable age."[93] Under Section 2243(a), a person is prohibited, while in the special maritime and territorial jurisdiction of the United States, or in a federally run or contracted prison, from knowingly engaging, or attempting to engage, in a sexual *act* with a child who is at least 12 years of age but younger than 16, and the offender is at least four years older than the child.[94] Violators of this section are subject to 15 years in prison.[95] If the offender initiates sexual *contact*, rather than engaging in a sexual *act*, with the child, that person will be subject to a maximum of two years imprisonment.[96] Under this section, the prosecution need not prove that the defendant knew the victim's age.[97] It is, however, a defense if the defendant can establish by a preponderance of the evidence that he "reasonably believed" that the victim was at least 16 years old or that the defendant and the victim were married at the time the act took place.[98]

Illegal Sexual Activity in Interstate Commerce

Dating back to 1910 with the Mann Act, Congress has outlawed certain sexual acts occurring in interstate commerce. For instance, under 18 U.S.C. Section 2423(a), it is unlawful to knowingly transport a minor (a person under the age of 18 years) in interstate or foreign commerce with the intent that the minor engage in prostitution or any other sexual activity[99] for which any person can be charged with a criminal offense.[100] The defendant need not know that the victim is under the age of 18 years when the crime is committed.[101] Moreover, the government need not prove that the illegal behavior was the "dominant purpose" for traveling, but only that it was a "motivating factor."[102] There is no limitation for when this crime may be prosecuted.[103] A violator of this statute may be imprisoned from a minimum of 10 years to life.[104] It is not a defense to a conviction under Section 2423(a) that the person whom the defendant attempted to transport across state lines was not actually a minor.[105] Rather, it is enough to sustain a conviction if the defendant had the requisite intent to transport a minor across state lines, even if the target was not actually a minor.

Additionally, any person who uses the mail or other facility of interstate commerce, or within a federal enclave, "knowingly persuades, induces, entices, or coerces" a minor under the age of 18 years to engage in "sexual activity for which any person can be charged with a criminal offense" can be imprisoned for 10 years to life.[106] Finally, it is a federal crime to knowingly transmit through the mail or other means of interstate commerce personal information (e.g., name, address, social security, e-mail address) about a minor under the age of 16 with the intent to entice or encourage any person to engage in any sexual activity for which any person can be charged with a crime.[107]

Other Sections Relating to Sexual Abuse

In addition to the specific criminal offenses, there are several corresponding penalty and procedural statutes. If in the course of committing any of the offenses previously mentioned, the offender murders the child, that person is subject to death or imprisonment for any term of years up to life.[108] If 18 U.S.C. Section 3559(e) (the "Two Strikes You're Out" provision)[109] does not apply, repeat offenders—persons previously convicted for an offense under chapter 109A of Title 18, or a state offense consisting of conduct that would be an offense if committed in the proper federal jurisdiction—shall be given a prison sentence twice the term that is already provided under each respective section.[110] If Section 3559(e) applies, repeat offenders may be sentenced to life imprisonment.[111] Finally, there is no statute of limitations for any of the offenses described above.[112]

Lesser Included Offenses for Child Sexual Abuse Crimes

Many of the child sexual abuse offenses have seemingly overlapping elements—that is, two offenses which have at least one similar element (e.g., sexual contact with a child through the use of force versus by threat of force). This overlap implicates the lesser-included offense doctrine, which permits a court to instruct the jury on not only the underlying offense charged by the government, but also a lesser offense that is "necessarily included" in that charged offense.

The lesser-offense doctrine was traditionally used to aid the government in achieving a conviction when the necessary proof for the primary offense was not attainable, but was sufficient to support a lesser charge.[113] It has also come to the aid of defendants, however, allowing the jury to use its nullification power to convict on the lesser included offense, and also provides a compromise conviction for a jury divided on the charged offense.[114]

Relying on language in Rule 31 of the Federal Rules of Criminal Procedure, the Supreme Court has adopted the "elements" test for determining whether the doctrine is applicable, requiring that the elements of the lesser included offense be a subset of the charged offense.[115] This requires the courts to focus objectively on the elements of the crime and not the actual facts of the crime allegedly committed.

A more straightforward application of the lesser-offense doctrine is displayed in *United States v. Boyles*, where the defendant argued that the court should have instructed the jury on the lesser offense of sexual assault under Section 2242(1), in addition to the charged offense of aggravated sexual assault under Section 2241(a)(1).

Aggravated sexual assault requires "knowingly causing another to engage in a sexual act *by using force against that person*," whereas general sexual assault requires "knowingly causing another to engage in a sexual act *by threatening them or placing them in fear*."[116] Noting this difference between the use of force on a victim as compared with using fear or threats, the court held that sexual assault under Section 2242(1) could not be a lesser-included offense of aggravated sexual assault, since the elements of the former were not a subset of the later.[117]

This doctrine becomes more difficult to apply when the elements are closer in nature. Take, for example, the split in the federal circuit courts of appeals over whether "sexual contact" under Section 2244 (abusive sexual contact) is "necessarily included" in the term "sexual act" under Sections 2242 (sexual abuse) and 2243 (sexual abuse of a minor or ward). The majority of the circuits hold that the inclusion of the intent requirement in Section 2244, the requirement that the prohibited act be coupled with "an intent to abuse, humiliate, harass, degrade, or arouse or gratify the sexual desire ...," which is not contained in Sections 2242 or 2243, necessarily requires that the lesser-included offense instruction *not* be given.[118]

The Eighth Circuit is the sole minority circuit holding that sexual contact under Section 2244 is a lesser included offense of both aggravated sexual abuse and sexual abuse of a minor.[119]

Appendix. Federal Child Sexual Abuse Laws

Offense	Code Section No.	Jurisdictional Clause	Prohibited Act	Penalty	Statute of Limitations
Aggravated sexual abuse of a child under 12 years	18 U.S.C. §2241(c)	Crossing a state line with the intent to engage in a sexual act or in the special maritime or territorial jurisdiction of the United States or in a federally run or contracted prison	Committing or attempting to commit a sexual act on a child under the age of 12 years	30 years–Life	No limitation
Aggravated sexual abuse of a child at least 12 years of age but younger than 16	18 U.S.C. §2241(c) & §2241(b)	Special maritime or territorial jurisdiction of the United States or in a federally run or contracted prison	Knowingly renders a child at least 12 years of age but younger than 16 unconscious or administers a drug to that child and engages or attempts to engage in a sexual act with that child	30 years–Life	No limitation
Aggravated sexual abuse of child at least 12 years of age but younger than 16	18 U.S.C. §2241(c) & §2241(a)	Special maritime or territorial jurisdiction of the United States or in a federally run or contracted prison	Knowingly causing a child at least 12 years of age but younger than 16 to engage in sexual act by using force or threat of death, serious bodily injury, or kidnapping	30 years–Life	No limitation

Offense	Code Section No.	Jurisdictional Clause	Prohibited Act	Penalty	Statute of Limitations
Sexual contact with a child under the age of 12 years through force or threat	18 U.S.C. §2244(c), §2244(a)(1), §2241(a)	Special maritime or territorial jurisdiction of the United States or in a federally run or contracted prison	Knowingly initiates sexual contact with a child under 12 years of age through use of force or threat to kill, seriously injure, or kidnap any person	20 year maximum	No limitation
Sexual contact with a child under the age of 12 years while unconscious or incapacitated	18 U.S.C. §2244(c), §2244(a)(1), & §2241(b)	Special maritime or territorial jurisdiction of the United States or in a federally run or contracted prison	Knowingly initiates sexual contact with a child under 12 years of age while child is unconscious or has been administered drugs	20 year maximum	No limitation
Sexual contact with a child under the age of 12 years through fear or threat	18 U.S.C. §2244(c), §2244(a)(2), & 2242(1)	Special maritime or territorial jurisdiction of the United States or in a federally run or contracted prison	Knowingly initiates sexual contact with a child under 12 years of age by threatening or placing child in fear	6 year maximum	No limitation
Sexual contact with child under 12 years of age who is incapacitated	18 U.S.C. §2244(c), §2244(a)(2), & 2242(2)	Special maritime or territorial jurisdiction of the United States or in a federally run or contracted prison	Knowingly initiates sexual contact with a child under 12 years of age who is incapable of understanding the situation or physically incapable of declining participation	6 year maximum	No limitation

Appendix. (Continued)

Offense	Code Section No.	Jurisdictional Clause	Prohibited Act	Penalty	Statute of Limitations
Sexual contact with a child under 12 years of age	18 U.S.C. §2244(c), §2244(a)(3) & §2243	Special maritime or territorial jurisdiction of the United States or in a federally run or contracted prison	Knowingly initiates or attempts to initiate sexual contact with a child at least 12 years of age but younger than 16	4 year maximum	No limitation
Sexual act with child at least 12 years of age but younger than 16	18 U.S.C. §2243(a)	Special maritime or territorial jurisdiction of the United States or in a federally run or contracted prison	Knowingly engaging, or attempting to engage in sexual contact with a child at least 12 years of age but younger than 16	15 year maximum	No limitation
Sexual contact with child at least 12 years of age but younger than 16	18 U.S.C. §2244(a)(3) & §2243(a)	Special maritime or territorial jurisdiction of the United States or in a federally run or contracted prison	Knowingly initiating sexual contact with a child at least 12 years of age but younger than 16	4 year maximum	No limitation
Sexual activity with a minor under the age of 18	18 U.S.C. §2422(b)	Use of mail or facility of interstate commerce, or special maritime or territorial jurisdiction of the United States	Knowingly persuading or inducing a minor under the age of 18 to engage in sexual activity when that act is a criminal offense	10 years–Life	No limitation

Offense	Code Section No.	Jurisdictional Clause	Prohibited Act	Penalty	Statute of Limitations
Transportation of minor under 18 years of age with intent to engage in sexual activity	18 U.S.C. §2423	Transport in interstate commerce	Knowingly transporting a minor under the age of 18 in interstate commerce with the intent that the minor engage in sexual activity when that act is a criminal offense	10 mandatory minimum	No limitation
Transmittal of information about minor to entice a sexual act	18 U.S.C. §2425	Use of mail or other facility of interstate commerce	Knowingly transmit personal information about a minor under 16 years with the intent to entice any person to engage in any sexual act for which any person can be charged with a crime	5 year maximum	No limitation
Sexual contact or act that results in death of child	18 U.S.C. §2245	Crossing a state line or in the special maritime or territorial jurisdiction of the United States or in a federally run or contracted prison	Child is murdered during the commission of a sexual offense as defined in Title 18, chapter 109, and §§2423.	Death or up to life imprisonment	No limitation

Appendix. (Continued)

Offense	Code Section No.	Jurisdictional Clause	Prohibited Act	Penalty	Statute of Limitations
Repeat Offenders	18 U.S.C. §2247	Special maritime or territorial jurisdiction of the United States or in a federally run or contracted prison	Second or subsequent offense committed under chapter 109A of Title 18	Twice the original sentence, or life if person was previously convicted of a sex offense against a minor	No limitation
Two sexual abuse offenses	18 U.S.C. §3559	—	A federal sex offense coupled with a prior sex conviction (under either applicable federal or state law).	Life, unless death penalty applies	No limitation

Source: Title 18 of the *United States Code*.

End Notes

[1] Adam Walsh Child Protection and Safety Act, P.L. 109-248, 120 Stat. 587 (2006).

[2] Child Abuse Prevention and Treatment Act, P.L. 93-247, 88 Stat. 4 (1974).

[3] CRS Report RL33967, *Adam Walsh Child Protection and Safety Act: A Legal Analysis*, by Charles Doyle; CRS Report R40899, *The Child Abuse Prevention and Treatment Act (CAPTA): Background, Programs, and Funding*, by Emilie Stoltzfus.

[4] Sexual Abuse Act of 1986, P.L. 99-646, §87, 100 Stat. 3592, 3620.

[5] Amber Hagerman Child Protection Act of 1996, P.L. 104-208, 110 Stat. 3009, 3009-031.

[6] Protection of Children from Sexual Predators Act of 1998, P.L. 105-314, 112 Stat. 2974.

[7] United States v. Lopez, 514 U.S. 549, 561 n.3 (1995) (quoting Brecht v. Abrahamson, 507 U.S. 619, 635 (1993)); *see also* Screws v. United States, 325 U.S. 91, 109 (1945) (plurality opinion) ("Our national government is one of delegated powers alone. Under our federal system the administration of justice rests with the States except as Congress, acting within the scope of those delegated powers, has created offenses against the United States.").

[8] Newberry v. United States, 256 U.S. 232, 258 (1921).

[9] Barnes v. Glen Theatre, Inc., 501 U.S. 560, 569 (1991).

[10] 1 WAYNE R. LAFAVE, SUBSTANTIVE CRIMINAL LAW §4.2(a) (2d ed. 2003). Congress's implied powers derive from the necessary and proper clause. U.S. CONST. art. I, §8, cl. 18 ("The Congress shall have Power ... To make all Laws which shall be necessary and proper for carrying into Execution the foregoing Powers....").

[11] "The Congress shall have Power ... To exercise exclusive Legislation in all Cases whatsoever, over such District (not exceeding ten Miles square) as may, by Cession of particular States, and the Acceptance of Congress, become the Seat of the Government of the United States...." U.S. CONST. art. I, §8, cl. 17.

[12] "The Congress shall have Power to dispose of and make all needful Rules and Regulations respecting the Territory or other Property belonging to the United States...." U.S. CONST. art. IV, §3.

[13] "The Congress shall have Power ... To exercise exclusive Legislation ... over all places purchased by the Consent of the Legislature of the State in which the Same shall be, for the Erection of Forts, Magazines, Arsenals, dock-Yards, and other needful Buildings." U.S. CONST. art. I, §8, cl. 17.

[14] 18 U.S.C. §7 (2006).

[15] *Id.*

[16] LaFave, *supra* note 10.

[17] U.S. CONST. art. I, §8, cl. 3.

[18] *See* United States v. Lopez, 514 U.S. 549, 558-59 (1995); United States v. Morrison 529 U.S. 598, 608-09.

[19] 18 U.S.C. §2261 (2006).

[20] 18 U.S.C. §2261A (2006).

[21] 18 U.S.C. §2241(c) (2006).

[22] *Lopez*, 514 U.S. at 551.

[23] Gonzales v. Raich, 545 U.S. 1, 22 (1995).

[24] *Id.*

[25] *See generally* KENNETH THOMAS, CONGRESSIONAL RESEARCH SERVICE, UNITED STATES CONSTITUTION: ANALYSIS AND INTERPRETATION 165 (2002), *available at* http://crs.gov/conan/default.aspx?mode=topic&doc=Article01.xml&t= 3|1|2&s=8&c=1.

[26] Pennhurst State Sch. & Hosp. v. Halderman, 451 U.S. 1, 17 (1981).

[27] South Dakota v. Dole, 483 U.S. 203, 211 (1987).

[28] Megan's Law, P.L. 104-145, 110 Stat. 1345 (1996).

[29] *See* W. Paul. Koenig, *Does Congress Abuse Its Spending Clause Power By Attaching Conditions on the Receipt of Federal Law Enforcement Funds to a State's Compliance with "Megan's Law"?*, 88 J. CRIM. L. & CRIMINOLOGY 721, 729-30 (1998).

[30] Child Abuse Prevention and Treatment Act, P.L. 93-247, 88 Stat. 4 (1974).

[31] S.Rept. 93-308, at 1 (1973).

[32] *See* CRS Report R40899, *The Child Abuse Prevention and Treatment Act (CAPTA): Background, Programs, and Funding*, by Emilie Stoltzfus.

[33] Child Welfare Information Gateway, Mandatory Reporters of Child Abuse and Neglect: Summary of State Laws, U.S. DEP'T OF HEALTH & HUMAN SERVICES, http://www.childwelfare.gov/systemwide/laws_policies/statutes/ manda.cfm. "Child abuse and neglect" was defined under CAPTA as "the physical or mental injury, sexual abuse, negligent treatment, or maltreatment of a child under the age of eighteen by a person who is responsible for the child's welfare under circumstances which indicate the child's health or welfare is harmed or threatened thereby, as determined in accordance with regulations prescribed by the Secretary." §3, 88 Stat. at 5. "Child abuse" was amended (to its present form) to mean "any recent act or failure to act on the part of a parent or caretaker, which results in death, serious physical or emotional harm, sexual abuse or exploitation, or an act or failure to act which presents an imminent risk of serious harm." 42 U.S.C. §5101 (2006).

[34] Victim's of Child Abuse Act, P.L. 101-647, §201, 104 Stat. 4789, 4806 (1990).

[35] 42 U.S.C. §13031 (2006).

[36] 18 U.S.C. §2258 (2006).

[37] *Hearings on Federal Rape Reform Law Before the Subcomm. on Criminal Justice of the H. Comm. on the Judiciary*, 98th Cong. 80 (1984) (statement of Rep. Steny Hoyer).

[38] White Slave Traffic Act, ch. 395, §4, 36 Stat. 825, 826 (1910). The Mann Act outlawed a person from enticing or coercing any female under the age of 18 to engage in "prostitution, debauchery, or any other immoral practice" while knowingly causing her to be transported in interstate commerce upon a common carrier. *Id.*

[39] White Slave Traffic Act, ch. 395, §4, 36 Stat. 825, 826 (1910).

[40] Sexual Exploitation of Children Act of 1977, P.L. 95-225, §3(a), 92 Stat. 7, 8 (codified at 18 U.S.C. §2423). The Child Sexual Abuse and Pornography Act of 1986, P.L. 99-628, §5, 100 Stat. 3510, 3511, amended the requirement that the prohibited sexual conduct "be commercially exploited," to its current form, which requires that the minor engage in sexual activity "for which any person can be charged with a criminal offense." 18 U.S.C. §2423(a) (2006).

[41] Sexual Abuse Act of 1986, P.L. 99-646, §87, 100 Stat. 3592, 3620; H.Rept. 99-594, at 6, 15 (1986).

[42] 18 U.S.C. §2241(c) (2006); 18 U.S.C. §2243(a) (2006).

[43] 3-61 MODERN FEDERAL JURY INSTRUCTIONS-CRIMINAL P 61.01 cmt. (2011).

[44] *Id.*

[45] 18 U.S.C. §§2242-43 (2006).

[46] 18 U.S.C. §2244 (2006).

[47] Sexual Abuse Act of 1986 §87.

[48] Amber Hagerman Child Protection Act of 1996, P.L. 104-208, §121(7), 110 Stat. 3009, 3009-31.

[49] Communications Decency Act of 1996, P.L. 104-104, §508, 110 Stat. 133, 137.

[50] Protection of Children from Sexual Predators Act of 1998, P.L. 105-314, 112 Stat. 2974.

[51] 18 U.S.C. §2244 (1994).
[52] 18 U.S.C. §2244(c).
[53] 18 U.S.C. §2244(a)(1).
[54] 18 U.S.C. §2244(c) (cross-referencing 18 U.S.C. §2244(a)(1)).
[55] §§102-3, 112 Stat. at 2975.
[56] 18 U.S.C. §2426 (2006).
[57] 18 U.S.C. §2425 (2006).
[58] Prosecutorial Remedies and Other Tools to end the Exploitation of Children Today Act of 2003 (PROTECT Act), P.L. 108-21, 117 Stat. 650.
[59] *Id.* §103, 117 Stat. at 652.
[60] *Id.* §106, 117 Stat. at 654.
[61] "Federal sex offense" is defined as "an offense under section 1591 (relating to sex trafficking of children), 2241 (relating to aggravated sexual abuse), 2242 (relating to sexual abuse), 2244(a)(1) (relating to abusive sexual contact), 2245 (relating to sexual abuse resulting in death), 2251 (relating to sexual exploitation of children), 2251A (relating to selling or buying of children), 2422(b) (relating to coercion or enticement of a minor into prostitution), or 2423(b) (relating to transportation of minors)[.]" 18 U.S.C. §3559(e)(2)(A) (2006).
[62] "Prior sex conviction" is defined as "a conviction for which the sentence was imposed before the conduct occurred constituting the subsequent Federal sex offense, and which was for a Federal sex offense or a State sex offense[.]" 18 U.S.C. §3559(e)(2)(C). "State sex offense" is defined as

an offense under State law that is punishable by more than one year in prison and consists of conduct that would be a Federal sex offense if, to the extent or in the manner specified in the applicable provision of this title—

(i) the offense involved interstate or foreign commerce, or the use of the mails; or

(ii) the conduct occurred in any commonwealth, territory, or possession of the United States, within the special maritime and territorial jurisdiction of the United States, in a Federal prison, on any land or building owned by, leased to, or otherwise used by or under the control of the Government of the United States, or in the Indian country (as defined in Section 1151)[.]

18 U.S.C. §3559(e)(2)(B).

Though beyond the scope of this report, there are specific sections of the United States Sentencing Guidelines Manual relating to sexual abuse of children. *See* U.S. SENTENCING GUIDELINES MANUAL §2A3.1 (2011); *see generally* CRS Report R41696, *How the Federal Sentencing Guidelines Work: An Overview*, by Charles Doyle.

[63] Adam Walsh Child Protection and Safety Act, P.L. 109-248, 120 Stat. 587 (2006).
[64] §204, 120 Stat. at 613, 18 U.S.C. §2423(a) (2006).
[65] §206, 120 Stat. at 613, 18 U.S.C. §2241(c) (2006).
[66] Sexual Abuse Act of 1986, P.L. 99-646, §87, 100 Stat. 3592, 3620.
[67] 18 U.S.C. 2241(c); United States v. Cryar, 232 F.3d 1318, 1322 (10th Cir. 2000); United States v. King, 604 F.3d 125, 139 (3d Cir. 2010). "Sexual act" is defined as

(A) contact between the penis and the vulva or the penis and the anus, and for purposes of this subparagraph contact involving the penis occurs upon penetration, however slight;

(B) contact between the mouth and the penis, the mouth and the vulva, or the mouth and the anus;

(C) the penetration, however slight, of the anal or genital opening of another by a hand or finger or by any object, with an intent to abuse, humiliate, harass, degrade, or arouse or gratify the sexual desire of any person; or
(D) the intentional touching, not through the clothing, of the genitalia of another person who has not attained the age of 16 years with an intent to abuse, humiliate, harass, degrade, or arouse or gratify the sexual desire of any person.
18 U.S.C.§2246(2) (2006).

[68] 18 U.S.C. §2241(c); *see* 3-61 MODERN FEDERAL JURY INSTRUCTIONS-CRIMINAL P 61.02 cmt. (2011).

[69] *Id.* (cross-referencing 18 U.S.C. §2241(a)(1)).

[70] *Id.* (cross-referencing 18 U.S.C. §2241(a)(2)).

[71] *Id.* (cross-referencing 18 U.S.C. §2241(b)).

[72] H.Rept. 99-594, at 16 (1986).

[73] H.Rept. 99-954, at 17 (1986).

[74] United States v. Two Elk, 536 F.3d 890, 899 (8th Cir. 2008) (holding that multiple counts under §2241(c) not prohibited under the Double Jeopardy Clause of the Fifth Amendment as the offense of aggravated sexual abuse is considered a "separate-act offense" and not a "course of conduct offense").

[75] 18 U.S.C. §2241(d); *see* United States v. Juvenile Male, 211 F.3d 1169, 1171 (9th Cir. 2000).

[76] 18 U.S.C. §3299 (2006).

[77] 18 U.S.C. §2241(c).

[78] *Id.*

[79] H.Rept. 105-557, at 10 (1998).

[80] Protection of Children from Sexual Predators Act of 1998, P.L. 105-314, §302, 112 Stat. 2974, 2979.

[81] 18 U.S.C. §2244(a)(1)-(4). Sexual contact is defined as the "intentional touching, either directly or through the clothing, of the genitalia, anus, groin, breast, inner thigh, or buttocks of any person with an intent to abuse, humiliate, harass, degrade, or arouse or gratify the sexual desire of any person...." 18 U.S.C. §2246(3) (2006).

[82] 18 U.S.C. §2244(c) (cross-referencing 18 U.S.C. §2244(a)(1) and 18 U.S.C. §2241(a)). One court has noted that an offender can be charged with the same conduct under both 18 U.S.C. §2244(a)(1) and §2241(b) combined with §2244(c). United States v. Johns, 309 F.3d 298, 301 (5th Cir. 2002). Section 2244(b) applies to all victims, regardless of age, thus is beyond the scope of this memorandum.

[83] 18 U.S.C. §2244(c) (cross-referencing 18 U.S.C. §2244(a)(1) and 2241(b)).

[84] *Id.* (cross-referencing 18 U.S.C. §2244(a)(1)).

[85] *Id.* (cross-referencing 18 U.S.C. §2244(a)(2) and §2242(1) (2006)).

[86] The mental state requirement of "knowingly" has been described in the sexual abuse context as follows: "[T]he defendant realized what he was doing and was aware of the nature of his conduct and did not act through ignorance, mistake, or accident. Knowledge may be proved by the Defendant's conduct and by all the facts and circumstances surrounding the case." United States v. Peters, 277 F.3d 963, 968 (7th Cir. 2002).

[87] §2244(c) (cross-referencing 18 U.S.C. §2244(a)(2) and 2242(2)).

[88] *Id.* (cross-referencing 18 U.S.C. §2244(a)(2)).

[89] *Id.* (cross-referencing 18 U.S.C. §2244(a)(3) and §2243(a) (2006)).

[90] *Id.* (cross-referencing 18 U.S.C. §2244(a)(3)).

[91] *Id.* (cross-referencing 18 U.S.C. §2243(b)).

[92] 18 U.S.C. §3299 (2006).

[93] H.Rept. 99-594, at 16 (1986).

[94] 18 U.S.C. §2243(a).

[95] *Id.* at (a)(2).

[96] 18 U.S.C. §2244(a)(3) (cross-referencing 18 U.S.C. §2243).

[97] 18 U.S.C. §2243(d).

[98] *Id.* at (c)(1).

[99] United States v. Cole, 262 F.3d 704, 708 (8th Cir. 2001) (holding that the application of a Florida law that prohibited a person from having sex with a person at least 12 years of age but younger than 16 was a proper predicate offense satisfying the "any other sexual activity" clause of §2423) (citing FLA. STAT. §800.04(4)(a) (2007)).

[100] 18 U.S.C. §2423(a) (2006).

[101] United States v. Hamilton, 456 F.2d 171, 173 (3d Cir. 1972).

[102] United States v. Garcia-Lopez, 234 F.3d 217, 220 (5th Cir. 2000).

[103] 18 U.S.C. §3299 (2006).

[104] 18 U.S.C. §2423(a).

[105] United States v. Morris, 549 F.3d 548, 550 (7th Cir. 2008) (sustaining conviction in which target was actually the mother of a 15-year-old girl).

[106] 18 U.S.C. §2422(b) (2006).

[107] 18 U.S.C. §2425 (2006).

[108] 18 U.S.C. §2245 (2006).

[109] 18 U.S.C. §3559(e); *see supra* note 60.

[110] 18 U.S.C. §2247 (cross-referencing 18 U.S.C. §2426(b) (2006)).

[111] 18 U.S.C. §3559(e).

[112] 18 U.S.C. §3299.

[113] 6 WAYNE R. LAFAVE ET AL., CRIMINAL PROCEDURE §24.8(d) (3d ed. 2007).

[114] *Id.*

[115] Schmuck v. United States, 489 U.S. 705, 716 (1989) (citing FED. R. CRIM. P. 31). Rule 31 states that a "defendant may be found guilty of ... an offense necessarily included in the offense charged." FED. R. CRIM. P. 31.

[116] United States v. Boyles, 57 F.3d 535, 544 (7th Cir. 1995).

[117] *Id.* at 544-45.

[118] United States v. Castillo, 140 F.3d 874, 886 (10th Cir. 1998); United States v. Torres, 937 F.2d 1469, 1477-78 (9th Cir. 1991).

[119] United States v. Demarias, 876 F.2d 674, 676-77 (8th Cir. 1989).

INDEX

#

A

B

C

D

E

F

G

H

M

N

R

S

T

U

V

W

Y

Z